Daniel

no **BLACK**, all WHITE

Nicole DiCenzo

To Manda,
Thanks for pushing me to teach a Bible Study on Daniel.
I thought there was nothing else to discover.
I was wrong.

All translations from NASB unless otherwise noted. *New American Standard Bible Giant Print Reference Edition* (Anaheim, California: Foundation Publications, Inc., 2002).

Unless otherwise noted, all Hebrew/Greek word definitions are from *The New Strong's Expanded Exhaustive Concordance of the Bible.* Strong, James. Published in Nashville, Tennessee by Thomas Nelson Publishers, 2010.
.

Scripture marked ESV comes from the *English Standard Version Study Bible* (Wheaton, Illinois: Crossway, 2008).

Scripture marked NIV comes from the *New International Version* (Grand Rapids, Michigan: Zondervan Publishing House, 1995).

Scripture marked NCV comes from the *New Century Version* of Scripture. *Mom's Bible: God's Wisdom for Mothers* (Nashville, TN: Thomas Nelson, Inc., 2005).

Scripture marked JNTP comes from *The Complete Jewish Bible* (Clarksville, Maryland: Jewish New Testament Publications, Inc., 1998). This is an English version of scripture translated by David H. Stern.

Scripture marked KJV comes from *The Comparative Study Bible* (Grand Rapids, Michigan: Zondervan., 1984).

Statue Art done by Sherry Kitts of Hixson, Tennessee. Thank you for everything you have done for this publication.

From the Author,

Daniel. He is amazing. I have loved this greatly esteemed man of God from afar for a long time. One day, one of my closest friends asked if I could teach a Bible Study on Daniel. I shrugged it off. There were already plenty of good studies on Daniel available. After all, I was not the only admirer. I thought there would be nothing else I could contribute to honor this man many other more capable teachers have honored by their words.

I was wrong. God gives each of His children unique perspective, and my perspective was different than all the other writers that have come before. This book is not about a man in the past – it is about men of the future – it is about us. We will walk the path Daniel walked. Many will shine like Daniel. Many others will fall. Which will you be? If you faithfully study Daniel, you will learn lessons that will help prepare your armor for the battle about to begin.

It's time to turn the page. It's time to prepare for war.

Nic

The Kings, Events, and Prophets of Daniel

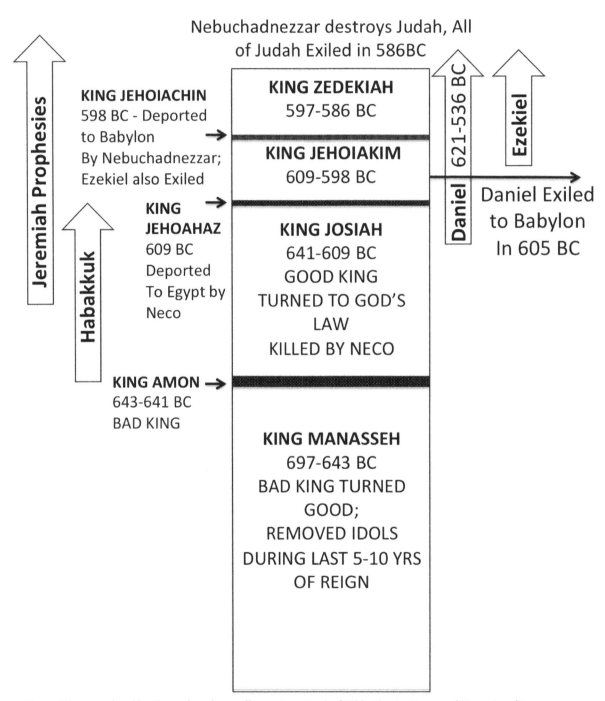

Notes: Kings are dated by time reigned according to *Rose Book of Bible Charts, Maps and Time Lines* (Torrance, California: Rose Publishing, 2005). Prophets (in arrows) are depicted by time prophesied according to the *English Standard Version Study Bible* (Wheaton, Illinois: Crossway, 2008) except Daniel – he is depicted by life.

Week One

Before him there was no king like him who turned to the Lord with all his heart . . . according to all the law of Moses . . .

2 Kings 23:25

Day One – The Stage
Josiah

Daniel is one of the most fascinating, action-packed, books of the Bible. It has been one of my favorites for years. Daniel is a man "greatly esteemed" by God and I am in awe of him whenever I study this book. Let's start off with some verses about Daniel.

Then the king ordered Ashpenaz, the chief of his officials, to bring in some of the sons of Israel, including some of the royal family and of the nobles, youths in whom was no defect, who were good-looking, showing intelligence in every branch of wisdom, endowed with understanding and discerning knowledge, and who had ability for serving in the king's court; and he ordered him to teach them the literature and language of the Chaldeans . . . Now among them from the sons of Judah were Daniel, Hananiah, Mishael, and Azariah.

Daniel 1:3-4, 6

Then at the end of the days which the king had specified for presenting them, the commander of the officials presented them before Nebuchadnezzar. The king talked with them, and out of them all not one was found like Daniel, Hananiah, Mishael and Azariah; so they entered the king's personal service. As for every matter of wisdom and understanding about which the king consulted them, he found them ten times better than all the magicians and conjurers who were in all his realm.

Daniel 1:18-20

Then King Nebuchadnezzar fell on his face and did homage to Daniel, and gave orders to present to him an offering and fragrant incense.

Daniel 2:46

There is a man in your kingdom in whom is a spirit of the holy gods; and in the days of your father, illumination, insight and wisdom like the wisdom of the gods were found in him. And King Nebuchadnezzar, your father, your father the king, appointed him chief of the magicians, conjurers, Chaldeans and diviners. This was because an extraordinary spirit, knowledge and insight, interpretation of dreams, explanation of enigmas and solving of difficult problems were found in this Daniel, whom the king named Belteshazzar. Let Daniel now be summoned and he will declare the interpretation.

Daniel 5:11-12

Then Belshazzar gave orders, and they clothed Daniel with purple and put a necklace of gold around his neck, and issued a proclamation concerning him that he now had authority as the third ruler in the kingdom.

Daniel 5:29

Then this Daniel began distinguishing himself among the commissioners and satraps because he possessed an extraordinary spirit, and the king planned to appoint him over the entire kingdom. Then the commissioners and satraps began trying to find a ground of accusation against Daniel in regard to government affairs; but they could find no ground of accusation or evidence of corruption, inasmuch as he was faithful, and no negligence or corruption was to be found in him.

Daniel 6:3-4

Gabriel, whom I had seen in the vision previously, came to me in my extreme weariness about the time of the evening offering. He gave me instruction and talked with me and said, "O Daniel, I have now come forth to give you insight and understanding. At the beginning of your supplications the command was issued, and I have come to tell you, for you are highly esteemed; so give heed to the message and gain understanding of the vision."

Daniel 9:21b-23

He said to me, "O Daniel, man of high esteem, understand the words that I am about to tell you and stand upright, for I have now been sent to you."

Daniel 10:11a

Everyone Daniel came across saw something special in him. From Ashpenaz, the chief of the officials who first took Daniel into the kings service, to Nebuchadnezzar the king, to Nebuchadnezzar's wife the queen, to Belshazzar the king's descendant, to the angel Gabriel, and to God Himself. Daniel stood out. Let's see why.

*But Daniel made up his mind that he **would not defile himself** . . . So Daniel was taken up out of the den and no injury whatever was found on him, because he had **trusted in his God** . . . When I, Daniel, had seen the vision, **I sought to understand it** . . . In the first year of his reign, I, Daniel, **observed in the books** . . . **I prayed to the Lord** my God . . . **and confessed** . . .*

Daniel 1:8, 6:23, 8:15, 9:2, 9:4

Daniel was outstanding because he decided on day one in a pagan land that he would not defile himself; he would trust God; he would seek understanding in the Word; and he would pray and confess his sins and the sins of the nation as a whole. Some good advice from the man God calls "highly esteemed." How did Daniel stay so strong? What influences did he have? We don't know too much about his history other than the fact that he was either of the royal family or one of the nobility (Daniel 1:3). Can we discern anything from the environment Daniel grew up in? Let's look at this.

Daniel was exiled to Babylon (more on this in a future lesson) in approximately 605 BC. The last vision that he received came in the third year of King Cyrus, which was approximately 536 BC.[1] We know that Daniel was a "youth" when he was taken to Babylon (Daniel 1:4). This probably meant he was a teenager, still young, but also budding into manhood because he was able to learn the ways of the Babylonians within three years and impress the king (Daniel 1:5). Many scholars believe Daniel was approximately 16 years old at the time of his exile, which would place the time of his birth at 621 BC.[2]

In order to better understand just who Daniel was at the time of his exile, we have to look at the kings who ruled when Daniel lived in Judah. Just what was the political environment like at the time of Daniel's upbringing?

Read Daniel 1:1. In what year of king Jehoiakim did Daniel get taken to Babylon? _____

Read 2 Kings 23:31. Before Jehoiakim, Jehoahaz was king. How long did he reign? _____

Turn back to 2 Kings 22:1. Who was king before Jehoahaz? _____
At what age did he become king? _____ How many years did he reign? _____

Daniel was approximately 16 years old when he went into exile. So, Jehoiakim was ruling Jerusalem when Daniel was between 13 and 16 years old. There was a brief three-month period where Jehoahaz reigned, but the majority of Daniel's young life was lived under the reign of Josiah. He grew up in the latter part of Josiah's reign, or the final 13 years.

Before we look at Josiah and what he did, we need to understand the overall religious environment of Israel. After the death of Solomon in approximately 931 BC, there was a split in the kingdom. Solomon's son Rehoboam did not listen to the pleas of the people for better treatment and ten of the twelve tribes of Israel separated and made Jeroboam their king (1 Kings 12).[3] Rehoboam ruled the southern area of Israel, which became known as Judah, and Jeroboam ruled the northern part of Israel. Jeroboam led the northern tribes into all out idolatry. He erected two golden calves for his people to worship so they wouldn't return to Jerusalem to worship God (1 Kings 12:25-29). He feared his people would turn back to Rehoboam if he allowed them to worship in Jerusalem. Jeroboam's idolatry caused a downward spiral in the northern tribes. No king of Israel that came after Jeroboam returned to the Lord. Every one of them was wicked, and led the northern nation into further sin. What was their judgment? God eventually sent the Assyrians to conquer Israel and take them into exile. This happened in approximately 722 BC.[4]

The story in Judah, where Daniel grew up, was a little different. Although many of the kings were wicked, there were some that were good. Before we look at Josiah, let me set the stage: Josiah's father was Amon and Amon only reigned two years in Jerusalem (2 Kings 21:19). Amon did evil in the eyes of the Lord, just like Manasseh his father before him who ruled for 55 years. Let's look to see what evil Manasseh committed.

Read 2 Kings 21:1-9. On top of all the other detestable things Manasseh did, what abomination is mentioned in verse six? _____ In verse nine what does it say Manasseh made Judah do? _____

Luckily, this is not the end of the story for Manasseh. This king actually turned to the Lord near the end of his reign. Manasseh reigned in approximately 697-643 BC, but something happened somewhere between 652-648 BC.[5]

Read 2 Chronicles 33:10-16. What did Manasseh do with the foreign gods? _____
_____ (verse 15)

Manasseh did a complete flip-flop during his final years, but it wasn't enough to affect his son (Josiah's father). Look at 2 Chronicles 33:22-23 in the margin.

Manasseh removed the idols, but he failed to destroy them. After Manasseh's death, his son brought those idols right back out. Josiah was eight years old when he became king (2 Kings 22:1). The prior two years before he was crowned, his father Amon had "multiplied guilt." But his grandfather Manasseh had removed the pagan gods and totally reformed approximately the time Josiah was born. Josiah started off with a good influence, and then proceeded to witness a downward plunge by his own father for the short two years of Amon's reign. Now let's read about Josiah.

> He did evil in the sight of the Lord as Manasseh his father had done, and Amon sacrificed to all the carved images which his father Manasseh had made, and he served them. Moreover, he did not humble himself before the Lord as his father Manasseh had done, but Amon multiplied guilt.
>
> 2 Chronicles 33:22-23

Read 2 Kings 22:1- 23:25

In 2 Chronicles 34, it gives us even more detail. Josiah sought the Lord in the eighth year of his reign and in his twelfth year he began to purge the land of false gods. Then in the eighteenth year of Josiah's reign, he found God's law and did some major reforming. He reigned 31 years, so that means the last thirteen years of his reign was marked by incredible reform in the land. This is approximately the same exact time Daniel was born. Daniel grew up under the influence of Josiah, and under the influence of God's laws.

> Before him there was no king like him who turned to the Lord with all his heart and with all his soul and with all his might, according to all the law of Moses; nor did any like him arise after him.
>
> 2 Kings 23:25

I want you to look again at 2 Kings 23:25 in the margin. Josiah was something else, a rare jewel in a long line of unfaithful kings. He reformed the land. He changed the religious environment of Israel. He turned with all his heart, all his soul, and all his might to God's law.

Daniel saw this. Daniel learned. And Daniel was of the "nobility" (Daniel 1:3). I would wager a pretty certain guess that Daniel knew Josiah, and Josiah's unwavering commitment to God and His laws influenced a young Daniel a great deal.

So Josiah had the good influence of his grandfather Manasseh who turned to the Lord in his old age, and the bad influence of his own father who followed Manasseh's reign. Similarly, Daniel had a good influence for the first thirteen years of his life in King Josiah and a bad influence in the latter years before his exile with Josiah's sons Jehoahaz and Jehoiakim who "did evil in the sight of the Lord" (2 Kings 23:32, 37). Both Josiah and Daniel could see the difference between the "good" and the "bad." Both chose the good. Both rejected the bad.

Now I want you to think about what the prophet Huldah said to Josiah about God's judgment. She informed Josiah that God was going to punish Judah for its idolatry. Even though Josiah's heart was pure, the people of the land were unfaithful and God knew they would go right back to their pagan ways. God then tells Josiah:

> *"Because your heart was penitent, and you humbled yourself before the Lord, when you heard how I spoke against this place and against its inhabitants, that they should become a desolation and a curse, and you have torn your clothes and wept before me, I also have heard you," declares the Lord. "Therefore, behold, I will gather you to your fathers, and you shall be gathered to your grave in peace, and your eyes shall not see all the disaster that I will bring upon this place."*
>
> *2 Kings 22:19-20 ESV*

God predicted disaster, but not in Josiah's day. If Daniel was of the nobility, did he hear this prophecy? Perhaps. Perhaps that is one of the reasons Daniel rejected the next king and retained his loyalty to God. Daniel could have been warned destruction was coming. He could have readied his heart for disaster.

Although Josiah "turned to the Lord with all his heart and with all his soul and with all his might" (2 Kings 23:25), he met with a tragic end.

Read 2 Chronicles 35:20-27. What happened to Josiah? _____
By what king? _____ In what plain was Josiah killed? _____

What familiar name do you see in verse 25, as in who was prophesying in Josiah and Daniel's day? _____

Now isn't that interesting. There is a lot going on in this passage, so let's break it down piece by piece. Josiah was killed by the Egyptian army, yet the king of Egypt told Josiah that he was not coming out against Judah (2 Chronicles 35:21). So why was Josiah insistent that he battle Neco? No one knows for sure.[6] But let me give you a little more information. There was a super power in the north whose power was coming to an end.

Turn to 2 Kings 23:29. What power was Neco riding to meet? _____

In Neco's day (approximately 609 BC),[7] Assyria was having problems with another super power – Babylon. Babylon and Assyria were fighting in the north and Neco was traveling through the valley of Megiddo on his way to help Assyria battle Babylon. Take note of these kingdoms, because as we move further into Daniel, all these powers will become incredibly important. Like I said, no one knows for sure why Josiah went to confront Neco, because Neco wasn't riding to war against Judah, but perhaps Josiah was siding with Babylon. Because Neco was opposing Babylon, Josiah might have wanted to try to destroy the Egyptian army before they could help Assyria. Why on earth would Josiah want to side with Babylon? I have a theory.

Read 2 Kings 17:6. What happened to the northern tribes of Israel? _____

Assyria was the super power that destroyed the northern tribes of Israel in 722 BC. That's not all.

Turn to 2 Kings 18:13. Who came up against Judah? _____

Assyria was also a bane in the side of Judah. Perhaps Josiah wanted to side with Babylon in order to crush the nation that had captured ten of the tribes and had also tormented Judah. After all, it seems Babylon had been friendly to Judah in the past. In approximately 710 BC when King Hezekiah had become sick, the king of Babylon sent him gifts and a letter (2 Kings 20:12), which prompted Hezekiah to show the envoys of Babylon all of his treasure.[8] Hezekiah's folly caused Isaiah to prophesy that all Hezekiah's treasure would be carried to Babylon (2 Kings 20:17). But up until this time, Assyria was the enemy of Judah, not Babylon.

But that was soon to change.

Let's get back to Josiah. He made a decision to march against Neco – even though Neco had warned him, and despite the fact that this warning was coming from God Himself (2 Chronicles 35:22). Josiah's decision met with fatal results. If you think about it, it probably would have been very easy to disregard Neco's words. Why should Josiah believe something coming from a king who didn't worship the one true God? But God can use anyone to bring His words. We need to remember that and test the spirits (Acts 17:11). Josiah was loved and "all of Judah and Jerusalem mourned for Josiah" (2 Chronicles 35:24). Even Jeremiah the prophet enters the scene by writing laments for the king.

The important thing to note here is that Jeremiah was walking in Jerusalem at the same time as Daniel. Daniel was sure to have heard Jeremiah prophesy. More on this as we continue our study.

The last thing I would like to point out about Josiah's death is something very interesting to me. Look at the verse in the margin. Josiah was killed in Megiddo, which is another name for the valley of Armageddon. Daniel is a book about end time events (Daniel 12:9), and the valley of Armageddon is where the armies of the world will gather to fight Jesus when He returns (Revelation 16:16). Josiah was the last good king in Judah. God told Josiah He would gather him to his fathers before he brought destruction on Judah (2 Chronicles 34:28). Josiah's death brought the decline of Judah and ultimately its deportation to Babylon. The end time system of Revelation, the ultimate kingdom that rises up to persecute both Christians and Jews, is referred to as Babylon in Revelation (Revelation 18:2). Although

In his days Pharaoh Neco king of Egypt went up to the king of Assyria to the river Euphrates. And King Josiah went to meet him, and when Pharaoh Neco saw him he killed him at Megiddo.

2 Kings 23:29

Babylon defeated Judah in Daniel's day, it will not succeed in the end. Although a good man fell in the valley of Armageddon in Daniel's day, bad men will be destroyed there in the end. We haven't seen the last of Babylon, or its kings. More to come tomorrow on the kings of Judah, but before we end for today, I want to point out one more thing.

> *"When the king heard the words of the book of the law, he tore his clothes . . . The king stood by the pillar and made a covenant before the Lord, to walk after the Lord, and to keep His commandments and His testimonies and His statutes with all his heart and all his soul, to carry out the words of this covenant that were written in this book. And all the people entered into the covenant."*
>
> *2 Kings 22:11, 23:3*

When the king heard the words of the law, he tore his clothes, and he led the people back into a covenant with God. Daniel knew the environment of Babylon, and he remembered Josiah. At the time of his exile he had a decision to make. Would he follow the Babylonian laws and gods? Or would he follow God and obey His laws like Josiah?

But Daniel made up his mind that he would not defile himself . . .
Daniel 1:8 NASB

If you were exiled into Babylon, what would you do?

In the end times, Babylon will come again (Revelation 17:5). It will be the greatest persecutor of Jews and Christians of all time (Revelation 6:9-10, 12:17). Will you stand firm when the Antichrist asks you to bow to him (Revelation 13:17)? Even if that means you will go hungry, or be beaten, or beheaded? Will you be resolved?

But Daniel resolved that he would not defile himself . . .
Daniel 1:8 ESV

Make up your mind. Be resolved. The Beast of Daniel is coming. Daniel foresaw it. By the end of this study, so will you.

More to come tomorrow.

1 *English Standard Version Study Bible* (Wheaton, Illinois: Crossway, 2008), 1581.
2 Hinnant, Greg. *Daniel Notes* (Lake Mary, Florida: Creation House Press, 2003). page xi.
3 *Rose Book of Bible Charts, Maps and Time Lines* (Torrance, California: Rose Publishing, 2005), 64
4 *Rose Book of Bible Charts, Maps and Time Lines* (Torrance, California: Rose Publishing, 2005), 65.
5 *Rose Book of Bible Charts, Maps and Time Lines* (Torrance, California: Rose Publishing, 2005), 65.
New American Standard Bible (Grand Rapids, Michigan: Zondervan, 1999), 626.
6 One-Volume Illustrated Edition of *Zondervan Bible Commentary* with General Editor F. F. Bruce (Zondervan, 2008), 386.
7 One-Volume Illustrated Edition of *Zondervan Bible Commentary* with General Editor F. F. Bruce (Zondervan, 2008), 386.
8 *English Standard Version Study Bible* (Wheaton, Illinois: Crossway, 2008), 686.

Day Two – The Stage
Jeremiah

To fulfill the word of the Lord by the mouth of Jeremiah . . .

2 Chronicles 36:21

We left off yesterday with the demise of Josiah, the last good king of Judah. Josiah went out against Pharaoh Neco and Neco killed him in the valley of Armageddon. Now let's continue the story of the kings Daniel witnessed ruling in Jerusalem.

After Josiah's death, his son Jehoahaz only reigned three months in Judah. Neco's campaign to help Assyria in the north only lasted three months.[1] On Neco's way back through Judah he dealt with Jehoahaz, apparently still infuriated that Josiah had tried to interfere with the war. Neco took Jehoahaz back to Egypt and imprisoned him (2 Kings 23:33).

Daniel has yet to be exiled. He witnessed Jeremiah's lament for Josiah and he saw Jehoahaz reign for three months. He also probably heard a prophecy by Jeremiah about Jehoahaz. Keep in mind when you read this next passage, that Shallum in verse 11 is another name for Jehoahaz.

Read Jeremiah 22:1-12

What did God command them to do (verse 3)? _____

If they did not obey what would happen (verse 5)? _____

What would God make them like (verse 6)? _____

What would He send against them (verse 7)? _____

What would happen to Jehoahaz (verse 12)? _____

Jeremiah's words proved true. Jehoahaz never saw Judah again. He died in Egypt (2 Kings 23:34). When Neco came and bound Jehoahaz, Neco made Josiah's son Eliakim king instead. Neco changed Eliakim's name to Jehoiakim. Jehoiakim then became Egypt's vassal and had to give tribute to Egypt. After all, Neco hadn't imprisoned him like he had Jehoahaz. Daniel was there for Jeremiah's prophecy, and he was there for Jehoiakim's newfound power. He was also there when Jeremiah was almost killed.

What did the people want to do to Jeremiah in verse 8? _____

What did Jeremiah prophesy against in verse 11? _____

What did Jeremiah tell the people to do in verse 13? _____

Read Jeremiah 26:1-15

Jeremiah narrowly escaped with his life when he warned the people – amend your ways! According to Jeremiah 26:1, this was at the beginning of Jehoiakim's reign. Daniel was still in Jerusalem. He would have been approximately 13 at the time. He might have even heard Jeremiah utter those words. If Daniel knew Josiah, he also knew his son Jehoiakim. Did Daniel watch the new king and compare him to his father? I would wager a bet he did.

In his *[Jehoiakim's]* days Nebuchadnezzar king of Babylon came up, and Jehoiakim became his servant for three years; then he *[Jehoiakim]* turned and rebelled against him.

2 Kings 24:1
explanation added

So at the time of Jeremiah's warning, Jehoiakim had an alliance with Egypt, which is probably where the trouble started. Because, if you recall, Egypt had sided with Assyria against the up and coming Babylon.

Here starts the beginning of the end for Judah. Take a look at 2 Kings 24:1 in the margin.

In approximately 605 BC Egypt and Assyria were defeated by Babylon at the battle of Carchemish.[2] Jeremiah even prophesied about this battle and predicted Egypt's defeat (Jeremiah 46:1-12). *(Note in Jeremiah, it says in the fourth year of Jehoiakim's reign, while Daniel indicates it was the third year. Jeremiah was probably using the Jewish system of dating which counted from the new year preceding the kings ascension, while Daniel was using the new year following the king's ascension which was the method used in Babylon).[3]*

After the battle of Carchemish in 605 BC, Nebuchadnezzar, king of Babylon, moved through Judah, after all they were the vassal of Egypt, Babylon's just defeated enemy. This changed Daniel's life forever. He was taken into exile. This was the same year Jeremiah wrote a prophecy in a scroll. The next year, it was read to the people.

Read Jeremiah 36:1-32

What did Jeremiah prophesy for Judah in verse 3?_____

Did the king care (verse 24)? _____

What did the king do in verse 23? _____

What would happen to Jehoiakim in verse 30? _____

What did Jeremiah say would happen to Judah in verse 29? _____

Now read 2 Chronicles 36:5-6. What happened to Jehoiakim? _____

Some scholars believe the invasion of 605 BC is probably the occasion where Jehoiakim was taken to Babylon.[4] Because Jehoiakim reigned eleven years (2 Kings 23:36) they believe he was allowed to return home. If this happened he would have obviously had to switch his allegiance from Egypt to

Babylon and become a subject of Nebuchadnezzar. If this is true, he rebelled after three years (2 Kings 24:1). There is another theory, however, that may be the truth. At the time of Nebuchadnezzar siege and Daniel's exile, Jehoiakim could have sworn loyalty to Babylon. Then, after three years, he rebelled and a few years after that Nebuchadnezzar came again to Judah where he "bound him with bronze chains to take him to Babylon." Notice it says, "to take him" to Babylon not that he "took him." Some believe that Jehoiakim died before Nebuchadnezzar could make the trek. 2 Kings 24:6 says Jehoiakim "slept" with his fathers" and doesn't say anything about him dying in exile. Jeremiah even prophesied what would happen to Jehoiakim's body. Look at Jeremiah 22:18-19 in the margin. It seems more likely to me that Nebuchadnezzar bound him with chains after he rebelled, which would be at the end of his reign, in approximately 598 BC.

Therefore thus says the Lord concerning Jehoiakim the son of Josiah, king of Judah: "They shall not lament for him, saying, 'Ah, my brother!' or 'Ah, sister!' They shall not lament for him, saying, 'Ah, lord!' or 'Ah, his majesty!' With the burial of a donkey he shall be buried, dragged and dumped beyond the gates of Jerusalem."

Jeremiah 22:18-19 ESV

Daniel was exiled three years into Jehoiakim's reign (Daniel 1:1), which means Jehoiakim reigned approximately eight more years in Jerusalem. Daniel was taken to Babylon when he was approximately 16. He would have been approximately 24 years old when Jehoiakim died outside the gates of Jerusalem, just like Jeremiah predicted.

Then Jehoiakim's son came to power. His name was Jehoiachin and he reigned in Jerusalem three months (2 Kings 24:8). Jehoiachin did "evil in the sight of the Lord, according to all that his father had done" (2 Kings 24:9). Let's read what happened to Jehoiachin.

Read 2 Kings 24:8-17

Jehoiachin along with a large group of Judah's inhabitants got exiled to Babylon, including Ezekiel (2 Kings 24:15-16, Ezekiel 1:1-2). But during this time, Jeremiah uttered a beautiful prophesy about the exiles. Take a look.

How did God say He regarded the captives of Judah in verse 5? _____

What did He promise in verse 6? _____
_____

Read Jeremiah 24:1-10

God declared those exiled "good" and He promised He would bring them back to the land of Israel. But God declared doom for the new king Zedekiah. When Nebuchadnezzar took Jehoiachin and the exiles back to Babylon, he appointed Jehoiachin's uncle Mattaniah king in his place and renamed him Zedekiah. Zedekiah was twenty-one when he became king and he reigned in Jerusalem eleven years (2 Kings 24:18). "He did evil in the sight of the Lord, according to all that Jehoiakim had done" (2 Kings 24:19).

Read 2 Chronicles 36:12-16. In verse 12, who did Zedekiah not humble himself before? _____ And in verse 13 who did Zedekiah turn against? _____

How were the people?_____(verse 14)

What did the people do to the messengers of God? _____(verse 16)

What did the nation of Judah provoke from God? _____(verse 16)

Zedekiah ignored Jeremiah's warnings and turned against the Lord. The people were unfaithful and mocked God's messengers. Let's see what Jeremiah warned them about in the first year of King Zedekiah.

Read Jeremiah 27:12-17. What did Jeremiah tell the people and Zedekiah to do?_____

Read Jeremiah 21:1-10. Judah's fate was sealed, but they had a choice. What was their choice (verse 9)?_____

God became wrathful, and God sent the Babylonians as Judah's judgment. After the rebellion of three kings, Nebuchadnezzar had had enough. He returned to Jerusalem in approximately 586 BC and conquered it.[5]

Did Jeremiah's warning about Zedekiah come true? Let's take a look.

Read 2 Kings 25:6-7. What happened to Zedekiah? _____

Again, this was when Daniel lived in Babylon. At Zedekiah's arrival Daniel would have been approximately 35. Did Daniel see Zedekiah? Did he speak with him? Let's see what else Nebuchadnezzar did to Jerusalem when he took Zedekiah captive.

Read 2 Kings 25:9. What did the Babylonians destroy?_____

Read 2 Kings 25:11-12. What happened to the people? _____

Read 2 Kings 25:13-17. What did the Babylonians take? _____

This is the end of Judah. The temple was destroyed. What treasure was left after the exile of Jehoiachin (2 Kings 24:13) was taken at the destruction of Judah in 586 BC. What people were not killed with the sword or taken at the exile of Jehoiachin, were taken at the destruction of Jerusalem in 586 BC (2 Chronicles 36:19-21). Only the poorest of the poor were allowed to remain in the land (2 Kings 25:12).

Daniel was in Babylon. He heard about Jerusalem being destroyed. He probably saw Zedekiah in prison. He could have seen the sacred objects of the temple being carried into Babylon. But before that, he heard the words of Jeremiah. "Do justice and righteousness . . . Or this house will become a desolation" (Jeremiah 22:3, 5) "Turn from your evil way . . . walk in My law . . . or I will make this city a curse to all nations" (Jeremiah 26:3-6).

Daniel sought to understand . . .
Daniel 8:15

The word of the Lord is here for the seeking. Do we seek to understand? Or do we think it is an outdated book?

In the end times, this question is critical. The beast of Daniel is already among us.

He will cause deceit to succeed by his influence . . .
Daniel 8:25

If we do not seek the truth, we could believe a lie.

For this reason God will send upon them a deluding influence so that they will believe what is false.
                                                                          2 Thessalonians 2:11

And what does Jesus say about the last days?

"At that time many will fall away . . ."
                                                                          Matthew 24:10

Some believers will be swayed. They will believe what is false. They will not seek to understand the truth.

Daniel sought to understand . . .
Daniel 8:15

Will you?

More to come tomorrow.

1 One-Volume Illustrated Edition of *Zondervan Bible Commentary* with General Editor F. F. Bruce (Zondervan, 2008), 386.
2 One-Volume Illustrated Edition of *Zondervan Bible Commentary* with General Editor F. F. Bruce (Zondervan, 2008), 444.
3 *English Standard Version Study Bible* (Wheaton, Illinois: Crossway, 2008), 1586
4 *English Standard Version Study Bible* (Wheaton, Illinois: Crossway, 2008), 797. One-Volume Illustrated Edition of *Zondervan Bible Commentary* with General Editor F. F. Bruce (Zondervan, 2008), 444.
5 *Rose Book of Bible Charts, Maps and Time Lines* (Torrance, California: Rose Publishing, 2005), 65.
New American Standard Bible (Grand Rapids, Michigan: Zondervan, 1999), 65.

The message which Jeremiah the prophet commanded Seraiah the son of Neriah, the grandson of Mahseiah, when he went with Zedekiah the king of Judah to Babylon in the fourth year of his reign. (Now Seraiah was quartermaster.) So Jeremiah wrote in a single scroll all the calamity which would come upon Babylon, that is, all these words which have been written concerning Babylon. Then Jeremiah said to Seraiah, "As soon as you come to Babylon, then see that you read all these words aloud, and say, 'You, O Lord, have promised concerning this place to cut it off, so that there will be nothing dwelling in it, whether man or beast, but it will be a perpetual desolation.' And as soon as you finish reading this scroll, you will tie a stone to it and throw it into the middle of the Euphrates, and say, 'Just so shall Babylon sink down and not rise again because of the calamity that I am going to bring upon her; and they will become exhausted.'" Thus far are the words of Jeremiah.

Jeremiah 51:59-64

Day Three – The Stage
Hope

Look at the words of Jeremiah in the margin. This was written in the fourth year of Zedekiah, which would have been approximately 593 BC. Daniel had been chosen in 605 BC to enter King Nebuchadnezzar's service. The next wave of exiles was taken in 598 BC, including King Jehoiachin and Ezekiel. But there was hope. Jeremiah said that Babylon would become a desolation. He told Seraiah to throw the scroll into the Euphrates. This is probably the area where the exiles lived. We know that Ezekiel lived by the river Chebar, an irrigation canal that channeled the Euphrates River to the surrounding area.[1] Jeremiah sent this to give the exiles hope. There is another prophecy we need to look at that Jeremiah uttered that will become very important to Daniel's life.

Read Jeremiah 29:4-13

This prophecy was spoken after Jehoiachin and Ezekiel were taken to Babylon (Jeremiah 29:2). God told His people in exile to get comfortable – they were going to be there a while.

How long were the people going to remain in Babylon (verse 10)?

_____

Then what would the people do (verse 12)?

_____

___

These words must have been like gold to the exiles. They would be in Babylon for some time, but in 70 years they would be allowed to return to the land of Israel. There was still hope to be had. With God, there is always hope.

What kind of future does God want for His people according to Jeremiah 29:11?

_____

God wants His people to have hope. Even when darkness falls there is still light, because He is the light (1 John 1:5). The exiles in Babylon could hold onto hope. There is another prophetic book that was written during this time – Habakkuk. It is one of my favorite books, because not only does it prophesy Babylon's doom, it is an end time prophecy for the return of the King – Jesus. It was probably written before the death of Josiah in 609 BC and possibly before Josiah even obtained the throne because it looks forward to the rise of Babylon and speaks about God's law.[2] If this is the case, a young Daniel could have read this prophecy before he was carried off to Babylon.

But before we look at Habakkuk, we need to remind ourselves of just what Judah and Israel were doing in the days of Daniel. If you recall, King Josiah did a huge reform, where he smashed all idols and had Judah return to the law of the Lord. But, this was after Israel had been taken captive by Assyria is 722 BC. Let's see why Israel was taken away.

Read Deuteronomy 28:58-59 and 64. What would the Lord do if they did not follow His commands? _____

Now read Jeremiah 3:6-10. In the days of Josiah, did Judah completely turn back to God? _____ What did they play? _____

Even though Josiah turned with all his heart, the heart of the people did not, which has been made clear when studying the kings. No other king after Josiah turned to the Lord. That is what Habakkuk saw. And that is why he lamented.

Habakkuk looks around at the nations and is disgusted. He can't believe God is allowing the falsehood to continue without doing something about it.

Read Habakkuk 1:1-2:1

What does Habakkuk cry out in 1:4? _____

The word "law" in this scripture is the Hebrew word *torah*. *Torah* refers specifically to the first five books of the Old Testament (Genesis – Deuteronomy), which is where God's rules were written. These were the laws Josiah realized were not being upheld when he "tore his clothes" and brought about reform (2 Kings 22:11-23:27). Habakkuk is grieved in spirit when he sees God's laws not being respected but is shocked when God answers him.

What does God say He is doing in Habakkuk 1:6? _____

How are they described in Habakkuk 1:7? _____

How do the Chaldeans bring men up? _____

God says the Babylonians (the Chaldeans) are coming and they will judge, not only the nations surrounding Judah, but also Judah herself. History attests that the Babylonians were feared. At times they took captives away by putting hooks in their noses (Habakkuk 1:15).[3] Habakkuk is shocked. Babylon? Babylon was *worse* than Judah! "Why are You silent when the wicked swallow up those more righteous than they" (Habakkuk 1:13)? Then Habakkuk sits and waits. He knows the Lord will answer. He knows God will reply. God does answer, and He declares, even though Babylon will come, He heralds five woes on the nation. Babylon will be judged. Then Habakkuk is given a vision about the end of Babylon, which will be fulfilled in the end times.

Read Habakkuk 3:3-15

If you haven't done my *Revelation in Black and White* study, I highly suggest you pick it up. The entirety of the book of Revelation will be too much to get into here, but we will be looking closely at many chapters of Revelation because they correlate with many chapters of Daniel. What I want you to realize is this: I wonder if Daniel read Habakkuk. He was of the nobility (Daniel 1:3). He was probably well read. Did Habakkuk's prophecy ignite his hunger for the end times? Did it influence him in his search for truth? I know when I was a young girl, reading Revelation sparked my interest in the end times that has never left me. Revelation is what prompted my study and quest for knowledge about Daniel and other books of scripture. I wonder if Daniel was the same way. Look at Daniel 9:2 in the margin.

> In the first year of his reign, I, Daniel, observed in the books the number of the years which was revealed as the word of the Lord to Jeremiah the prophet for the completion of the desolations of Jerusalem, namely, seventy years.
>
> Daniel 9:2

We know Daniel read Jeremiah. I would wager a pretty good guess that he read Habakkuk. We have established that Habakkuk was talking about Babylon. Let's look at a few verses more closely.

In Revelation 18:2, name the empire that will rise and fall in the end times?_____

In Habakkuk 3:3-4, God (Jesus) is coming. What covers the heavens? _____ What is His face like? _____

Compare to Revelation 1:16. What did His face look like? _____ In Revelation 19:11 what was open? _____

Read Habakkuk 3:6. What shattered and collapsed? _____ In Revelation 16:20, what happens?_____

In Habakkuk 3:8, what was He riding on? _____ In Revelation 19:11? _____

In Habakkuk 3:9 what is discussed?_____ In Revelation 19:15?_____

In Habakkuk 3:13 what did He come for? _____ And what did He strike? _____ What is the purpose of His second coming in Revelation 12:10? _____ And who did He strike in Revelation 19:20? _____

Habakkuk predicted woe to Babylon, but his final chapter foreshadows Jesus' second coming.

Daniel probably didn't live in the time of Habakkuk, but Habakkuk's writings had probably been circulated in the time of Daniel. Daniel sought to understand; therefore, Daniel would have read his book.

Daniel observed in the books . . .
Daniel 9:2

In the last days, there will be many voices, and one of those voices will be the voice of the Antichrist. He will cause "deceit to succeed by his influence" (Daniel 8:25).

Blessed is he who reads and those who hear the words of the prophecy, and heed the things which are written in it; for the time is near.

Revelation 1:3

Jesus is the Word (John 1:1) and He is the truth (John 14:6). When deceit is running rampant, you need the truth, and if the truth is in the Word, you have to know it, which means, you have to read it.

Daniel observed in the books . . .
Daniel 9:2

Read. Hear. Heed.

1 Butler, Trent C. et al.,eds. *Holman Illustrated Bible Dictionary* (Nashville, Tennessee: Holman Bible Publishers, 2003), 53.
2 *English Standard Version Study Bible* (Wheaton, Illinois: Crossway, 2008), 1719.
3 *English Standard Version Study Bible* (Wheaton, Illinois: Crossway, 2008), 1722.

> "The prophet who prophesies of peace, when the word of the prophet comes to pass, then that prophet will be known as one whom the Lord has truly sent."
>
> Jeremiah 28:9

Something interesting happened at the beginning of Zedekiah's reign in approximately 597 BC, eight years after Daniel was exiled and at the time of Jehoiachin (and Ezekiel's) trek to Babylon. We have just read prophecies from Jeremiah about Jerusalem being destroyed by Babylon. We have also heard Jeremiah say that the exiles would be in Babylon for 70 years (Jeremiah 29:10). About the same time Jeremiah uttered this prophecy, someone else uttered another prophecy.

Read Jeremiah 28:1-17

How many years did Hananiah specify (verse 3)? _____

Who was going to come back (verse 4)? _____

I want you to look at verse two again and really let its words sink into your brain. Hananiah claimed he was speaking *for the Lord*. I want you to get the gravity of this. He was standing up and declaring to the people *on behalf of the Lord* that Babylon would be broken in two years. This is serious stuff, and for his lie, Hananiah died.

This is the environment Daniel grew up in. Different voices were everywhere. Do you remember Jeremiah chapter 26? Jeremiah spoke to the people at the beginning of Jehoiakim's reign, when Daniel was still in Judah. He told them that if they didn't turn back to God's laws, the city would be desolate. Jeremiah was telling the truth. He was pleading with the people to turn back to the Lord. What happened? The people wanted to kill him! Look at Jeremiah 26:8 in the margin.

> When Jeremiah finished speaking all that the Lord had commanded him to speak to all the people, the priests and the prophets and all the people seized him, saying, "You must die!"
>
> Jeremiah 26:8

Jeremiah narrowly escaped with his neck and he was speaking on behalf of the Lord.

Look back at Jeremiah 28:15. Did Hananiah convince the people of his lie?

_____

Do you remember the passage we looked at in Jeremiah that was specifically written to the exiles in Babylon? This was the same passage that prophesied that they would be there 70 years. I want you to turn there again.

What did Jeremiah warn them about in Jeremiah 29:8-9? _____

False prophets were also with the exiles. Ezekiel was one of the exiles. Let's see what Ezekiel had to say about them.

Read Ezekiel 13:1-10

What were the prophets prophesying from (verse 2)? _____

What were they following (verse 3)? _____ What had they seen? _____

False prophets were making the people's hopes "pretty" by covering them with whitewash. False prophets were everywhere, both before and after Daniel was exiled. You had to discern just what the truth was, and you had to trust in God whether or not the truth was good or bad. The people didn't want to believe Jeremiah because the future looked grim for 70 years. They wanted to believe Hananiah. They wanted the yoke of Babylon to be broken. They wanted the exiles to come home. But that was not the truth.

Read Jeremiah 14:14. Had God even spoken to the false prophets? _____

What had convinced them to speak? _____

True or false? The truth of false prophets scares me today. I see multitudes in churches believing their pastor when he says something false. I see multitudes looking on the Internet, believing what they read because, well, they like the guy who wrote it. What people today aren't doing is what is praised and acclaimed in scripture.

Read Acts 17:11. What did these people do? _____ How often? _____

What does scripture call them? _____

They examined the scriptures making sure what Paul told them was true! They listened to Paul, they wanted to believe, but they would not commit until they read the word of the Lord. They would not commit until the Spirit told them the truth. They examined the scriptures, not once a month, or sitting in church once a week, but daily. Do you know why I put so many scripture references in my studies? I want you to examine the scriptures – daily. I want you to see for yourself if what I am saying is true. Look at 1 John 4:1 in the margin. This is what the Lord wants us to do – test what we hear and see.

Beloved, do not believe every spirit, but test the spirits to see whether they are from God, because many false prophets have gone out into the world.

1 John 4:1

Look up Jesus' words in Matthew 24:11. In this scripture He is talking to His disciples about the last days. What will happen in the last days?

_____

There are true teachers and false teachers all around us – all around us.

Look at Peter's words in the margin. Many will follow false teachers because of their "sensuality." It is interesting the NASB uses this word. The word in the original Greek is *apoleia* (Strong's 684) and it means "loss of well-being. It is used of things to signify their ruin, or of persons signifying their spiritual and eternal perdition." Basically false teachers will lead the flock down a path of ruin because of their greed. Their greed does not necessarily have to mean monetary greed. It wasn't with the false teachers of the past. It can be greed to be recognized, to be popular, to be followed, and to be, in a way, worshiped for their words. Notice 2 Peter 2:1-3 says the false teachers deny the Master who "bought them." Jesus blood buys everyone, but it is up to you whether or not you choose to be purchased. Jesus death was known from the beginning, so if you deny God, you deny His salvation. And those who deny Him will be under God's judgment. 2 Peter 2:1-3 says their destruction is not asleep – meaning it is coming.

> But false prophets also arose among the people, just as there will also be false teachers among you, who will secretly introduce destructive heresies, even denying the Master who bought them, bringing swift destruction upon themselves. Many will follow their sensuality, and because of them the way of the truth will be maligned; and in their greed they will exploit you with false words; their judgment from long ago is not idle, and their destruction is not asleep.
>
> 2 Peter 2:1-3

Read Matthew 7:15. What do false prophets wear (symbolically)? _____

Turn to Revelation 13:11. This passage is describing the false prophet of Revelation 19:20. What two animals are used to describe this human beast? _____ and _____.

The dragon of Revelation is found in 12:9. Who is the dragon? _____ And what does the dragon do? _____

How does Jesus describe Satan in John 8:44? _____

False prophets look harmless (like a lamb). They sometimes disguise themselves as true followers of the Lamb of God. They claim to speak for God like the prophet Hananiah, but they are false, and there is deception in them. They speak like their father – Satan, the liar, the father of lies, and the dragon of Revelation.

Daniel was surrounded by false prophets and false teachers before he went into exile, and also after. Daniel was commanded to learn the ways of the Babylonians. Don't you think he learned about their false gods? Don't you think he had to walk a line between being supportive of his king and being loyal to his King? Daniel had to make a choice. What did he do?

Daniel trusted in his God . . .
Daniel 6:23

What will you do in the last days? Jesus has warned us many false prophets will appear. They will disguise themselves as heralds of good, but they will be following the dragon. Because of them the truth will be maligned. If you don't know the Truth (Jesus – John 14:6), you will not recognize falsehood. If you don't examine the word (the Truth – Jesus – John 1:1), then you will be unable to make a sound judgment. Look at Psalm 119:160 in the margin.

The sum of Your word is truth, and every one of Your righteous ordinances is everlasting.

Psalm 119:160

What is the truth?_____

Faithful friends, you can't just take one scripture and declare it the whole truth. The sum of the Word is the truth because Jesus is the entire Word! Let me say that again: Jesus is the entire Word!

Daniel wasn't swayed by false teaching. He grew up under the reign of Josiah who went back to God's laws. He knew God's ways, and he recognized those walking in falsehood. He studied the words of Jeremiah and knew their truth. He believed their truth, even though he went into exile . . . even though it seemed God had given up on the Jews . . . even though he had to leave his family . . . even though he probably became a eunuch . . . even though he was thrown into the lions' den . . .

Daniel trusted in his God . . .
Daniel 6:23

In the last days, when things get bad, and the beast of Daniel starts persecuting the Christians and the Jews (Daniel 7:25, Revelation 12:14-17) will you be like Daniel?

If you go into exile, will you believe? If your children die, will you trust? If you go hungry, will you continue to stand firm? Or will you fall away? Will you believe a lie? Will you turn to falsehood if that means you remain alive?

The beast is already among us. It is disguising itself like a lamb, but it speaks like a dragon. One day it will issue a mark. If you do not take it, you will not be able to buy or sell (Revelation 13:17).

Will you trust the mark? Or will you be like Daniel?

Daniel trusted in his God . . .
Daniel 6:23

Day Five – The Stage
Babylon

The beginning of his kingdom was Babel . . . in the land of Shinar . . . from that land he went forth into Assyria, and built Nineveh . . .

Genesis 10:10-11

In order to study Babylon, we have to go back to Genesis, because the beginnings of Babylon were started near the beginning. Take a look at Genesis 10:10-11 in the margin. After the flood, one of Noah's descendants started, not only the ancient city of Babel, but also the great city of Assyria – Nineveh. His name was Nimrod, and he was the son of Cush, the son of Ham, the son of Noah. Let's look at a brief snippet of Ham's life that may indicate what kind of people his descendants would be.

Read Genesis 9:20-27. Were Ham's actions honorable? _____

Ham's descendant Canaan was cursed by Noah. What is extremely interesting to me is that it was Ham that brought forth many of the archenemies of God: Canaan, Assyria, and yes, Babylon. The descendants of Ham's son Canaan settled in the land God called Abraham to inhabit (Genesis 12:4-7) and they were the people the Israelites were called to destroy (Numbers 13:2). Nimrod, Ham's grandson, started the ancient city of Babel, which would ultimately become the kingdom of Babylon. He also started Nineveh, which was the capital of Assyria, the empire that exiled the northern kingdom of Israel. Nineveh was also the wicked city where Jonah went to preach.

But back to Babel and the founding of what would be the territory of Babylon. Before you read this next passage, keep in mind that the flood had happened only about 100 years prior.

Read Genesis 11:1-9

In Genesis God told Adam and Eve to "fill the earth." Yet the people who where building the tower of Babel wanted to stay in one place. After the flood, the people had decided they needed to band together. They were defying God's express command. They wanted to build a tower that would "reach into heaven" and they wanted to "make a name for themselves." The tower of Babel was a tower of human pride and rebellion.[1]

Years later, Babylon became a kingdom. The city of Babylon itself is on the Euphrates River about 50 miles south of modern day Baghdad. Actually, in Daniel's day, the Euphrates River actually ran though the city. This will be very important when we study Daniel chapter five.

At the Battle of Carchemish where Nebuchadnezzar defeated Egypt and Assyria, he was the crown prince of Babylon. After this battle Nebuchadnezzar went to Judah and took Daniel and his friends back to Babylon. Nebuchadnezzar would have probably stayed around and advanced on more territory, but he got word that his father, Nabopolassar, had died – he was now king. He went home to claim the throne only a few months after the defeat of Egypt and Assyria.[2] In fact, Nebuchadnezzar may not have been too much older than Daniel in 605 BC. We know he ruled from 605 to 561 BC, which would be 43-year reign.[3]

We have been over many dates and names, so before we move forward, let's recap what we have learned.

Kings/Events	Dates
Josiah rules Israel	641-609 BC
Josiah dies at the hand of Pharaoh, Jehoahaz becomes king	609 BC
Jehoahaz exiled to Egypt, Jehoiakim becomes king	609 BC
Prince Nebuchadnezzar defeats Egypt and Assyria at Battle of Carchemish	605 BC
Daniel taken to Babylon, Jehoiakim becomes subject to Babylon	605 BC
Nebuchadnezzar returns to Judah, Jehoiakim dies Jehoiachin crowned but he surrenders Jerusalem to Babylon Many exiled (including Ezekiel). Nebuchadnezzar crowns Zedekiah king	598 BC
Nebuchadnezzar returns and destroys Judah Zedekiah and rest of population (other than the poorest of the land) taken to Babylon	586 BC

In Daniel's time, an eleven-mile wall surrounded Babylon encasing the suburbs and Nebuchadnezzar's palace. Babylon was famous for its Hanging Gardens, one of the seven wonders of the ancient world. Nebuchadnezzar would go down in history as being the best and greatest ruler of Babylon. Babylon had to have impressed the Jews and provided them with many economic activities, which was probably why many remained in Babylon even after they were allowed to return home after the 70-year exile.[4]

Babylon had many gods, but the main one was Marduk, otherwise known as Bel or Baal (meaning "lord"). Baal was believed to be the author of creation and ultimately became known as the lord of the heavens. Babylon's inhabitants also worshiped Ishtar who was known as the "Queen of Heaven." She was thought to have betrayed her lover Tammuz, who was the god of vegetation. As a result of the betrayal, Tammuz was thought to die each autumn.[5]

Before Judah was exiled by Nebuchadnezzar in 586 BC, Israel was exiled by Assyria in 722 BC. Let's remind ourselves of just why the nation of Israel was taken from their land.

Read 2 Kings 17:15-17. Whom did the Israelites serve? _____

They served Baal. They also made an Asherah, which was an object that provided a way to worship the mother of Baal.[6] To make matters worse, they made their children pass through the fire. The point? The Israelites were being affected by the surrounding nations for hundreds upon hundreds of years. They had ample time to repent; yet they chose not to. They rejected God's statutes and His laws. Now look at something else with me.

Turn to Ezekiel 8:14. Who were the women weeping for? _____

This vision came after King Jehoiachin, Ezekiel, and other Israelites had been deported (but before the destruction of Jerusalem in 586 BC). The people left behind in Jerusalem still hadn't learned. They were weeping for Tammuz, Ishtar's lover. They were not turning back to God.

The Babylon we will read about in Daniel will fall, but it will rise again in the shape of another kingdom, then another, and finally another. This final system will become the beast of Revelation and will be the biggest persecutor of Jews and Christians the world has ever seen (Revelation 6:10, 12:17). We need to take a lesson from the people we read about in the scriptures. God warned them, yet they did not take heed. God sent prophets to plead with them, but the people did not listen. God sent them great men as examples, but they did not take notice.

> Blessed is he who reads and those who hear the words of the prophecy, and heed the things which are written in it; for the time is near.
>
> Revelation 1:3

I want you to notice something with me. Look at Revelation 1:3 in the margin. There were many in Judah who knew Josiah's heart and knew the laws of God. There were many people in Judah who heard Jeremiah's warnings. They heard them, but they did not heed them. How can you be blessed? According to Revelation 1:3, you have to heed the words, not just see or hear. You have to heed, because only if you heed God's words are you truly with Him.

Babylon is seductive, and with the spirit of tolerance we have in today's world, if anyone has doubts of Babylon's intentions, they will sweep them under the rug in order to appear amicable. But Jesus was offensive. He urged people to turn from their sin. He spoke the words of truth. He walked the narrow road. Let's take a look.

Read John 8:3-11. What did Jesus tell the woman to do? _____(verse 11)

Read John 5:39. You can search the Words, but what do the scriptures declare?_____
And what is He (John 14:6)? _____

Read Matthew 7:14. What does the narrow road lead to? _____

Jesus loved everyone, but He didn't pat people on the heads and say, "No problem. Keep on sinning." That is the way of destruction. He told people to turn from their sin. There is a narrow road leading to the life (Jesus) and that is for someone who is truly trying to follow Him, which means turning from everything evil. Let me say that another way.

In order to follow Jesus, you must turn from Babylon.

Babylon is already among us. It is everything against God. Babylon shakes its fist at God. It defies Him. We are all living in a type of Babylon. If we want to remain in Him, we have to recognize Babylon for what it is and what it can do to our lives. Let's search scripture to see if we know of a way to fight Babylon.

Read Hosea 4:6. How are the people destroyed? _____

You are destroyed if you fail to have knowledge. What knowledge are we talking about?

Drop back to Hosea 4:1. What knowledge are we talking about? _____

Without the knowledge of God, you will be destroyed by the false system of Babylon. And how do we get the knowledge of God? Look at Acts 17:11 in the margin.

To be nobleminded, you have to examine the scriptures, because in them is the knowledge of God.

Babylon is anti-God. It may be seductive, but it is against the Almighty, and if you side with it, you are siding against the Savior.

> Now these were more nobleminded than those in Thessalonica, for they received the word with great eagerness, examining the Scriptures daily to see whether these things were so.
>
> Acts 17:11

If you fail to be resolved, like Daniel, you could fall prey to its charms. If you fail to seek understanding in the Word, you could fall prey to Babylon's false truth. If you fail to trust God despite Babylon's persecutions, you could fall away (Matthew 24:10-11).

Even when surrounded by the falsehood of Babylon, even when surrounded by their gods, even when immersed by its sedeuction . . .

Daniel prayed to the Lord his God and confessed . . .
Daniel 9:4

What will you do when the beast rises up? Will you be resolved? Or will you falter?

Will you seek to understand? Or will you accept Babylon's lies?

Will you continue to trust? No matter Babylon's persecutions? Or will you do anything to escape the sword?

Daniel prayed to the Lord his God and confessed . . .
Daniel 9:4

1 Butler, Trent C. et al.,eds. *Holman Illustrated Bible Dictionary* (Nashville, Tennessee: Holman Bible Publishers, 2003), 155.
2 Butler, Trent C. et al.,eds. *Holman Illustrated Bible Dictionary* (Nashville, Tennessee: Holman Bible Publishers, 2003), 157. *One-Volume Illustrated Edition of Zondervan Bible Commentary* with General Editor F. F. Bruce (Zondervan, 2008), 386.
3 Hinnant, Greg. *Daniel Notes* (Lake Mary, Florida: Creation House Press, 2003), 1. Butler, Trent C. et al.,eds. *Holman Illustrated Bible Dictionary* (Nashville, Tennessee: Holman Bible Publishers, 2003), 159.
4 Butler, Trent C. et al.,eds. *Holman Illustrated Bible Dictionary* (Nashville, Tennessee: Holman Bible Publishers, 2003), 158-159. *One-Volume Illustrated Edition of Zondervan Bible Commentary* with General Editor F. F. Bruce (Zondervan, 2008), 449.
5 Butler, Trent C. et al.,eds. *Holman Illustrated Bible Dictionary* (Nashville, Tennessee: Holman Bible Publishers, 2003), 160, 843, 1076, 1556.
6 Butler, Trent C. et al.,eds. *Holman Illustrated Bible Dictionary* (Nashville, Tennessee: Holman Bible Publishers, 2003), 125.

Week Two

> He brought them to the land of Shinar, to the house of his god, and he brought the vessels into the treasury of his god.
>
> Daniel 1:2b

Day One – Chapter One
The Vessels

Read Daniel 1:1-2

It is 605 BC and Nebuchadnezzar comes to Judah in order to lay siege to Jerusalem because King Jehoiakim is in allegiance with Egypt. King Jehoiakim surrenders. He becomes the servant of Babylon, but that is not all. Nebuchadnezzar takes some of the treasures of God's house back to Babylon. This was not unorthodox. It was customary for a conquering nation to do so. The treasures were a tribute to the conquering nation's gods.[1]

I want you to think about this both from the perspective of Babylon, and from the perspective of the Israelites. God's vessels were taken – they were put into the treasury of a false god. What was Babylon saying? We defeated you; therefore, our god is better than your God. Our god is **higher** and **greater** and **mightier** than yours. What did this say to the Israelites? Those who knew God would have perhaps thought that He had left them or rejected them. They may have thought God hated them. The morale in the city would have been extremely low. The Babylonians knew exactly what they were doing when they took some of God's vessels. It was a show of strength.

Read Exodus 30:22-29. After the vessels were consecrated, what did they become?

_____

The vessels were holy. They were set apart for God's service. Exodus 30:29 says, "whatever touches them shall be holy." This almost sounds like if you touched them, you would be made holy, but the better translation is probably whatever touches them has to be holy – or set apart. As in, you had to be consecrated to God – like the priests – in order to touch the holy vessels in the temple. That is why there were strict rules about just who got to help out in the temple. Let me prove it to you.

Turn to Numbers 4:5. Who could go into the tabernacle and touch the holy objects? _____ In Numbers 4:12, did this include the vessels (utensils)?_____

Now look at Numbers 4:15. What would happen if others touched them? _____
What would happen if they looked at them (Numbers 4:20)? _____

The Levites were one of the tribes of Israel and they were the tribe in charge of God's tabernacle. Levi had three sons: Gershon, Kohath, and Marari (Exodus 6:16). These three families had different duties in and around the tabernacle. Aaron was a grandson of Kohath. Only Aaron's sons could enter the tabernacle and touch the holy things, but the line of Kohath were the ones allotted to carry the holy objects once they had been covered by Aaron's descendants. But even the line of Kohath (besides the line of Aaron) could not directly touch or look at the holy objects or they would die. Why? The holy vessels were reflecting God's brilliance. The vessels in the tabernacle were also foreshadowing another tabernacle.

Read Exodus 33:20. What happens when you see God? _____

Read John 2:19. What temple is Jesus talking about? _____

Think about that for a minute. No one could touch them – or even look at them, yet the Babylonians did – and Nebuchadnezzar took them away and brought them "to the house of his god." Think about the message this sent to the people of Israel. Think about what message this sent to the Babylonians. Their god had conquered. Their god had triumphed. Their god was superior.

Also think about this: every object in the temple was a representation of Jesus' sacrifice. That is why those objects were so holy, and that is why you had to be consecrated and deemed holy before you touched them. They were foreshadowing the true temple that would be destroyed for the sake of the entire world.

Eventually, everything was taken. # Read 2 Kings 25:13-17

The entire temple was taken to Babylon – the entire temple. That which represented Jesus – God Himself – was taken to Babylon and placed in a temple of a false god.

Think about how serious the situation had become for God to allow this. God had warned them but they had not listened (2 Kings 20:12-21, Jeremiah 27).

Israel had left Him. They had played the harlot with other gods. They had put their sons into the fire (2 Kings 21:2-9). The temple is taken away – not a piece of it – but eventually all of it. And so were the people. The first wave left with Daniel, but eventually Judah as a whole was exiled (2 Kings 25:11).

There is a lesson here.

Even though the people were taken into exile, God was right there with them.

Isn't that so like our God? He wants to be with us despite the mess we have gotten ourselves wrapped up in. No matter what He has to do, or where He has to go – He will go with us. He will even go all the way to Babylon.

Let's see what eventually happens.

Read Ezra 1:1-11

What prophet's name do we see in Ezra 1:1? _____

What did Cyrus command in verse 3? _____

In what year did this happen (based on the king)? _____

What else did the exiles take in verse 4? _____

Now turn to Daniel 10:1. Did Daniel see this happen?_____

All the treasure of the house of the Lord returned to Judah. The exiles who left Babylon carried God's house with them! Cyrus even commanded his citizens to be favorably inclined to the exiles. In other words, foreigners gave the Israelites silver, gold, goods, cattle, and freewill offerings to take to the house of God in Jerusalem. Cyrus was a leader of the Medo-Persian Empire that conquered Babylon (we will learn about this later in our study) in 539 BC.[2] He came to power about 23 years after Nebuchadnezzar's rule came to an end.

Now look at Isaiah 44:28 in the margin. Isaiah prophesied between 760 and 673 BC, at least 134 years before Cyrus issued the decree for the exiles to return to Judah.[3] That means, Cyrus hadn't even been born when Isaiah wrote that prophecy. The historian Josephus reported that Cyrus read the prophecy in Isaiah and was so impressed that he was eager to fulfill God's words.[4] We don't know if that is true, but it is interesting to think about.

> "It is I who says of Cyrus, 'He is My shepherd! And he will perform all My desire.' And he declares of Jerusalem, 'She will be built,' and of the temple, 'Your foundation will be laid.'"
>
> Isaiah 44:28

I want you to consider for a minute what this meant to the exiles. They were going home. And they were taking the temple of their God with them. Perhaps they were thinking – God didn't desert us – look at what He has done! Not only that, but they were able to transport Him home. Daniel didn't go with the exiles. By this time he was over 80 years old and he was in the service of Cyrus. But can you imagine how Daniel was feeling? He had to be ecstatic. He also had to feel somewhat honored. He was seeing the prophecies he had read about in Jeremiah and Isaiah come to pass right before his eyes.

We have yet to move past the first few verses of Daniel, but I want you to think about something with me. A good portion of Daniel is about end-time events. Let me prove it to you.

Read Daniel 12:4. For what appointed time did the book of Daniel's visions pertain?
_____

As we continue to study Daniel, we will soon see that we too will be seeing prophecy come to fruition. We are walking in a time just like Daniel. We are walking into the time of the end. And here is the other thing we need to come to grips with: We will also be walking into the spirit of Babylon according to Revelation 17. Let's look at a few verses that tell us what will happen to the saints in the last days.

Read Matthew 24:9. What will they deliver us to? _____ What else will happen? _____ What will the nations think of us? _____

According to Daniel 7:25 what will the Antichrist do to the saints? _____
How long will this last? _____

But as we have learned today. God goes with us into Babylon. He will not leave us. No matter if we are taken out of our homelands (Daniel 1:3), or our heads are threatened (Daniel 2:13), or we are thrown into a fiery furnace (Daniel 3:20) – our God goes with us. Let's close by looking at some verses that emphasize this.

Read Matthew 28:20. How long will Jesus be with us? _____

Look at Isaiah 43:2-3 in the margin. If we are with God, will life overwhelm us? _____

How often is God with us according to Psalm 73:23? _____

No matter what happens in Babylon, God will be with us. More on Babylon tomorrow.

"When you pass through the waters, I will be with you; and through the rivers, they will not overflow you. When you walk through the fire, you will not be scorched, nor will the flame burn you. For I am the Lord your God, the Holy One of Israel, your Savior."

Isaiah 43:2-3a

1 One-Volume Illustrated Edition of Zondervan Bible Commentary with General Editor F. F. Bruce (Zondervan, 2008), 883.
2 Rose Book of Bible Charts, Maps and Time Lines (Torrance, California: Rose Publishing, 2005), 65.
3 Rose Book of Bible Charts, Maps and Time Lines (Torrance, California: Rose Publishing, 2005), 65.
4 English Standard Version Study Bible (Wheaton, Illinois: Crossway, 2008), 1322.

Youths in whom was no defect, who were good-looking, showing intelligence in every branch of wisdom . . .

Yesterday we studied the vessels that were carried to Babylon, but that is not all that Nebuchadnezzar took. He carried away something else very dear to God's heart – he carried away Daniel.

Read Daniel 1:3-7

Daniel 1:4

Ashpenaz, chief of the officials (eunuchs) is ordered to take some beautiful unblemished youths. They were to have noble blood running through their veins, and they were supposed to be intelligent and discerning. Daniel met the cut. So did his three friends Hananiah, Mishael, and Azariah.

It was customary for a conquering nation to adopt some of the higher-class citizens into the court of the conqueror. This would indoctrinate the royal line into the culture of the foreign land. It would also serve to leave the conquered nation without rising royalty, which would in turn make the nation more subservient to its conqueror. God had warned them this would happen.

Read 2 Kings 20:12-18. What did God tell Hezekiah in verse 18?_____

We don't know the heritage of Daniel or his three friends, but they were all of noble blood. We don't know if they were descendants of Hezekiah but it seems fairly likely. Rest assured, they were important youths. They were taken away from their family and their land. Pause here and really think about that. They were stripped of stability and love. Can you imagine when the youths were chosen? Did Daniel's parents fall to their knees and beg the Babylonian King not to take him? Or did they keep their mouths shut, knowing that if Daniel did get chosen, he would enter the king's service and be treated fairly? What were they thinking? What was the scene like?

If you recall from a previous lesson, after Nebuchadnezzar's battle with Egypt and Assyria in 605, he got word that his father had died. Nebuchadnezzar was the crown prince during the battle. At this point, he could have been king even though he had not yet traveled back to Babylon. His reign was approximately forty-four years. Nebuchadnezzar was born in approximately 630 BC, which would make him approximately 25 when he came to power.[1] He may not have been much older than Daniel. When a new king comes to power, normally a lot of the cabinet members get replaced. After all, would you want to use the same men your father used to make decisions? Let's see what happened in the history of Israel.

Read 1 Kings 12:6-11. Did he consult with his father's advisors? _____ Did he listen to them? _____ Who did he listen to? _____

This may have been another reason Nebuchadnezzar took some intelligent noble youths back to Babylon. He wanted to train his new counselors himself.

Look again at Daniel 1:4. When Nebuchadnezzar specified "youths," what were the first two qualities they had to have? They had to have _____ and they had to be _____.

Ah, Babylon. The king didn't want to look at some unattractive intelligent people, or people with defects (blemishes). I mean, he was the king, and it was Babylon. Only the best and the prettiest were welcome. Let's see what scripture says about the end time system of Babylon.

Read Revelation 17:4-5. Describe the woman._____

Read Revelation 18:9. What did the nations commit with her? _____

Babylon is a hub of sensuality and immorality. She seduces those in the earth to commit acts of immorality with her. That is exactly what Nebuchadnezzar wanted to do with Daniel and his friends. He wanted to seduce them into converting to the ways and customs of the "better and mightier" Babylon. He ordered that Daniel and his friends be taught in the "literature and the language" of Babylon. This would mean that they would be educated in Babylonian gods and indoctrinated into a pagan culture.

Not only were they to be educated, they were also to be fed from the king's choice food and wine. This was the best food and wine in the province of Babylon. It was what the king ate and drank.

Nebuchadnezzar wanted to erase all history and culture from these exiles. Their people were gone, their home was gone, their things were gone, and even their names were changed. Names were very important in middle-eastern culture. When you were named, your name declared something about you, something about the circumstances you were born into, or something that your parents wanted you to become. Names not only had a meaning (like ours), names were the meaning. For example, my name is Nicole but it means "victory." In the middle-eastern culture, you wouldn't call me Nicole, you would literally call me "Victory." Sometimes two words were put together to form a name, sometime the name was a derivative of a particular word, but if you knew the language and you knew a person's name, you wouldn't have to ask them its meaning because you would be saying the meaning when you said their name. Here is an obvious example.

Turn to Matthew 1:21. What were they to call Him? _____ Why? _____

Jesus is the Greek word for the Hebrew word Yeshua, and what does Yeshua mean? You guessed it – salvation or God saves. As in, Jesus' name was the word salvation! When Mary called to Him, she was calling to *Salvation*, when the people bowed at His feet, they were bowing at the feet of *Salvation*, when the Pharisees plotted to kill him, they were plotting to kill *Salvation*. It was and always will be His name.

When you know this, you should realize that Jesus' name is written all over the Old Testament. Look at Isaiah 12:2 in the margin. Now doesn't that just knock your socks off? God is Yeshua (Jesus). God is salvation (Yeshua – Jesus). I mean, you can't get any clearer that that. Jesus name is all over the Old Testament because the word "salvation" is all over the Old Testament and He is **Salvation** – it is His **NAME.**

Let's look at Daniel and his friends' names one at a time.

Daniel

Read Genesis 30:6 in the margin. Rachel named him Dan. What do you think Dan means?_____

> Behold, God is my salvation *[Yeshua – Jesus]*, I will trust and not be afraid; for the Lord God is my strength and my song, and He has become my salvation *[Yeshua – Jesus]*.
>
> Isaiah 12:2

> Rachel said, "God has judged me innocent . . ." so she named him Dan.
>
> Genesis 30:6 NCV

If you said "judge" you would be right. Dan means judge, which is part of Daniel's name. But there is another word in Daniel's name. It is *El.*

What does "El" mean (see Genesis 17:1 in margin)? _____

> "I am God *[El]* Almighty; walk before Me, and be blameless."
>
> Genesis 17:1b

El can mean any god but it is often used in scripture to name God Himself. Daniel's name can be interpreted "judge of God" or "God's judge."[2] Remember that I said you grew into your name? What would become of Daniel? His name became his legacy, did it not? He was taken to Babylon and became "God's judge" in a foreign land. He interpreted dreams for kings, and declared prophecy for his time and the time of the end.

Hananiah

Hananiah is better translated from the Hebrew as Chananyah. Let's see what it means. Look at Psalm 102:13 in the margin.

> "You will arise and have pity on Zion; it is the time to favor *[Chanan]* her.
>
> Psalm 102:13 ESV

What does Chanan – part of Hananiah's name mean?

_____

Look at the last part of Hananiah's or Chananyah's name. It is made up of three letters: *Yah.* Does that sound familiar to you? It is the shortened form of Yahweh, or the sacred name of God. There is a variation of this word, and it is one you might be familiar with – Jehovah.

So Hananiah's name means "Yah has favored."[3] Now think about what happened to Hananiah. He was chosen to be in the king's service. Do you think God had shown him favor?

Mishael

Do you recognize a word in Mishael's name that we have just discussed? If you said, *El* you got it right. "God" is also in Mishael's name. The beginning of Mishael's name is made up of a few pronouns linked together. The best translation of Mishael's name is "who is what God is?"[4] Let's think about this for a minute. Mishael found himself in Babylon and there were a few tests that he had to endure in order to stand up for God. God came through miraculously in both circumstances. Mishael would learn the answer to that question, "Who is what God is?" The answer would be, "No one is like Him!"

Azariah

If you are tracking the Hebrew, you may recognize something else here. Just like Hananiah is better translated Chananyah, so is Azariah better translated as Azaryah. There is the same ending here. Again, the "iah" or the "yah" in Azariah's name is the shortened form of the sacred name of God – Yahweh. Look at Isaiah 41:10 to see what *azar* means.

What does "azar" mean? _____

So Azariah's name means "Yah has helped."[5] And help God did, both at the time of the exile by choosing Azariah to be in the royal court, and at the time of testing which we will read about in chapters one and three.

> "Do not fear, for I am with you; do not anxiously look about you, for I am your God. I will strengthen you, surely I will help [azar] you, surely I will uphold you with My righteous right hand."
>
> Isaiah 41:10

What is very important here is the fact that God is in the names of the Jewish exiles. Whenever they heard their names they heard *El* or *Yah*.

Nebuchadnezzar wanted to indoctrinate them with the god's of Babylon. He couldn't have their names bearing praises to the God of Israel, after all Nebuchadnezzar's "gods" had conquered the God of Judah. No, he had to strip even their names from Daniel, Hananiah, Mishael, and Azariah. Look at who they became.[6]

Daniel or *God's judge*   **Belteshazzar** or *Bel will protect*
Hananiah or *Yah has favored*   **Shadrach** or *Inspired of Aku*
Mishael or *Who is what God is*   **Meshach** or *Belonging to Aku*
Azariah or *Yah has helped*   **Abednego** *Servant of Nebu*

Now, when their names were called, they heard the names of Babylonian gods. They were stripped of everything – even their names. They were all alone, in a foreign land, and they didn't even have their names.

More to come tomorrow.

1 http://www.biography.com/people/nebuchadnezzar-ii-9421018 (this was Neb birth year)
http://www.keyway.ca/htm2002/nebuch.htm
2 *The New Strong's Expanded Exhaustive Concordance of the Bible*. Strong, James. Published in Nashville, Tennessee by Thomas Nelson Publishers, 2010. Hebrew #1840.

3 *The New Strong's Expanded Exhaustive Concordance of the Bible*. Strong, James. Published in Nashville, Tennessee by Thomas Nelson Publishers, 2010. Hebrew #2608.

4 *The New Strong's Expanded Exhaustive Concordance of the Bible*. Strong, James. Published in Nashville, Tennessee by Thomas Nelson Publishers, 2010. Hebrew #4332.

5 *The New Strong's Expanded Exhaustive Concordance of the Bible*. Strong, James. Published in Nashville, Tennessee by Thomas Nelson Publishers, 2010. Hebrew #5838.

6 *The Complete Word Study Old Testament* with Warren Baker, D.R.E. as the General Editor (Chattanooga, Tennessee by AMG Publishers, 1994), 2096.

Day Three – Chapter One
The Decision

> But Daniel made up his mind that he would not defile himself . . .
>
> Daniel 1:8

We left off yesterday looking at Daniel and his friends' names. Nebuchadnezzar gave them a name change, knowing full well that their original names honored the Hebrew God Yahweh. He wanted to immerse Daniel and his friends into the culture, literature, language, and customs of Babylon; he also wanted them to convert to his gods.

Daniel and his friends had another idea.

Read Daniel 1:8-21

Daniel decided that he didn't want to defile himself. He made a decision on day one that he would not become integrated into the system of Babylon. He would retain his identity. He would stand firm for his God. Daniel understood what Jesus declared before His crucifixion in prayer to His Father.

Read John 17:14 -17. Are we of the world? _____ But did Jesus call us out of the world? _____ How are we sanctified? _____

We are not of the world, but in the same vein, Jesus did not call us out of the world. In order to shine our light to Babylon, we can't hide in a corner or bury our heads in the sand. We need to be sanctified. That word means to "make holy" or to be "set apart." Do you remember those vessels that were taken to Babylon and placed in the treasury of Nebuchadnezzar's gods? They were sanctified, but they were hidden. Daniel knew he could not hide. He had to be loyal to the king of Babylon, but he also had to be loyal to his King. Daniel and his friends could have become Babylonianized. They could have thrown their hands up in the air and said, "Oh well, we have to become Babylonians." But they did not; they chose to be like those vessels – they chose to be "set apart." And the way they were set apart? They were sanctified by His Word – they obeyed His laws. One of those laws is found in some Old Testament scriptures that Daniel and his friends would have been very familiar with. It is found in Leviticus 11 and Deuteronomy 14. God gave specific laws about the meat the Israelites could and could not eat. Some animals were declared "clean" and others were declared "unclean." Take a look at Leviticus 11:24 in the margin.

> "By these, moreover, you will be made unclean: whoever touches their carcasses becomes unclean until evening."
>
> Leviticus 11:24

At this point in time, Daniel and his friends were under strict orders to eat the choice food the king ate. Daniel and his friends had not yet been presented to the king or gained any recognition of being "set apart." They were served what they were served. Daniel knew the dangers of being

Babylonianized. He knew the seduction of the pagan land in which he found himself and he recognized the fact that if he didn't do something about it, he was in trouble.

He had no parents. He had no land. He had no name. He only had his integrity. So Daniel "made up his mind that he would not defile himself with the king's choice food or with the wine which he drank."

Let's pause here to say this: all meat was not considered "unclean." As a matter of fact, in a later chapter of Daniel, it hints to the fact that this resolution to refrain from eating Babylonian meat was not a forever commitment.

Read Daniel 10:1-3. What did Daniel say he refrained from here? _____
In what year? _____

If Daniel refrained from meat and wine and choice food in Daniel 10:2-3, then at some point in the past he had once again partaken of meat, wine, and choice food. Had Daniel broken his vow? No. There are two explanations as to why Daniel turned from his initial commitment. Let's explore these two options.

First, look up Psalm 141:4. What does this say about eating?_____

Now isn't that interesting. This Psalm tells us not to eat of the delicacies of those who do iniquity. This probably means both physical eating and the "eating" of their ideology. We know that Daniel would put Babylon in the "those who do iniquity" category. But if you notice in Daniel 10, he had been eating meat and drinking wine in the third year of Cyrus king of Persia. Cyrus is the king who conquered Babylon in 539 BC. In his first year as king, Cyrus let the Jews return to Israel (Ezra 1:1). This would have put Cyrus in the "good" category, don't you think? Daniel knew his scripture. He probably knew this Psalm. He may have tied his food choice to the king on the throne. In the last days, we need to be very aware of this warning.

Read Revelation 18:2-3. What have the nations done with Babylon?_____

This means that they are buying into her falsehood and immorality. As God's people in the last days, we need to understand this. We cannot take one sip of Babylon's wine and retain our commitment to God. She will seduce us into a relationship if we allow her to do so.

Secondly, the Levitical law restricted some meat, like I said previously, but it in no way restricted wine. In fact, God had indicated that wine was for happiness and celebration. Look at Deuteronomy 14:26 in the margin.

> "You may spend the money for whatever your heart desires: for oxen, or sheep, or wine, or strong drink, or whatever your heart desires; and there you shall eat in the presence of the Lord your God and rejoice, you and your household."
>
> Deuteronomy 14:26

Some scholars believe that Daniel knew the wine would have been offered to some Babylonian gods, but if that is the case, so would some grains and also some vegetables. Obviously, Daniel ate vegetables so this is not a satisfactory answer.[1]

What is the best answer? Like I said previously, Daniel knew if he let down his guard while he was learning the Babylonian system, then he was in severe danger of falling prey to it. Would it have been wrong for Daniel to eat of the clean meat and drink the king's wine? No, but it wouldn't have been wise, not at this point in Daniel's life. He was young, and he knew through his studies he would be immersed in the culture and seductions of Babylon. He knew the Psalm that said to refrain from eating the delicacies of those who do iniquity. He understood he and his friends were in serious trouble if they "gave in" to Babylon. Take the following thought to heart:

Daniel wanted to be set apart, but he also needed a reminder that he was set apart.

Take a lesson in this: not all things are wrong – but not all things are wise. Daniel was wise. He knew the dangers Babylon would hold, and he wanted to prepare himself. So did his friends. They needed a reminder everyday that they were the lights of the One true God. Their food was a reminder of this. They were Israelites. They were Jews. They followed Yahwah. Not Bel. Not Aku. Not Nebo. They were Daniel, and Hananiah, and Mishael, and Azariah. They were not Belteshazzar, and Shadrach, and Meshach, and Abed-nego. They worshiped El the God of Israel. They worshiped Yah.

Do you see it? They were in Babylon, but they were not of Babylon. They new God's law, but they also knew the dangers of being seduced by the enemy. Daniel 10:2 confirms that meat and wine weren't "wrong." But at the time, it was wrong for Daniel, Hananiah, Mishael, and Azariah. They were young and impressionable and they knew it. They were wise. Know this:

Some things may not be wrong; but some things may not be wise.

It was not that they were unconcerned about the Levitical law and God's rules about the clean and unclean – of course they were. In fact, that law is what first prompted their concern. They did not want to touch, or have any of their foods touch something unclean, but not all meat was wrong for them to eat. They did not want to be tempted in any way to conform to the luxuries of Babylon.

You are in your own Babylon. The world itself is a form of it. Where in your life are you making unwise choices? Remember, all things are not wrong, but all things are not wise. There are times in your life where you should walk away from something like Daniel did in Daniel chapter one. In other seasons of your life you may be able to allow those same things in (when you are strong in your faith) like in Daniel chapter 10. Your past will influence whether certain things are wise or unwise. You present circumstances will determine whether certain things are wise or unwise. And your future hope will determine whether certain things are wise or unwise. Look at Ephesians 5:15-16 in the margin.

Therefore be careful how you walk, not as unwise men but as wise, making the most of your time, because the days are evil.

Ephesians 5:15-16

Why should we walk as wise men? _____

Because, essentially, we are all walking in Babylon.   Be wise.

Let's get back to Daniel. Daniel was resolved not to eat the choice food, but he still had to pass that by Ashpenaz, the commander of the officials, the one who had chosen him for service in Babylon.

Read Daniel 1:9. Did Ashpenaz like Daniel? _____

Read Daniel 1:10. But what and who did Ashpenaz fear?_____

Ashpenaz feared for his head. He was under orders to feed these youths and if some of them looked haggard, then his head would roll.

Read Daniel 1:11. This was not Ashpenaz, who was the "commander." Who was this? _____

The first time Daniel asked, he was denied. But Daniel didn't stop. He knew what he had to do. Instead of pleading with Ashpenaz, he inquired of the man Ashpenaz had put in charge of them – the one who was actually bringing them the food. Sometimes when we get an answer that is contrary to what we want we throw up our hands and give up. But sometimes, it is just not the person we need to see about the problem. Sometimes, the way God works is not the way we expect for Him to work. Sometimes He chooses people we wouldn't think He would choose. Yes, it would have been easier if Ashpenaz had agreed, but he wasn't really needed. Daniel went to the one who would truly be serving them, the one that had been put in charge of them.

What did Daniel tell him in Daniel 1:12-14? _____

This person listened to Daniel and gave Daniel what he requested. What prompted him to do so? I mean, his commander Ashpenaz was unwilling to risk his head. Why was this man? Did this man see something in Daniel that convinced him? We can't be sure, but it is interesting to think about. This person would see Daniel day in and day out. Perhaps he though if the situation looked grim, he would break his commitment. But he did not. He gave Daniel ten days.

Many translations of scripture use the word "vegetables" for what Daniel requested to eat. The King James Version of scripture translates the Hebrew word correctly as "pulse." Pulse is a term that is used to describe anything that is sewn. This would have probably included fruits and grains as well as vegetables.

Daniel and his friends had ten days, and at the end of the ten days "their appearance seemed better and they were fatter than all the youths who had been eating the king's choice food." God blessed their faithfulness so that the overseer "continued to withhold their choice food." Not only that, but God gave them "knowledge and intelligence in every branch of literature and wisdom; Daniel even understood all kinds of visions and dreams."

So what happened after the three years of training?

Read Daniel 1:19. Who stood out to the king? _____

Read Daniel 1:20. How much better than others did the king find them? _____

There was no one like Daniel, Hananiah, Mishael, and Azariah. They entered the king's personal service. Nebuchadnezzar did not find anyone else that matched their wisdom in all of his realm.

The servants of the One true God stood out. Look at Daniel 12:3 in the margin.   Daniel and his friends shone like the stars.

This was one of Israel's darkest days. Daniel and his friends were taken away from their homes, and their temple was eventually destroyed; yet God reserved some of His faithful ones to shine like the stars. There is a lesson here:

Even in the darkest day, God will raise up those who will shine for Him. The brightest of lights are reserved for the darkest of days.[2]

When the end times begin, we need to be resolved, like Daniel, and we need to be wise. We cannot fall prey to the Babylonian system. We cannot be seduced by its charms. We need to pray for "wisdom and understanding" so that we can "lead many to righteousness."

"Those who have insight will shine brightly like the brightness of the expanse of heaven, and those who lead the many to righteousness, like the stars forever and ever."

Daniel 12:3

1 *English Standard Version Study Bible* (Wheaton, Illinois: Crossway, 2008), 1587.
2 Hinnant, Greg. *Daniel Notes* (Lake Mary, Florida: Creation House Press, 2003), 5.

Day Four – Chapter One
Wisdom

The fear of the Lord is the beginning of knowledge; fools despise wisdom and instruction.

Proverbs 1:7

In yesterday's lesson we said that some things aren't wrong, but they are unwise. We also said that in one of Israel's darkest hours, God raised up individuals to shine for Him. I don't think we are done with the discussion, because we are living in dark times right now. We want to be God's light to Babylon, just like Daniel, Hananiah, Mishael, and Azariah. We want to be known as those who worship Yahweh and do not compromise His Word. Look at Proverbs 1:7 in the margin. If you stand in fear of God – if you revere Him and His laws – this is the beginning of wisdom. If you fear God, you will listen to Him.

Let's look at some stories in scripture. The first one is about David, who is called "the man after God's own heart" (Acts 13:22).

Read 1 Chronicles 21:1-7. What did David do? _____

Did God approve? _____ Who told David not to do this? _____

This is an incredible story to me. David, a man after God's own heart, ordered Joab to count the people. Now, in and of itself, a census is not wrong to do. God told Moses to take a census of Israel's fighting men in Numbers 1:1-54. David was just doing the same. But Joab was not a man after God's own heart. He was the commander of David's army and had done great evil. Joab killed David's ally for the sake of vengeance (2 Samuel 3:27). When David replaced Joab with another commander, Joab murdered his replacement (2 Samuel 20:10). Joab wasn't a wise man, according to Proverbs 1:7. Joab didn't really fear the Lord. David did. Although David made some mistakes, he always repented and turned back to the right path. Let's get back to the census. Counting people isn't wrong, so what is happening here?

There are few ways to look at this. First, what prompted David to take a census? God didn't prompt him. Could it have been pride?[1] Did David want to see how strong he was? Some scholars think so. There is something else we need to consider as well.[1]

Read Exodus 30:12. What was supposed to be done at a census? _____What would break out if this did not happen?_____

Now Read 1 Chronicles 21:14. What happened as a result of the census? _____

David was probably prideful, but he also disobeyed the law of the Lord. But here is something interesting to note: Joab warned him. Joab said to David, "Why does my lord seek this thing? Why should he be a cause of guilt to Israel?" Something about this census wasn't quite right, and Joab knew it. Although Joab didn't fear the Lord, the Lord used him to warn David, just like God used Pharaoh Neco to warn Josiah to turn back from his pursuit (2 Chronicles 35:20-24). Look at the two verses from Proverbs in the margin.

The first step to knowledge is the fear of the Lord. But to be wise the rest of your days, you must listen to counsel. If you trust in your own heart, you can be foolish. If you walk wisely, you will be delivered. How can we apply this to David? He was walking the path of his own heart. He wanted to see how powerful his nation had become. When Joab warned him, he brushed the counsel aside instead of taking a step back and really thinking about what he was doing and why he was doing it. Don't rush into something others have warned you about. You need to sit back and search your heart to see if what you are doing is right.

> Listen to counsel and accept discipline, that you may be wise the rest of your days.
>
> Proverbs 19:20

> He who trusts in his own heart is a fool, but he who walks wisely will be delivered.
>
> Proverbs 28:26

Read Daniel 1:8. Who made up his mind? _____

Here is something I want you to take to heart. It never says anything about Hananiah, Mishael, or Azariah being resolved – it only speaks about Daniel's resolve. It never says anything about Hananiah, Mishael, or Azariah talking to Ashpenaz or the person overseeing the delivery of food. Did Daniel give his friends wise council? If that is the case, they were wise enough to take it. Surround yourself with people who fear God, and the advice you receive will be sweeter than the advice of many counselors you could retain. A wise friend's advice may not always be the correct path for you, but you need to listen and then seek the Lord for His will in your life.

That being said, I want you to read another story I find extremely disturbing.

Read 1 Kings 13:1-32

Does anyone else feel as horrified as I do?

Look at verse 18 again. What did the second "prophet" do to the first? _____

He lied. He claimed to be a true prophet, but he was false. He claimed that an angel had spoken with him, but an angel had done no such thing. The first prophet had been told by the Lord not to eat or drink there, but the first prophet listened to the second, and it cost him his life. This is the very reason false prophets are so dangerous. They claim to speak for the Lord, and if you believe them, it could cost you your life. We need to know with whom we are speaking before we turn a blind eye to God's express command for our life. We have to be wise, examining what our next step should be and not be convinced by someone who is false. The first prophet didn't take the time to seek the Lord on the matter, he just blindly followed the second. This was where he was wrong. Remember the people of Berea in Acts 17? They heard what Paul was saying, but they still sought the truth in God's Word. They "examined the scriptures daily." They sought the Lord.

So what should we do? This is why it is so important to be in a relationship with God. If you only seek Him once a week at church, you could be fooled by others claiming to know Him. What should we do? Be like the Bereans – examine the scriptures daily.

On that note, I want to look at one other story.

Read Nehemiah 6:1-14

We don't know exactly how Nehemiah recognized the deception, but he did. The word "perceived" in verse 12 might give us a general clue as to why Nehemiah was so wise. That word in the Hebrew is *nakar* (Strong's 5234) and it means "to scrutinize, look intently at, pay attention to." Nehemiah knew the enemy was out to disrupt his plans, and unlike the story of the prophet in Kings, he didn't immediately trust what Shemaiah was saying. He scrutinized the man's words. He looked intently at him and paid attention to the situation. Another thing we can glean from Nehemiah was that he was in constant prayer with the Almighty. If you read Nehemiah from the beginning you see Nehemiah always praying to God (Nehemiah 1:5, 2:4, 4:4, 5:19, 6:14). Nehemiah was in constant prayer, as we should be. If we are in constant communication with God, His spirit should be able to warn us if something is amiss. We will end today with this thought in mind.

Read 1 Thessalonians 5:17. How are we to pray? _____

Be like the Bereans and Nehemiah. Be like Daniel. Examine the scriptures daily, and pray without ceasing. Then when false prophets come, you will be equipped to recognize them.

1 *English Standard Version Study Bible* (Wheaton, Illinois: Crossway, 2008), 732.

Then Daniel replied with discretion and discernment . . .

We looked at wisdom yesterday, and today, you will see Daniel answer with great wisdom.

Daniel 2:14

Read Daniel 2:1-18

Before we get into the story, we need to pause here and explain something unique to Daniel.

Read Daniel 2:4. What language did the Chaldeans speak? _____

Until this verse, the book of Daniel has been recorded in Hebrew, the language of the Jews. Beginning in Daniel 2:4 the language abruptly changes to Aramaic, the language of Babylon. Why would Daniel do this? If you look ahead in Daniel, the language shifts again in Daniel 8:1 and becomes the language of the Jews again. Scholars believe that Daniel shifts languages here in order to inform the reader that the messages in Daniel 2:4-7:28 pertain to "the times of the Gentiles" (Luke 21:24) or the Gentile nations. But in Daniel 8:1, the focus is once again on the nation of Israel.[1] We will see this clearly as we move forward in Daniel.

So, in Daniel chapter two, the king has a dream and it greatly disturbs him. Let's focus for a minute on one verse. Please read Daniel 2:5 in the margin.

The king replied to the Chaldeans, "The command from me is firm: if you do not make known to me the dream and its interpretation, you will be torn limb from limb and your houses will be made a rubbish heap."

Daniel 2:5

I would not want to be a wise Chaldean at this moment. The command is a little rash, don't you think? This dream came in the second year of Nebuchadnezzar (Daniel 2:1). Like we have said previously, the king may not have been too much older than Daniel. Consider for a moment Nebuchadnezzar's anger. This dream must have really disturbed him. In verse one it says, "his spirit was troubled." He wanted answers, and he wanted them quickly. No one knows whether Nebuchadnezzar wanted his dream told to him in order to verify the interpreter's accuracy or whether he didn't remember much of the dream when he woke. It is anyone's guess. But his command was "firm." The Chaldeans had to tell him his dream and then interpret it. They argued with him, exclaiming that his command was "difficult." You think so? Impossible, as a matter a fact!

Nebuchadnezzar does not yield. He is so disturbed by the dream that he becomes angry when his wise men tell him what he asks is ridiculous. He flies into a rage and orders the execution of every wise man in Babylon. This goes to show you how irrational someone can be when they are angry. We need to keep a calm head when something disturbs us, or we very well may issue a demand like Nebuchadnezzar and regret it later.

We know from scripture that Daniel, Hananiah, Mishael, and Azariah were not among those called forward to interpret the dream. Why do you think this would be?

Take another look at Daniel 2:1. In what year did Nebuchadnezzar have his dream?_____

Turn back to Daniel 1:5. How long was Daniel's education? _____

If you recall Babylon numbered the years of the king's reign starting with the new year after he came to power. So in our method of counting, this is probably right at Nebuchadnezzar's third year. But what is important to note is that Daniel and his friends had probably barely completed their training. They had "just graduated college" and were probably still "unpacking their bags" at their new homes. They had been declared "wise" but had not yet proven their wisdom to their peers. There is something we can learn from this:

Once you have completed your training, God will not waste one moment before giving you an opportunity to shine.

Daniel's bags had yet to be unpacked when Arioch came marching through the hallway with an ax. Can you imagine what Daniel was thinking? "I just got here!" Even though they were considered "ten times better" than all other wise men in Babylon, obviously the other wise men didn't think so (their heritage could have had something to do with this – more on that in a future lesson). They were not taken to the king. But Daniel 2:13 tells us that the guards were on the hunt for Daniel and his friends in order to kill them with the rest of the wise men from Babylon.

Read Daniel 2:14. How did Daniel reply? _____

Daniel could have flipped out and lost his wits. But he did not. He remained strong and steady. Daniel probably remembered a very important fact.

Read Proverbs 3:25-26. When something goes wrong, who helps us?_____

Daniel answered Arioch wisely because He knew the king's rash command didn't take the Lord of the universe by surprise. Daniel knew his God, and he knew what his God was capable of doing. The NASB translates Daniel 2:14 by saying that Daniel used "discretion and discernment." The word translated "discernment" is very interesting to me. Some other interpretations translate this word as "wisdom" or "tact" or "discretion" but when you look at the Aramaic word *tem* it gets fascinating. It is Strong's number 2942 and it means "flavor." It is equivalent to Strong's 2941 *taam,* which means "taste." This same word used in Daniel 2:14 (Strong's 2942) is used in its exact form later on in Daniel.

Look at Daniel 5:2 in the margin.

Now, back in chapter one, we learned that Daniel refrained from tasting some of the king's food, did we not? Belshazzar now "tastes" the Babylonian wine Daniel refused to drink in chapter one. Belshazzar even tries to "taste" the heathen wine using God's vessels! Can you imagine the arrogance? The wine of Babylon was going to be poured into God's vessels. We learned earlier that God's vessels were "set apart" and "holy." Yikes. We will see the outcome of that choice in chapter five, but for now, let's get back to our word *tem* or "taste" which can also be translated "wisdom" or "discernment." Because if you have "taste" you have "wisdom" and we know that "wisdom" is the fear of the Lord (Proverbs 1:7). I just find this fascinating that the word used to describe Daniel's "wisdom" can also be translated "taste." There are many other Hebrew words for wisdom God could have used to tell us about Daniel's character, yet God uses a word that means "taste." Daniel had good taste, both in decisions, and character.

Here is another thought we need to ponder.

Belshazzar, while he tasted *[tem]* the wine, commanded to bring the golden and silver vessels which his father Nebuchadnezzar had taken out of the temple which was in Jerusalem; that the king, and his princes, his wives, and his concubines, might drink therein.

Daniel 5:2 KJV

Read Daniel 2:16. Who went to the king to request some time for interpretation?_____

Daniel went to the king himself! Arioch didn't venture into the king's chambers. I wonder if Arioch was thinking his head would roll if he even tried to approach the king about delaying the dream's interpretation. Anyone with me? If I were Arioch, I don't know if I would be too excited about running that errand. He let Daniel go himself. We don't know why Nebuchadnezzar granted Daniel's request, but perhaps it was the save reason Arioch gave him leave to speak to the king. Daniel had "discretion and taste." Perhaps, Nebuchadnezzar was curious. This was one of those Jews he had taken from Babylon – the same one he had found "ten times better" than his other wise men. Perhaps Nebuchadnezzar was so impressed with Daniel's confidence that he hoped if given some time Daniel could describe the king's dream and provide the interpretation. Or perhaps Nebuchadnezzar had cooled off a bit and realized his order to kill all the wise men was a little senseless. Whatever the case, Daniel's request was granted.

So now we know that Daniel wasn't only wise, he was also brave. He faced an angry king that had just commanded the death of all the wise men. Daniel had some guts.

Then what does Daniel immediately do?

Read Daniel 2:17. What did Daniel do? _____

Yesterday we looked at wisdom, and we said it was wise to seek counsel. Daniel immediately went to Hananiah, Mishael, and Azariah about the matter. Then what did they do? They prayed. They sought the compassion of God. My faithful friends, Daniel, Hananiah, Mishael, and Azariah fell to their knees. This is another thing we need to seek – the King's face. We need to seek Him not only in the Word, or from the counsel of His followers; we also need to seek Him face to face in prayer if we are to be truly wise or have *tem*. Look at Jeremiah 29:12-13 in the margin. Call. Pray. Seek.

That is what Daniel and His friends did. And the Lord rewarded them. God revealed the dream and its interpretation. We will look at God's response and Daniel's prayer over the next few days. Today, I want to wrap up with another thought.

"Then you will call upon Me and come and pray to Me, and I will listen to you. You will seek Me and find Me when you search for Me with all your heart."

Jeremiah 29:12-13

Take another look at Daniel 2:18. What was one of the reasons Daniel and his friends prayed?_____

Notice it says "so that Daniel and his friends would not be destroyed with the rest of the wise men of Babylon."

Were some of the wise men destroyed before Daniel made the request of Arioch? It seems from this text that Arioch had gone forth to slay the wise men in Daniel 2:14. Perhaps he was rounding Daniel and his friends up when Daniel made his request.[2] Daniel stopped him at some point, but how many were killed before Daniel headed (no pun intended) off the king's bodyguard? And in the same vein, did it stop the killing? Daniel made a request for "him," not for all the wise men of Babylon.

Read Daniel 2:24-25. What did Daniel say to Arioch? _____

How did Arioch react? "Then Arioch _____ brought Daniel into the king's presence . . ."

Arioch seemed a little frazzled. We don't know for sure what happened to the wise men, but we do know not all of them were destroyed.

Look forward to Daniel 2:48. Who was Daniel in charge of? _____

Daniel got promoted to be over all the wise men of Babylon. Quite an honor, don't you think? So in the end, Daniel saved at least some of the wise men. But Daniel 2:18 seems to indicate that some heads had rolled. It might even mean that heads were rolling while Daniel and his friends prayed. Wise men were dying. The decree had been sent. The order had been given.

Daniel and his friends were on their knees. If God didn't reveal the dream – their heads were next.

More to come next week.

1 Hinnant, Greg. *Daniel Notes* (Lake Mary, Florida: Creation House Press, 2003), 21.
English Standard Version Study Bible (Wheaton, Illinois: Crossway, 2008), 1588.
2 Hinnant, Greg. *Daniel Notes* (Lake Mary, Florida: Creation House Press, 2003), 29.

Week Three

"I thank and praise you, God of my ancestors, for giving me wisdom and power, and revealing to me what we wanted from you, for giving us the answer for the king."

Daniel 2:23 JNTP

Day One – Chapter Two
Daniel's Prayer

We left off last week with head's rolling. Daniel and his friends had every faith in God, but can you imagine the time ticking away as they prayed? I sure can. Let's see what happens next.

Read Daniel 2:19-23

Can you feel Daniel's excitement? It leaps off the page like sunshine off water. God revealed the dream to Daniel in a night vision. This is amazing to think about. Daniel had no idea what the king had dreamed, but he saw it clearly. Let's look at a few other places in scripture where God revealed something in a vision.

Read Acts 10:1-23. Were these visions beneficial immediately? _____

This is one way God uses visions, to provide us with an immediate answer. Some visions pertain to "now." God gave Cornelius a vision in order to send word to Peter; in return He provided Peter a vision that prompted him to take the good news to the Gentiles. "What God has cleansed, no longer consider unholy."

Read 2 Corinthians 5:15. For whom did Jesus die? _____

The Savior cleanses even the Gentiles. Now, let's read about another way God uses visions.

Read Ezekiel 37:1-14

Who said the Bible wasn't exciting? God showed Ezekiel a valley of dry bones. Ezekiel prophesied and the bones stood on their feet. He prophesied again and breath came into them.

What did God tell Ezekiel the bones were in verse 11? _____

What did God tell the bones He would do in verse 14? _____

Turn to Ezekiel 37:24. Who would rule them? _____

Ah faithful friends! This vision is for a time far in the future. This is the Messianic Age – the Millennial Kingdom of Christ! This is what much of the book of Daniel is predicting and something we will study in chapter two. This is another reason God gives visions – for a future time, a time far off, but notice what the vision intends to provide for the reader.

What had the people lost in Ezekiel 37:11? _____

The prophecy was for the people to have hope. Ezekiel was exiled only a few years after Daniel – and then all of Judah a few years later. They were in a strange land, away from the land God had promised them, their temple was destroyed, and their king was gone. God told them one day they would be back in the land of Israel, His Spirit would be with them, and David would be their king: David, the great king, the king after God's own heart (Acts 13:22). Don't you think this would have given the exiles hope? You bet it would. One day, they would be great again because their God would be with them back in their homeland (Ezekiel 37:27).

Let's get back to Daniel. God reveals the king's dream. Then Daniel says a beautiful prayer of praise. Let's look at some aspects of this prayer.

What did Daniel say belongs to God in Daniel 2:20? _____

What did Daniel say God gave him in verse 23? _____

In verse 21, what does God give to the wise? _____ To men of understanding? _____

Don't you find this powerful? We have already looked at wisdom. "The fear of the Lord is the beginning of knowledge" (Proverbs 1:7). This is powerfully displayed in Daniel chapter two. God is the only One who is powerful and wise. Only if we are with Him can we be like Him. He gives the wise (those who fear the Lord) wisdom and men of knowledge (those who fear the Lord) understanding.

Read 1 Corinthians 3:19: What is foolishness before God? _____

Read Romans 1:18-32. What do men suppress (verse 18)? _____

When men of this world claim to be wise what are they (verse 22)? _____

There is one way to be wise, and that is if you are with God, because if you are with Him, you will know the truth (Jesus – the Word) and you will become wise like Daniel, Hananiah, Mishael, and Azariah. This prayer is saying, "Bless you God, because you bestowed on your servant some of who You are!"

Let me share with you a scripture that I recently rediscovered. Look at 2 Chronicles 6:41 in the margin. Do you remember when I said that Yeshua's (Jesus') name is the word "salvation?" His name shows up once again in 2 Chronicles 6:41. The priests, those who could enter the Holy Place to attend the holy vessels, were clothed with salvation, because they had been "set apart" and "sanctified." Everything they did in that tabernacle represented Jesus. In order to be with the living God, you have to be clothed with Jesus because He is the only sacrifice for sin. When you are with Him, you are clothed with Him, and because you are clothed with Him, you can obtain some of His gifts – wisdom and understanding. Glory!

"Now therefore arise, O Lord God, to Your resting place, You and the ark of Your might; let Your priests, O Lord God, be clothed with salvation *[Yeshua]* and let Your godly ones rejoice in what is good."

2 Chronicles 6:41

Look up Galatians 3:27. Who are we clothed with?_____

You bet. The only way we can enter eternity is if we are clothed with Christ. When God looks at us, He sees the perfect sacrifice of His Son. That is the only way we can get wisdom and knowledge – if we walk with Him. Have you ever tried to explain God's ways and His wisdom to someone not walking with Him? They don't get it, do they? They can't get it. They reject the truth. Like Romans chapter one says, "They suppress the truth." Until they acknowledge God for who He is and accept His Son as their Savior, they are blind.

Let's get back to Daniel's prayer. Do you remember when I said Daniel knew scripture? We just looked at where Daniel praises God for His wisdom and power and then praises Him for bestowing on His faithful wisdom and power. But let's see where Daniel could have coined his language.[1]

53

Read Job 12:13 and compare to Daniel 2:21 and 23.   What similarities do you find?
_____

Read Psalm 31:15. What similarities do you find to Daniel 2:21?_____

Read Psalm 75:6-7. What similarities do you find to Daniel 2:21? _____

Daniel knew the Word, and because he knew the Word, the words of the Word spilled from his lips during his prayer. The more you study God's Word, the more it will be engrained in your mind and tumble from your lips when you speak. Let's look at verse 21 a little more closely.

Daniel 2:21: He changes _____ and _____. He removes _____ and establishes _____.

If you have read anything about the statue of Daniel chapter two, you might understand why Daniel was praising God for this particular matter. The dream Daniel witnessed was a great statue, and that statue represented kingdoms. God revealed to Daniel the order of the kingdoms that would rise after Babylon until the end of time, and Daniel praises God for doing so. God changes the "times and the epochs," or the "times and the seasons." God is in control of the future, not Nebuchadnezzar, not the next kingdom that comes, or even the next. Daniel has witnessed the future and seen when and where God will end the reign of kings. Despite being in captivity, and being threatened to have their heads removed, God was in control. Praise the Lord!

"He reveals mysteries from the darkness and brings the deep darkness into light."

Job 12:22

Next Daniel thanks God for revealing "profound and hidden things." You can say that again. God revealed something extraordinary to Daniel. Daniel didn't just get to interpret dreams like Joseph; he had to recall the dream himself! This is remarkable. Look at Job 12:22 in the margin.

God "knows what is in the darkness and light dwells with Him" (Daniel 2:22). Who is the light? You should know the answer to that, but we have to take a look at another verse.

For with You is the fountain of life; in Your light we see light.

Psalm 36:9

Read John 1:1-9. Who is the light? _____
The life? _____ So the light is the life!

Now read Psalm 36:9 in the margin. This seems odd until you realize to "see light" is another way of saying "to experience life." Jesus is the light and only in Him is the life. Amen and amen. We will look at the answer to Daniel and his friends' prayer tomorrow.

1 Leupold, H.C. *Exposition of Daniel* (Grand Rapids, Michigan: Baker Book House Company, 1969), 98-99.

Day Two – Chapter Two
The Dream and the Stone

"Thou, O king, sawest, and behold a great image. This great image, whose brightness was excellent, stood before thee; and the form thereof was terrible."

Daniel 2:31 KJV

Yesterday we looked at Daniel's prayer. Today we will look at the dream itself.

Read Daniel 2:24-35

Arioch "hurriedly" took Daniel to the king when Daniel declared he could interpret the dream. The word "hurriedly" or "haste" in some interpretations is the Aramaic word *bhal* (Strong's #927), which corresponds to the Hebrew word *bahal* (Strong's #926). This means to "tremble inwardly or palpitate, be alarmed or agitated." This word has been translated, "trouble, haste, afraid, vexed, affrighted, thrust him out, rash, speedily." Like we studied a few days ago, Arioch may have already taken some heads. He may have had some friends who were "wise men." He was anxious to halt the killing and that word says it all. He was alarmed, agitated, trembling inwardly, and he basically thrust Daniel into the king's chambers. Think about this scene for a moment with me. Imagine Daniel being shoved into the king's chambers. Imagine Arioch holding his breath, praying to whatever god he prayed to that Daniel could do as he claimed. Imagine Nebuchadnezzar slowly turning to Daniel and asking, "Are you able to make known to me the dream which I have seen and its interpretation?" You probably could have heard a pin drop.

How did Daniel respond in Daniel 2:27? Could he?_____

But who could in Daniel 2:28? _____

Can you imagine Nebuchadnezzar's face when Daniel first started speaking? Can you imagine Arioch standing behind him biting his nails? This had to be a sight to see. I hope God has a big movie theater in heaven where we will be able to witness the reenactment. But here is one lesson we need to take from this:

When God gives you a revelation – you give Him the glory.

Daniel gave the glory to God – all of it – every last bit. He didn't stand before the king like he alone was able to declare the vision. He knew he was not to be praised for revealing the secret of this dream because "there is a God in heaven who reveals mysteries." We need to remember, when God gives us a revelation, it comes from Him and Him alone – not us. We need to keep our pride in check or God could be revealing the next revelation to someone else.

Read Daniel 2:31 and write here a one word interpretation of the statue._____

The NASB says the statue was "large and of extraordinary splendor . . . and its appearance was awesome." The NIV says the statue was "large . . . enormous, dazzling . . . awesome in appearance." The NCV says the statue was "huge, shiny, and frightening." Based on the Aramaic words, the KJV says it best. Look at Daniel 2:31 on the previous page. This is probably why Nebuchadnezzar was so riled up over this dream. Even though the statue was exceedingly bright, it was also "terrible." The word terrible in Daniel 2:31 is *dechal* (Strong's #1763) and it means "to slink." It corresponds to the Hebrew word *zachal* (Strong's #2119), which means "to crawl." Isn't that fascinating? The word *dechal,* meaning "to slink," implies "fear, to be formidable, to make afraid, and dreadful." Have you ever been so terrified that your skin was crawling? Well, that is what the statue did to the king – and to Daniel. No wonder the king was so shook up. The statue was dreadful and terrifying and formidable. *It slinked.* Is anyone getting chills right now? I sure am. The statue slinked.

Now let's look at the statue's attributes.

What was the head made of? _____ The chest and arms? _____

Belly and thighs? _____ Legs?_____ Feet?_____

What do you notice about this? The metals depicted in the statue have less value the lower they go, but each new metal has increased strength and endurance.[1] There is something else interesting we can observe about this statue.

Read Daniel 2:32. How is the gold described? _____ Are any of the other metals in the statue depicted as such? _____

Not only does the statue get less valuable, it also get's less refined.[2] We will see tomorrow that each metal represents a different kingdom. So, taking all of this into consideration, the latter kingdoms will be less refined, but more strong. Today I want to focus on Daniel 2:34-35 in the margin.

There is a stone. How is it cut out? _____

What did it strike? _____

What fell? _____

What was left to be found of them? _____

What did the stone become? _____

What did it fill? _____

"You continued looking until a stone was cut out without hands, and it struck the statue on its feet of iron and clay and crushed them. Then the iron, the clay, the bronze, the silver and the gold were crushed all at the same time and became like chaff from the summer threshing floors; and the wind carried them away so that not a trace of them was found. But the stone that struck the statue became a great mountain and filled the whole earth."

Daniel 2:34-35

Understand this: the focus on Daniel 2:34-35 shouldn't be on the statue and its metal parts, but on the stone. I'm not saying the pieces of the statue aren't important, they are of great importance, but the true focus, the true message, the true meaning behind the vision is the stone. The importance of the stone is what God wanted to hammer into Nebuchadnezzar's head. This is the message Daniel already knew. This is the power, the dominion, and the glory forever and ever – amen.

Let's look at this stone.

Read 1 Peter 2:6. Who is the cornerstone? _____

Read Romans 9:33. Who is the stone? The rock?_____

Read 1 Corinthians 3:11. What is Jesus? _____
What are foundations laid with? _____

Read Matthew 7:24-25. What was the rock/the foundation Jesus referred to here?_____ The rock is compared to hearing the word; who is the Word (John 1:1)? _____

Read Psalm 18:2 in the margin. Who is our rock?_____

> The Lord is my rock and my fortress and my deliverer, My God, my rock, in whom I take refuge; My shield and the horn of my salvation, my stronghold.
>
> Psalm 18:2

Jesus is the stone in Daniel. He is cut out by no human means (without hands). He comes freely and with power. He crushes the final kingdom that is depicted in Daniel (the toes of iron and clay) and breaks them. This is our focus – Jesus' return. Do you see it? It is not the gold, or the silver, or the bronze, or the iron, or even the iron and the clay – it is the stone. Let me prove to you that this is depicting the second coming of Christ.

Read Psalm 2:8-9. What is shattered? _____ Shattered how? _____

Read Revelation 19:11-15. With what does Jesus' rule? _____(vs. 15)

> O my God, make them like the whirling dust, like chaff before the wind.
>
> Psalm 83:13.

The stone depicts Jesus' second coming. When He returns His coming not only breaks the final kingdom depicted in the statue, it breaks the entire statue apart, and all the kingdoms of the world disappear like chaff. Pause here and look at Psalm 83:13 in the margin. This is a verse that depicts what will happen in the latter days. The kingdoms will be like chaff before the wind.

According to Daniel 2:28, these events will take place in the latter days. The stone will come in the latter days. The rod of iron will descend in the latter days. It will shatter the kingdoms on the earth – not just the final system – but all the other kingdoms that have come before. Jesus will rule, and His reign will be secure.

What did the stone become in Daniel 2:35? _____

Look at Zechariah 8:3 in the margin. Who will return to Zion? _____ What will the city/mountain be called? City of _____ Who is the truth (John 14:6)?_____

Now read Isaiah 2:2-4. When will this come to pass? _____

What will be established? _____

Who will stream to it? _____

What will they say? _____

Where is this mountain established? _____

Will there be peace? _____

> Thus says the Lord, "I will return to Zion and will dwell in the midst of Jerusalem. Then Jerusalem will be called the City of Truth, and the mountain of the Lord of hosts will be called the Holy Mountain."
>
> Zechariah 8:3

The stone, the cornerstone, the rock, the foundation, our hope will return. He will crush every single man-made system that was in the past; He will rule with truth and there will be peace in His reign during the Millennium.

That is our focus. No matter the gold, the silver, the bronze, the iron, or the iron and the clay, the stone is the focus. Do not forget this as we begin to discuss the kingdoms tomorrow.

The stone is coming.

1 *English Standard Version Study Bible* (Wheaton, Illinois: Crossway, 2008), 1590.
2 Hinnant, Greg. *Daniel Notes* (Lake Mary, Florida: Creation House Press, 2003). 34.

Day Three – Chapter Two
The Kingdoms

"You, O king, are the king of kings . . . You are the head of gold . . . After you there will arise another kingdom inferior to you . . . then another third kingdom . . . then there will be a fourth kingdom as strong as iron . . ."

Daniel 2:37-40

We looked at the statue yesterday, but we mainly focused on the stone, our rock, our foundation and our hope. Today we are going to look at the metals in the statue and explain what they mean.

Read Daniel 2:31-43

Do you see Nebuchadnezzar's head growing big about now? I sure do. Daniel told him, "You, O king, are the king of kings, to whom the God of heaven has given the kingdom, the power, the strength and the glory . . . You are the head of gold."

We said yesterday that the gold at the top of the statue was "fine." No other metal in the statue is described this way. The king was the "head of gold" and he was "fine." This might have something to do with Nebuchadnezzar's ego boost in the next chapter (not that he was lacking in ego before). We will soon see his ego overload, but for now let's focus on the statue. The gold is the most valuable metal in the statue.

What did Nebuchadnezzar rule over according to verse 38?_____

Read verse 39. When the next kingdom arises what will it be compared to Nebuchadnezzar's kingdom? _____

Now, I want you to keep in mind, this is Nebuchadnezzar's dream. He thought himself extremely "fine," "refined," and "superior." Even though God gave Nebuchadnezzar this dream, He used images that Nebuchadnezzar would most identify with. If God had shown the king something less than gold, I just don't know if it would have made a lasting impact on Nebuchadnezzar. Nebuchadnezzar thought himself superior in every way.

I want you to take note that this image is of a man.

What three ways is this statue described in Daniel 2:31: _____
and _____ and _____.

This stands for and depicts not only the pride of man, but also the pride of Nebuchadnezzar.[1] This depiction was self-worshiping, but it also stood for mankind's continued rebellion against God. This reminds me of another image of pride.

Read Genesis 11:3-4. What did the people try to do? _____

Note something with me in verse 3. What did they substitute for stone? _____
Who is the stone? _____

You can't do it. You can't substitute anything for Jesus and be with God. The people of Babel fell far short. They could only make bricks. You can't make or substitute anything for the stone. You have to humble yourself, not build a tower whose top will reach to heaven. You can get to heaven by no other way but the stone. You have to have His foundation and then and only then will you be able to enter the free gift of "forever."

Nebuchadnezzar had pride in mankind, himself, and his kingdom. This is depicted in the "head of gold."

Daniel says, "After you there will be another kingdom inferior to you." Although God doesn't name this kingdom here, it is named many other times in Daniel. In fact, this is the kingdom that came and conquered Babylon in Daniel's day.

Let's find out the identity of the next kingdom in the statue, the silver kingdom, which is represented by the chest and arms.

Read Daniel 8:20. What kings are named here? _____

Read Daniel 5:30-31. Who was slain? _____ the _____ and _____ the _____ received the kingdom.

The kingdom of Medo-Persia is represented as the silver kingdom. Medo-Persia defeated Babylon in one night and took over the Babylonian empire in one day. We will study this more in chapter five. What is important to note here is that Daniel actually saw this kingdom come to power and served under its leadership. Medo-Persia let the Jews return to rebuild their temple and wall (see Ezra and Nehemiah). It is depicted as less refined than Babylon, but also stronger. This probably means Medo-Persia had more military might than Babylon – it was "stronger" in that sense, but it may have been considered "inferior" because the Medo-Persian power wasn't as concentrated as Babylon. Persia was actually part of the Median kingdom but Cyrus II rose up and captured the king of the Medes, which gave Cyrus control of the Median kingdom. The Medes and the Persians were never really a united people, and two thousand years of Babylonian influence ultimately outweighed the two hundred years of Medo-Persian dominion.[2] The "inferior" nature of this kingdom may be its lack of total unity and also its shortened reign. It could also mean the morals of this kingdom were even less than that of Babylon.

The next kingdom depicted in the statue was the bronze kingdom. This one is also named in Daniel.

Read Daniel 8:21. What is this next kingdom? _____

Greece is the kingdom described in Daniel chapter two as ruling "over all the earth." Greece, under the leadership of Alexander the Great, conquered the land spanning into the northern regions of India and also Syria, and Egypt. The land mass acquired by Alexander was unmatched by his predecessors.[3]

Daniel then goes on to say that a fourth kingdom will come to power. It would be as strong as iron and like iron it would crush and shatter "all these in pieces." We have to pause here and ask a very simple question.

Look again at Daniel 2:40. What will the fourth kingdom crush? _____

The fourth kingdom will crush all the other "kingdoms" in the statue. How will it do that, you might ask, because only the last one will exist at the time of the fourth? Good question.

First we need to ask ourselves another simple question.

Who is having the dream? _____

What is he concerned about? _____

Nebuchadnezzar is concerned about Babylon – the empire he controls. He is concerned about the territory in his possession. Without getting too in-depth here (we will go deeper in future chapters), when Medo-Persia conquered Babylon it was an empire in its own right. When Medo-Persia conquered Babylon, its territory grew. When Greece conquered Medo-Persia, its territory grew. The same thing happened when the fourth empire rose up. It would crush and break all the other territories that the statue depicted, meaning it would be the largest of them all – encompassing all of Greece, which took in Medo-Persia, which took in Babylon.

Here is what we need to understand. Scripture does not state the identity of the fourth kingdom, unlike the first three. The fourth kingdom is a mystery. Here is another thing we need to understand: the fourth kingdom is not necessarily the next kingdom that rose up. It has to do with territory – specifically Nebuchadnezzar's territory.

What different substance is identified in Daniel 2:33? _____

The iron kingdom is slightly different from the other kingdoms. In the latter days, another form of the iron kingdom would grow, and instead of being totally "iron" it would become "iron mixed with common clay" (Daniel 2:41). So what is the identity of the iron in the statue? Here is where it gets a little tricky. Two kingdoms arose after Greece. The first empire you are very familiar with. It was in power in Jesus' day. This kingdom nailed the Son of God to the cross.

What was the name of this kingdom? _____ (Acts 23:11)

Most scholars believe the Roman Empire is the fourth empire depicted in Daniel (the iron kingdom) so most theories about end time events have been written around the revived Roman Empire (the toes of iron and clay) and a Roman Antichrist. But Daniel makes it clear that the fourth kingdom would "crush and break all these in pieces." Did Rome crush all the empires depicted in the statue? Remember each empire grew in landmass. Rome never conquered all the regions Greece conquered. Rome was predominately a western empire, not a Middle Eastern empire. Greece spread out well east of the Euphrates River (into the region of the Persians – our Iran). Let me say that another way – Rome never conquered all of Babylon. Rome never touched some of Nebuchadnezzar's land. It came to the Euphrates, but never past it. The fourth kingdom of Daniel is supposed to encompass all the other kingdom's territories – especially all of Babylon.[4]

Was there another kingdom that arose that would fit the description in Daniel? Yes, it was called the Turkish Ottoman Empire. The Turkish Ottoman Empire was a Middle Eastern Empire, just like Babylon, Medo-Persia, and Greece. It crushed and broke all the landmasses that are depicted in the statue, and much more. Can we see this clarified in scripture? Yes we can. Look at Revelation 17:8 in the margin. I don't want to get into Revelation in-depth here because we will do so when we study chapter seven of Daniel, but for now know that the 10 toes (the iron and clay) that Jesus (the stone) crushes will be the final kingdom of the last days. Remember, Daniel's vision is about the latter days (Daniel 2:28), and the stone is the return of the King (Revelation 19).

In Revelation 17:8 an angel is speaking to the apostle John about the end time kingdom (the toes of Daniel) and is trying to get John to understand the identity of this kingdom. So, I want you to pause here and recall just what kingdom was in power in John's day. What kingdom crucified Jesus and oppressed the saints in the apostles' day? This would be the kingdom who "is" according to Revelation 17:8.

"The beast that you saw was, and is not, and is about to come up out of the abyss and go to destruction. And those who dwell on the earth, whose name has not been written in the book of life from the foundation of the world, will wonder when they see the beast, that he was and is not and will come."

Revelation 17:8

Which kingdom? _____

We will go much deeper in a future lesson, but for now we just need to know the identity of the fourth kingdom – is it Rome or the Turkish Ottoman Empire? I have rewritten Revelation 17:8 with an explanation inserted with what we know from Daniel so far.

*The beast that you saw was **[Babylon, Medo-Persia, and Greece]**, and is not **[Rome]**, and is about to come up out of the abyss and go to **destruction [Turkish Ottoman Empire]**. And those who dwell on the earth, whose name has not been written in the book of life from the foundation of the world, will wonder when they see the beast, that he was **[Babylon, Medo-Persia, and Greece]** and is not **[Rome]** and will come **[Turkish Ottoman Empire]**.*

Rome is not depicted in the beast of Daniel because it is Nebuchadnezzar's dream. He does not care about Rome if it doesn't conquer his territory. He was dreaming about future kingdoms that would arise in the Middle East and conquer the entirety of Babylon. The beast of Revelation, on the other hand, is from Satan's point of view. Because he raised up Rome to oppress the Jews, it is depicted in the beast of Revelation. But it is not the beast. It is not the fourth kingdom in Daniel -- the Turkish Ottoman Empire, or the iron kingdom. It was destroyed in 1924 after World War one, but what is it doing today? It is regrouping. Soon it will form the ten toes.

The beast is already among us faithful friends, and the church as a whole is blind to its existence.

1 Hinnant, Greg. *Daniel Notes* (Lake Mary, Florida: Creation House Press, 2003), 41-42.
2 Leupold, H.C. *Exposition of Daniel* (Grand Rapids, Michigan: Baker Book House Company, 1969). 116.
3 Butler, Trent C. et al.,eds. *Holman Illustrated Bible Dictionary* (Nashville, Tennessee: Holman Bible Publishers, 2003), 45.
4 Shoebat, Walid, written with Joel Richardson. *God's War on Terror* (Top Executive Media, 2008. Also check out Joel Richardson's *Antichrist Islam's Awaited Messiah* published in 2006. Both are well worth the read.

Day Four – Chapter Two
The Statue's Demise and Daniel's Promotion

Yesterday we looked at the statue and the identity of the kingdoms represented. We have also studied the stone, but we will revisit the stone here. Let's revisit what happens to the statue when the stone descends upon it.

The statue never stood a chance. Jesus, the stone, the rock, our foundation, and our Savior has told us He will return. And when He returns, all kingdoms of the earth will be broken. His kingdom will never be destroyed. It will "endure forever." Let's look at this.

Read Daniel 2:44-45

Read Isaiah 9:6-7. Who are we talking about? _____ He will be called
_____, _____, _____ and
_____.

What will never have an end? _____ or _____

How long will this last? _____

What will accomplish this? _____

Someone needs to say, "Hallelujah!" There will be no end to His government and no end of peace. He will uphold His kingdom with justice and righteousness. The zeal of the Lord will accomplish this. I want to focus in on that word "zeal." It is a very interesting Hebrew word, and just reading it as "zeal" does not give the full impact as to why the Lord will establish His kingdom. The word "zeal" is the Hebrew word *qinah* (Strong's #7068). I want to look at some other scripture to see how that word is used.

> *How long, O Lord? Will You be angry forever? Will Your jealousy [qinah] burn like fire?*
>
> *Psalm 79:5*

> *For jealousy [qinah] enrages a man, and he will not spare in the day of vengeance.*
> *Proverbs 6:34*

> *Put me like a seal over your heart, like a seal on your arm. For love is as strong as death, jealousy [qinah] is as severe as Sheol; its flashes are flashes of fire, the very flame of the Lord.*
>
> *Song of Songs 8:6*

A tranquil heart is life to the body, but passion [qinah] is rottenness to the bones.

Proverbs 14:30

"Therefore wait for Me," declares the Lord, "For the day when I rise up as a witness. Indeed, My decision is to gather nations, to assemble kingdoms, to pour out on them My indignation, all My burning anger; for all the earth will be devoured by the fire of My zeal [qinah].

Zephaniah 3:8

Therefore thus says the Lord God, "Surely in the fire of My jealousy [qinah] I have spoken against the rest of the nations, and against all Edom, who appropriated My land for themselves as a possession with wholehearted joy and with scorn of soul, to drive it out for a prey." Therefore prophesy concerning the land of Israel and say to the mountains and to the hills, to the ravines and to the valleys, "Thus says the Lord God, 'Behold, I have spoken in My jealousy [qinah] and in My wrath because you have endured the insults of the nations.'"

Ezekiel 36:5-6

"In My zeal [qinah] and in My blazing wrath I declare that on that day there will surely be a great earthquake in the land of Israel."

Ezekiel 38:19

Qinah means "ardor, zeal or jealousy." It is translated more in the King James version of scripture as "jealousy" (25x) than "zeal" (9x). Rightfully so, because the word *qinah* is derived from Strong's #7065 *qana* which means "to be zealous (in a bad sense), jealous, or envious." Think about that for a minute and you might understand what I am getting at. In Isaiah 9:7, He is establishing His kingdom forever and His "zeal" will accomplish it. God is jealous for us! He wants us to be His – forever – and the world is leading some of us astray. He is filled with passion for us, like a husband is jealous for his wife. Zephaniah 3:8, Ezekiel 36:5-6 and Ezekiel 38:19 (the last three scriptures written above) have to do with the last battle – the battle known to us as Armageddon. This battle is detailed out in Revelation, but in Daniel it is depicted by a stone. That stone strikes the statue and that stone is coming in *qinah* because the Lord is jealous for His people, His nation, and His earth. He will set things right. The word *qinah* is associated with His wrath and that wrath will be the stone's decent. Glory!

Daniel 2:45 says that the vision that Daniel saw was "true" and its interpretation was "trustworthy. The King James version of scripture translates this phrase as "certain and sure." The first word is *yatstsiyb* (Strong's #3330) and it means "fixed or certain" and can be translated as "true." The second word is *aman* (Strong's #540) and it means "faithful and sure." So another way to say that phrase is "faithful and true." Why is this vision and its interpretation "faithful and true?" Well, Jesus is the stone descending. Jesus is the One who will lay claim to the kingdoms of the earth. Jesus' reign will be the kingdom that will grow into the large mountain. Look at Revelation 19:11 in the margin. The vision is faithful and true because He is faithful and true! He will come. He will reign. He will be with His people forevermore. Amen!

And I saw heaven opened, and behold, a white horse, and He who sat on it is called Faithful and True, and in righteousness He judges and wages war.

Revelation 19:11

Read Daniel 2:46-49

The king is ecstatic his dream is interpreted. He is in no way upset that more kingdoms will arise. Why is this?

Turn back to Daniel 2:39. When does it say the second kingdom will arise? _____

Nebuchadnezzar is in the clear. His kingdom will endure. Only after him will another kingdom arise. This is good news for the king. He rewards Daniel with gifts, makes him ruler over the whole province of Babylon, and chief over all the wise men. Daniel is promoted, and he has just finished his training! Daniel didn't have to say anything to the king about his friends, but Daniel was loyal: he did not forget Hananiah, Mishael, or Azariah. Per Daniel's request, his friends were promoted to extremely high positions as well.

What are Hananiah, Mishael, and Azariah promoted to? _____
But where does Daniel stay? _____

This will be important when we look at chapter three. Although all four are promoted, Daniel stays at the king's court while the others oversee the administration of the province of Babylon. Another way to say "the king's court" is the "king's gate." This was the most important place to be in the entire kingdom.[1] It was a position with unmatched authority. This was where the king conducted state business and received guests. For Daniel to be in the king's gate is extremely significant. He probably saw the king's face daily. He was an advisor to the very man who took him captive. Now I want you to focus a minute on Nebuchadnezzar's words.

Fill in the blanks. Nebuchadnezzar said in verse 47, "Surely your God is a _____ of _____ and a _____ of _____."

I want to draw your attention to that last blank. Nebuchadnezzar could have said, "God of gods, and Lord of lords," but he did not. Daniel's God is the Lord of kings. For a brief moment Nebuchadnezzar realizes that Daniel's god is Lord over **him.** This is very important. Daniel's God is above all other gods, and all kings – Nebuchadnezzar included. Nebuchadnezzar pays homage to Daniel, but who he was truly honoring was God Himself. Honoring the man with God's message was the pagan way of showing homage to the God the man represented. This is emphasized by Nebuchadnezzar's words. He doesn't praise Daniel's wisdom; instead he praises the God that bestowed on Daniel the dream and its interpretation.[2]

You would think Nebuchadnezzar would start to worship Daniel's God, but he does not. In fact, he does something quite remarkable after Daniel's revelation. See what he does tomorrow.

1 Hinnant, Greg. *Daniel Notes* (Lake Mary, Florida: Creation House Press, 2003)., 54.
2 Hinnant, Greg. *Daniel Notes* (Lake Mary, Florida: Creation House Press, 2003), 48-49.

Nebuchadnezzar the king made an image of gold . . .

Yesterday we saw Nebuchadnezzar exclaiming that God was a "God of gods and a Lord of kings." So, did Nebuchadnezzar humble himself? Did he start worshiping the one true God? Did he become a fair and just king because he followed God's laws and obeyed His commands? Let's find out.

Daniel 3:1

Read Daniel 3:1-8

Oh, Nebuchadnezzar, you could have turned around. You could have recognized the hour of your visitation (Luke 19:44). But no, you just had to build a statue. This event probably occurred about 16 years following the king's dream or approximately 18 years into his rule. This is noted in the Septuagint, or the Greek version of the Hebrew scriptures written in approximately the third century.[1] If this was according to the Babylonian method of timekeeping, this would have been approximately 586 BC – the year Nebuchadnezzar destroyed Jerusalem. So some time had past between chapter two and chapter three.

We could go through this section rather quickly, but I want to pause here and really do a thorough job of discussing a subject that is probably fairly painful to all of us . . .

Pride.

What metal symbolized Nebuchadnezzar's kingdom in Daniel 2:36-38? _____

What metal did Nebuchadnezzar build the image out of in Daniel 3:1? _____

If a cubit is approximately 1.5 feet, how tall was the statue?[2] _____

We can safely say that Nebuchadnezzar wasn't just prideful; his pride was off the charts. Do you concur? The statue was approximately 90 feet tall. That is the approximate size of an eight-story building. Can you imagine this for a minute? Ninety feet tall! Nebuchadnezzar thought he was hot stuff. After all, he was the head of gold in the dream, and only "after him" did another king dare to take over the kingdom of Babylon. After the dream about the statue, Nebuchadnezzar could have gone the other route – the route of submission and worship – but he did not. He went the route of Satan.

Read Ezekiel 28:13-17. In verse 17, how does God describe Satan's heart? _____
Because of what? _____

The phrase "lifted up" (also translated "proud") is the word *gabahh* and it means "to soar" (Strong's #1361). Satan's heart was "soaring" because he thought he was beautiful. I do believe Nebuchadnezzar's heart was "soaring" because he was the head of gold.

Read Ezekiel 28:14. What is Satan called in this scripture? _____ What did he walk among? _____

Satan is called a "cherub" who walked among fiery stones or stones of fire. In Ezekiel chapter one, you meet creatures called "the cherubim" (Ezekiel 10:2). These creatures carry the throne of God on top of their heads (Ezekiel 1:26-28).

Read Ezekiel 1:13. What was darting between the living beings or the cherubim? _____

Doesn't this sound very similar to fiery stones? Think about this with me. Satan was the "anointed cherub" according to Ezekiel 28:14. He walked in the midst of the stones of fire, meaning he was either one of the cherubim who held up the throne of God or he was allowed entrance into that space under the throne like the angel in Ezekiel 10:2. What did Satan have to do to see God? If he was below the throne, he had to look up. Pride filled his heart and he fell. He wanted to be on the throne and not under the throne. Nebuchadnezzar had the same thought. Instead of bowing to the God who had revealed the dream, he wanted to show the world how great he had become. Although the people were bowing down to an image, the people were really bowing down to Nebuchadnezzar. *"You are the head of gold."*

Look at Proverbs 16:18-20 in the margin.

> Pride goes before destruction, and a haughty spirit before stumbling. It is better to be humble in spirit with the lowly than to divide the spoil with the proud. He who gives attention to the word will find good, and blessed is he who trusts in the Lord.
>
> Proverbs 16:18-20

What goes before destruction? _____

Who is blessed? _____

This is important. If you are prideful, destruction is coming because you are trusting in yourself and not in the Lord. You are putting yourself before God. You are like Satan: you want to sit on the throne, not be under it. You want control of your own life, not let God lead your steps. Nebuchadnezzar was proud, and destruction was coming. We will see his destruction in the next chapter. Although the head of gold will remain, Nebuchadnezzar himself will be humbled. But today, let's continue to talk about pride.

Read Mark 7:14-23. What familiar word does Jesus mention in verse 22? _____

What does this thing do to a man according to verse 23? _____

The word "defile" means "unclean." When you are prideful, when you put yourself in God's place, you are defiled.

Read Titus 1:15-16. If you are prideful (defiled) nothing is pure. Who do the defiled profess to know? _____ But by their deeds what do they do? _____

Look back at Daniel 2:47. Who did Nebuchadnezzar profess to know? _____
But what did he do in Daniel 3:1? _____

Nebuchadnezzar professed God, but by his deeds he denied God. How many in the church today do this? How many profess, yet by their deeds deny? Let's look at another scripture.

Read Romans 1:18-23. According to verse 20, is God clearly seen?_____

Did they know God according to verse 21? _____ Did they honor Him? _____

What did they profess to be (verse 22)? _____ What did they become? _____

What did they exchange the glory of God for in verse 23? _____

They are prideful. They think they are wise. They clearly see God, yet they deny Him. They exchange God for *an image of corruptible man.* Nebuchadnezzar sure did. So do we. This reminds me of a church in Revelation.

Read Revelation 3:14-17

The church of Laodicea was rich. She didn't need anything – even God. Her deeds were lacking. She had no fire for the Lord anymore because she was content in herself.

What does Jesus say to her in verse 16? _____

Jesus says, "I will spit you out of My mouth." Laodicea had seen the Lord, yet she denied His power. She didn't need Him anymore. She was happy the way she was. She was prideful.

I need you to pause here and think about your life. Where are you in relation to the throne? Are you trying to claw your way into it? Or have you given God complete access to your life? Is He the leader of all you do? Do you consult Him in all areas of your life? What about your church? Your nation? Can you see the sin of Laodicea surrounding you?

"But whoever does not fall down and worship shall immediately be cast into the midst of a furnace of blazing fire."

Daniel 3:6

Let's look at one more thing before we close for the day. Look at Daniel 3:6 in the margin.

Read Isaiah 13:11. What are the ruthless considered? _____

Read Psalm 86:14. What is proud (or arrogant) man paired with? _____

When you are proud or haughty, you are ruthless and violent. When you are prideful, you tend to want to destroy anyone in your path that disagrees with you in any way. Nebuchadnezzar will be "filled with wrath" tomorrow when three of the faithful do not bow down to the image he had set up. This is a sign of pride – when you want the destruction of any who stand firm in their convictions.

Look at Proverbs 6:16-19 in the margin. What is the first thing listed that the Lord hates? _____

Search your own life and see if there is any desire to destroy others who rise against you, and when you see others who seek to destroy you, understand the root of their problem is pride.

If the Septuagint, or the Greek version of the Hebrew Scriptures, is correct when it notes that the statue was built approximately 18 years after Nebuchadnezzar's ascension to the throne, this would place the building of the statue with the destruction of Jerusalem.

What do you think Nebuchadnezzar was saying to God?

"I got your people, Yahweh. I took your lands. I destroyed your temple. I'm not just the head of gold; I am the entire statue. I am the man. I am the king. I am the statue of gold!"

I am quite certain Nebuchadnezzar is about to be humbled, don't you?

There are six things which the Lord hates, yes, seven which are an abomination to Him: haughty eyes, a lying tongue, and hands that shed innocent blood, a heart that devises wicked plans, feet that run rapidly to evil, a false witness who utters lies, and one who spreads strife among brothers.

Proverbs 6:16-19

1 Hinnant, Greg. *Daniel Notes* (Lake Mary, Florida: Creation House Press, 2003), 59.
2 Butler, Trent C. et al.,eds. *Holman Illustrated Bible Dictionary* (Nashville, Tennessee: Holman Bible Publishers, 2003), 372.

Week Four

"Let it be known to you, O king, that we are not going to serve your gods or worship the golden image that you have set up."

Daniel 3:18b

Day One – Chapter Three
The Stand

We looked at pride last week; we will see it manifested here with striking ramifications.

Read Daniel 3:8-18

We have witnessed the rising of a statue dripping with pride. We now see the prideful revenge of some men. Let's look closely at the Chaldeans' words.

In verse 12, what people group is named? _____ Who appointed them? _____ Who have these men disregarded? _____

If you recall from the end of chapter two, Daniel became "ruler over the whole province of Babylon and chief prefect over all the wise men" and Hananiah, Mishael, and Azariah were appointed "over the administration of the province of Babylon." These men were Jews, as was so clearly revealed in the Chaldeans' words. These Jews were "over" the other Chaldeans, they were more "important" in the affairs of Babylon. Can you feel the Chaldeans' envy? Can you sense their animosity? They wanted the Jews out. They wanted Babylonians to be in those offices. They appealed to Nebuchadnezzar's arrogance. They said that Shadrach, Meshach and Abed-nego had "disregarded" Nebuchadnezzar. They were trying to stroke the king's pride. The king fell for it. He calls the faithful three in to see him.

What does he do in verse 15? _____

I don't think the king was unaware of the intentions of the Chaldeans. Nebuchadnezzar was no fool. He gives Hananiah, Mishael, and Azariah another chance. There is a lesson here:

The Devil will always give you another chance to sin.[1]

Satan is no fool. Neither was Nebuchadnezzar. He offers the faithful three another chance to bow down. After all, the fire was right there, crackling and popping. Will the fire of persecution persuade them? We need to understand that in the end times, there will be a great persecution of the faithful. Once your faith is discovered, you will probably be given a chance to convert. The fire, or the ax, or the gallows will be right there, trying to persuade you. We need to stand firm in our faith and not be tempted to deny the One true God. We need to be like Hananiah, Mishael, and Azariah.

Nebuchadnezzar wanted to see for himself if the Chaldeans were telling the truth. He probably didn't expect his three servants to deny him. I mean, if you were faced with a fiery furnace, not many would have the guts to stand firm. Before we go any further, we need to ask a question. Where is Daniel? He is clearly absent, and there is no reason to think that Daniel was among those who fell to their knees because his integrity is never in question. He is just not among those assembled. Perhaps he was out of the city, doing a task for the king, or perhaps the Chaldeans targeted Daniel's three friends because the king would take issue with them accusing Daniel. We have no idea how close Daniel had become to his captor. He was perhaps with the king more than any other official in Babylon. There is really no reason to speculate. Daniel wasn't there, which brings to mind another point:

God will isolate you at some point in your life in order to test your faith.

Daniel was the leader. He was the one who "made up his mind that he would not defile himself." Daniel is the one who got Hananiah, Mishael, and Azariah their powerful positions. Daniel probably provided these faithful friends with a sense of security. Now God takes away their leader. These faithful three have to go it alone. Would they break if Daniel wasn't there? Or would they rely on God?[2]

Nebuchadnezzar tells the three friends to "fall down and worship" the image he has set up. This sounds suspiciously like someone else we read about in scripture. Look at Matthew 4:8-9 in the margin. The devil said the same thing to Jesus. He wants our worship, no matter if it is through actual idol worship, the worship of self-pride, or the worship of the world. Satan is the prince of this world (John 14:30), and he will do anything to take your worship away from the one true God. He will do so again in the last days – through the Antichrist, or the man of lawlessness – he will demand that we fall to our knees and worship.

Again, the devil took Him to a very high mountain and showed Him all the kingdoms of the world and their glory; and he said to Him, "All these things I will give You, if You fall down and worship me."

Matthew 4:8-9

Read 2 Thessalonians 2:1-4. Who will be revealed (verse 3)? _____

And who will he claim to be in verse four? _____

The Antichrist, or the man of lawlessness, will claim to be God. And Satan, the beast of Revelation, is behind his declaration (Revelation 12-13). Nebuchadnezzar's pride foreshadows the pride and arrogance of the Antichrist.[3] He will demand our worship. We have to prepare our hearts like Hananiah, Mishael, and Azariah. We have to stand firm.

Notice what Nebuchadnezzar says at the end of verse 15: "What god is there who can deliver you out of my hands?" Can you hear the pride dripping off of his tongue? I mean, Nebuchadnezzar may worship pagan gods, but he felt like he was above them! As the years had passed, he had forgotten about the God who he declared to be "the God of gods and a Lord of kings and a revealer of mysteries." I imagine our three friends were saying under their breath, "You don't know our God!"

Although they had been deported, Hananiah, Mishael, and Azariah had seen God reveal the king's dream and save the wise men. They had heard about His miracles of old: parting the Red Sea, providing manna in the wilderness, crumbling the walls of Jericho, having the sun stand still in the sky, and raising the dead to life. Nebuchadnezzar had no idea who he was up against, but Hananiah, Mishael, and Azariah did. Look at their reply in the margin.

Their first statement sounds a little arrogant until you take the passage as a whole. What they were saying was this, "We don't need a lengthy discussion, king. Our answer is final. We will not bow down." They weren't being arrogant; they were being firm. Nothing was going to persuade them, even the threat of death.

> "O Nebuchadnezzar, we do not need to give you an answer concerning this matter. If it be so, our God whom we serve is able to deliver us from the furnace of blazing fire; and He will deliver us out of your hand, O king. But even if He does not, let it be known to you, O king, that we are not going to serve your gods or worship the golden image that you have set up."
>
> Daniel 3:16-18

Fill in the blanks. "If it be so, our God whom we serve is _____ to deliver us from the furnace of blazing fire; and He _____ deliver us out of your hand, O king. But even if He _____ _____, let it be known to you, O king, that we are not going to serve your gods or worship the golden image that you have set up."

They knew God was able to save them, but they didn't know if He would. They had every faith in Him, but they hadn't had a dream, a vision, or a word from the Lord telling them they would be all right. They didn't know if they would survive, but they would not yield. They knew a truth Paul revealed centuries later.

Read 2 Timothy 3:12. Everyone who lives godly lives will be _____

If we are walking with God, that does not mean we will have a smooth life, in fact, the very opposite is true.

Read John 15:18-20. How does the world feel about us? _____ What will the world do to us? _____

The world hates us so that means the world will persecute us. Look at Jesus' own words about the last days in the margin.

"Then they will deliver you to tribulation, and will kill you, and you will be hated by all nations because of My name."

Turn to Revelation 2:13. What had happened to Antipas? _____

Matthew 24:9

Even though this happened, what did the other saints do? _____

A saint name Antipas was killed, yet the others did not break the faith. They would not deny the one true God. They looked into a fiery furnace of their own and they stood firm, just like Hananiah, Mishael, and Azariah. In the last days, we will need to do the same.

Read 1 Peter 1:6-7. How are we tested? _____

Read 1 Peter 4:12. How is testing described here? _____

But who can endure the day of His coming? And who can stand when He appears? For He is like a refiner's fire and like fullers' soap.

Malachi 3:2

Isn't it interesting that our testing is depicted as being "tested by fire" and portrayed as a "fiery ordeal." Being tested is painful, because without pain there is no growth. If we aren't put into the fire we cannot be refined. Look at Malachi 3:2 in the margin. Jesus is compared to a refiner's fire and fullers' soap. Fire will burn you if you are apart from Him, but if you are with Him, fire refines you. Through testing, He is growing you to be more like Him. He is causing you to shine.

Read Exodus 34:29. What happened to Moses?_____ Why? _____

Read Matthew 17:2. What did Jesus look like? _____

Read Matthew 5:14-16. What are we to do? _____ What do you think we are shining? _____

When we are with Him, we shine Him, and the more our faith grows (through the fire), the more we shine. I want you to revisit the response of the faithful three. They said that God could save them, but then they said, "if he does not." Between those two phrases they say something else interesting. They say, "He will deliver us out of your hand, O king." Although they were unsure whether or not they would be delivered from the fire, they did tell Nebuchadnezzar that God would absolutely deliver them from the king's hand. This is interesting. Either way, God would deliver them.

There were only two ways this could go: they could be thrown into the fire and die; they could be thrown into the fire and survive. Either way, God would deliver them. Do we have this kind of faith? Do we understand that even if God doesn't save you from the fire, that He still saves you? This is where I feel the church is lacking today. We don't realize that death is not death, but life – because He is the life. There are a lot of walking dead out there because if you are apart from Him, you are dead, even if you are alive! Only in Him is life. Death is not death to the faithful. Either way, God would deliver Hananiah, Mishael, and Azariah. They would either be thrown into the fire and live through it, or they would be thrown into the fire and live in another place. But either way: God would deliver them. They would live. Take this truth to heart:

You can walk into the fire, or walk through the fire. Either way, you live.

Before we end for today, I want you to think about Hananiah, Mishael, and Azariah. They were standing before the flames, firm in their faith. We may know the end of their story, but they did not. They had no idea if God was going to miraculously intervene. As they stood there, they knew one thing: fire was coming. If you had a choice, would you be able to stand the flames?

In the last days, you will be presented with a question: Will you bow down? This question shouldn't be a hard one to refuse. Yes, there may be pain in the flames if you refuse to bow, but on the other side of those flames is life. If you bow, you may be saved from immediate pain, but you have given up your life.

Life or death? The choice is really simple.

1 Hinnant, Greg. *Daniel Notes* (Lake Mary, Florida: Creation House Press, 2003), 70.
2 Hinnant, Greg. *Daniel Notes* (Lake Mary, Florida: Creation House Press, 2003), 61-62.
3 Hinnant, Greg. *Daniel Notes* (Lake Mary, Florida: Creation House Press, 2003), 58.

Day Two – Chapter Three
The Flames

"Was it not three men we cast bound into the midst of the fire?"

Daniel 3:24b

We left off yesterday with Hananiah, Mishael, and Azariah standing firm before a blazing fire. They told Nebuchadnezzar to take a hike – they would not bow down. Let's see what happens.

Read Daniel 3:19-25

There are just no words to do this story justice. Imagine watching this on the big screen and just when you think there is no hope – they walk out of the fire! Can you imagine Nebuchadnezzar's face? Speaking of the king's face, take another look at verse 19. He was "filled with wrath." Scripture says his face was changed toward Hananiah, Mishael, and Azariah. There is something interesting in those words. The word for "face" or "facial" or "form" is *tselem* (Strong's #6755). It is the same word used all throughout Daniel chapter three. Look at Daniel 3:1 in the margin for another way *tselem* is translated.

Nebuchadnezzar the king made an image *[tselem]* of gold . . .

Daniel 3:1

The word used for Nebuchadnezzar's face can also be translated "image." The image of gold was set up. Nebuchadnezzar commands everyone to bow down. Hananiah, Mishael, and Azariah refuse. Nebuchadnezzar's personal image becomes changed and altered. Herein lies a very important lesson:

You become what you worship.

Do you remember our discussion yesterday about being tested through the flames? The more you grow in Him, the more you will reflect His glory – just like Moses' face in the wilderness. Your face (or image) can shine Him or it can radiate something else. You become what you worship. Nebuchadnezzar had treated Hananiah, Mishael, and Azariah with respect and honor in the past. Now, in a flash, his respect is taken away. The image towering over him is turning Nebuchadnezzar's heart to stone. You become what you worship. Look at your life and see what you bow down to. If it is anything besides God, it is affecting your testimony. Be strong and stand up. You don't want to become anything other than a light for Christ.

Nebuchadnezzar ordered the furnace heated seven times hotter. I don't know how they measured this, but it is very significant that Nebuchadnezzar ordered it heated seven times hotter. Seven is the number of perfection in scripture: seven days of creation, seven years of plenty, seven years of famine, seven times around the walls of Jericho. Yesterday we looked at purification through fire. This trial by fire was the perfect trial by fire. After this chapter, we hear nothing else about Hananiah, Mishael, or Azariah. When they came out of those flames, at this stage of their walk, their faith had been perfected.[1]

Scripture says Nebuchadnezzar commanded certain "valiant warriors who were in his army." The King James Version says he commanded "the most mighty men that were in his army." The word translated "most" is *chayil* (Strong's #2429) and it means "army" or "strength." The word for "mighty" is *gibbar* (Strong's #1401) and it means "valiant" or "warrior." It is interesting to note that the word *chayil*, which is translated as "most" here, is also translated as "army" in that very same verse. So, what we have is an emphasis on the army-like attributes of these men. The verse could literally be translated "the army mighty men that were in his army." As in, these were the main men of the army, the best of the best, the cream of the crop, the stud muffins of the mix, the "do-not-mess-with-me-or-your-face-will-be-punched-in bad boys." Anyone with me? These were the tip of the top. These were Nebuchadnezzar's go-to warriors.

Fill in the blanks of Daniel 3:22. For this reason, because the king's command was _____ and the furnace had been made extremely hot, the flame of the fire _____ those men who carried up Shadrach, Meshach and Abed-nego.

These men died a tragic, needless death because of Nebuchadnezzar's rage. This leads us to conclude another important lesson:

When we are angry, we need to pause before we do anything rash.

Anger is not an "evil" emotion, but when it is ignited by the wrong reasons or with the wrong motivation, it can lead to catastrophic results. We need to be angry about rape, abuse, persecution, and all sorts of evil things in the world today, but we need to check our pride at the door and examine our hearts to see if we are angry for the right reasons. Nebuchadnezzar's prideful anger caused some of his best men to be killed.

We don't know exactly how it happened, the text is unclear, but it is quite possible the very act of throwing the faithful three into the flames caused a surge of fire to come forth, killing the soldiers in a heartbeat. This seems the best explanation and if this is so, it could have been God's way of punishing those who followed the king's orders to depose of Hananiah, Mishael, and Azariah. Don't mess with the faithful because at some point you will get burned. This also foreshadows what will occur in the last days. Fire comes down from heaven to punish the wicked that have persecuted those faithful to God. Fire is coming, and if you attempt to kill the faithful, you will be burned. It may not be immediately, like the fate of the soldiers in Daniel, but God's wrath will fall. Look at Isaiah 66:15-16 in the margin.

> For behold, the Lord will come in fire and His chariots like the whirlwind, to render His anger with fury, and His rebuke with flames of fire. For the Lord will execute judgment by fire and by His sword on all flesh, and those slain by the Lord will be many.
>
> Isaiah 66:15-16

God is patient with the world today, wanting no one to perish (2 Peter 3:9), but one day His patience will come to an end. He will answer with fire.

Read Daniel 3:21. What was tossed into the fire with the faithful three? _____

In ancient times, people were "stripped" of their fine apparel before any type of punishment was inflicted, but the king's order was "urgent" so all clothing remained on Hananiah, Mishael, and Azariah when they were thrown into the flames.[2] That is a lot of combustible material and it makes the miracle all the more amazing. Let's take a look at the details.

In verse 23, how were they thrown into the fire? _____

How were they described in verse 25?_____

Hananiah, Mishael, and Azariah were tossed into the flames with bindings, but when Nebuchadnezzar saw them in the midst of the fire, they were loosed and "walking about." Not only that, there was another person in the flames that looked like "a son of the gods." So just who was this fourth individual in the flames? It could be an angel as Nebuchadnezzar says in verse 28, but most scholars tend to believe this is Jesus Christ Himself. I tend to concur, because later in Daniel, Jesus is described in a very similar way. Also, Daniel deals with end time events. Many things in Daniel, like the fiery furnace, foreshadow the end of times, and Jesus will return in the end to save the faithful in the fire. Let's look and see where we see Jesus reappear in Daniel.

Read Daniel 7:9-14. What attends the Ancient of Days in verse 10? _____

In Revelation 5:11, what attends Him? _____

Who came before Him in verse 13?_____

What did this Son of Man come with?_____

How is Jesus said to come in Acts 1:11?_____

Will His kingdom pass away? _____

The Son of Man is walking around in the fire with Hananiah, Mishael, and Azariah. If you notice, the three faithful were not running for the nearest exit.[3] They were calm in the midst of the fire, no doubt because of the man walking with them. This again, leads us to a valuable lesson:

Even if the flames of persecution surround you, God is right there with you.

Look at Psalm 46:1-3 in the margin. God is our refuge and help. We should not fear persecution or fiery trials. Jesus told us they would come (Matthew 24:8, John 15:20). Our eyes always need to be focused on the One who can help us, the One who can save us, and the One who has already saved us, even if the flames surrounding us lead to death in the here and now.

God is our refuge and strength, a very present help in trouble. Therefore we will not fear, though the earth should change and though the mountains slip into the heart of the sea; though its waters roar and foam, though the mountains quake with its swelling pride.

Psalm 46:1-3

Let's pause here and consider that Hananiah, Mishael, and Azariah probably saw Jesus long before He was born in Bethlehem. Did they speak to Him? What did He say? What did they say? What we can know for sure is this:

If Jesus is in our midst, there is salvation, because He is the salvation and the life.

Do you remember back in a previous lesson where I said Jesus' name is Salvation, well, here is an absolutely beautiful picture of what Jesus does for us. We are in the fire of life. We are bound in sin. We are on the path of death by the eternal flames (Revelation 20:10). Yet, if we invite Jesus into our lives, we are set free of sin's bindings and we can walk into freedom and life. Yes, Jesus is beautiful, is He not? He set us free. We are free. And even in the flames, we have the life.

So if the Son makes you free, you will be free indeed. (John 8:36)

You are free, faithful friends. The flames can't touch you. You already have "the life" (John 14:6). More to come tomorrow.

1 Hinnant, Greg. *Daniel Notes* (Lake Mary, Florida: Creation House Press, 2003), 77.
2 Leupold, H.C. *Exposition of Daniel* (Grand Rapids, Michigan: Baker Book House Company, 1969), 155.
3 Leupold, H.C. *Exposition of Daniel* (Grand Rapids, Michigan: Baker Book House Company, 1969), 157.

Day Three – Chapter Three
Promotion Through Pain

Nor had the smell of fire even come upon them.

Daniel 3:27b

Yesterday we saw Jesus saving Hananiah, Mishael, and Azariah. Today, we see the result of their faithfulness.

Read Daniel 3:26-30

What did Nebuchadnezzar immediately recognize in verse 26? _____

Nebuchadnezzar doesn't stutter like he is unaware of what is happening. He has already encountered Daniel and his friends' God in chapter two. He knows exactly who he is dealing with: the Most High God, the only One he should worship. If the Most High God can save the faithful from the flames, He alone should be worshiped. Nebuchadnezzar recognizes he is standing before greatness. He calls Hananiah, Mishael, and Azariah out of the flames. They walk out completely unharmed.

According to verse 26, were their bodies harmed? _____ Were their clothes or their hair? _____ Did they even smell like smoke? _____

Nothing was harmed: not their bodies, or their hair, or their clothes. They were in the midst of a blazing fire, heated to an extraordinary degree that killed the men that had bound them, and they were unharmed. I don't know if we can even wrap our minds around this miracle. It is amazing. But here is the really amazing thing: they didn't even smell like smoke. When you are surrounded by fire, you smell like smoke. Think about sitting around a campfire. You may not be touching the flames, but the smoke is all around you. You can't walk away from a campfire without smelling like smoke. It gets in your hair and your clothes. When you leave you can still smell it. These men didn't even smell like fire. If you hadn't seen them walk away from the flames, you would have never believed the tale. This brings us to another important take away:

If you are with Jesus, you can walk out of a trial by fire without any negative effects.

You can be delivered to such a degree that no one would guess you had gone through the trial at all. Have you met anyone that just wears their burdens? I am sure you have. They are the negative Nellies of your life, the ones that bring up their problems over and over again. They take what has happened in their past and put it on like a cloak of depression. They can barely smile. They limp around like they will die if you push them with your little finger. These people didn't look to Jesus in their fires, they concentrated on the flames, on the hurt, and on the ones who inflicted it. They pointed their fingers at their Nebuchadnezzars, blamed the soldiers, and feared the flames.

But then there are the warriors. You know them, the ones that have been thrown into the flames and have come out unscathed. At one point you may have looked at them and wondered what was so special about their life. Then you find out that they have been through one of the worst trials anyone could walk – yet they don't wear it like a cloak of depression. They barely even talk about it. They don't talk about it because Jesus was with them in the fire, and when they walked out, they didn't even smell like smoke. They clung to Him through the flames and they walked out without a burn. They looked to the One and not their problems. They relied on the One and not the flames. They knew that only He could be their salvation. They didn't blame their Nebuchadnezzar, or the soldiers who threw them into the flames, or the flames themselves. They stood firm.

In the last days, there will be many fires.

Turn to Revelation 6:3-4. What does this horseman bring? _____

What about Revelation 6:5-6? _____ Revelation 6:7-8? _____

What about Revelation 6:9? _____

There will be the fire of terror, the fire of famine, the fire of death, and the fire of martyrdom. Will we be Hananiah, Mishael, and Azariah in the flames? Will we look to the One and not our circumstances? Ready your hearts, my faithful friends. Ready your hearts.

When Hananiah, Mishael, and Azariah walk out of the flames, Nebuchadnezzar says something profound. Look at Daniel 3:28 in the margin. He sees it all clearly, and he praises them for violating his command and yielding their bodies to the flames.

Scripture says we are to obey human authority until it conflicts with God's authority.

Read Matthew 22:21. What are we to do? _____

The first and second commandments tell us to not have any other god before God, and to never make a graven image (Exodus 20:3-6). The Word of God is above Nebuchadnezzar, and the faithful three cannot disobey it. They had to violate the king's command in order to obey God. They yielded their lives to do so and trusted the outcome of their decision to the hands of God.

"Blessed be the God of Shadrach, Meshach and Abed-nego, who has sent His angel and delivered His servants who put their **trust** in Him, **violating** the king's command, and **yielding** up their bodies so as not to serve or worship any god except their own God."

Daniel 3:28, emphasis added

What does Jesus say in Revelation 2:10. If they are faithful to the point of death, what do they receive? _____

Read John 11:26. What does Jesus say here? _____

Hananiah, Mishael, and Azariah believed this. No matter if death came, so did the life. They violated the king's command because they had to yield to a higher authority and trust all would be well.

Because of what he has seen, Nebuchadnezzar dose something surprising.

What does he do in verse 29?_____

Oh, you just have to love old Neb! He goes to extremes all the time, does he not? Off with their heads! No, God is a revealer of mysteries. Raise up a statue to worship! No, issue a decree that if anyone says anything bad about God, then they should be torn limb from limb. I love it. I just love it. He is black and then he is white. I kinda like old Nebuchadnezzar. You have to hand it to him: he isn't boring. He issues a decree that hinders anyone from saying anything against the God of Hananiah, Mishael, and Azariah without fear of death. Think about the ramifications of this: the Jews were in exile, in a foreign land, with foreign gods and people who perhaps persecuted them for their beliefs. Then the king of Babylon says you can't speak out against the God of the Jews. This is huge for the Jewish remnant in Babylon. Their sense of security increased greatly because they could now worship Yahweh without fear of persecution.[1]

Look at Daniel 3:27. Was it just Nebuchadnezzar that witnessed the trial by fire?_____

In Daniel 3:2 it says that Nebuchadnezzar assembled "all the rulers of the provinces to come to the dedication of the image" he had set up. Many were gathered. We do not know how many remained when Hananiah, Mishael, and Azariah were singled out, but there were many present. Verse 27 says "the satraps, the prefects, the governors and the king's high officials gathered around" Hananiah, Mishael, and Azariah. They all saw them walking around in the fire unscathed with one that looked like "a son of the gods," and they witnessed the three faithful coming out without even the smell of smoke. These were the high officials of Babylon. They saw it all.

Read Psalm 40:1-3. What does the end of verse three say? _____

Do you think God was showing off in order to touch some hearts of the "high officials" in Babylon? God does not want any to perish, but for all to come to repentance (2 Peter 3:9). Don't you think that even means those in Babylon? I sure do. In the last days, Babylon will return. There is a reason why God's wrath falls over a period of time and doesn't occur all at once – repentance. He wants those in Babylon to repent. In Revelation, there is a critical verse that we would call "the point of no return." It is only after this point that the final wrath of God is unleashed.

Read Revelation 9:20-21. What did mankind not do? _____

This is announced at the end of trumpet number six, one of the judgments of Revelation. But with the blowing of the seventh trumpet, the bowls are unleashed and the bowls are the final wrath of God pouring down on the earth in very quick succession. You could say that Jesus comes with the bowls. Jesus returns only when no one else repents. This leads us to a very important lesson:

God wants to convert even our enemies.

Even though Babylon was used as a destructive tool, it had another purpose. God's people tend to seek Him more when they are in pain. With pain there is growth and repentance. God was trying to get His people's attention. "Then you will call upon Me and come and pray to Me, and I will listen to you" (Jeremiah 29:12). And when Judah finally acknowledged God in Babylon, Judah's light shone. Daniel's light shone. Hananiah, Mishael, and Azariah's light shone. And all the "high officials" in Babylon saw that light. Did some of them repent? I bet they did. Just like Psalm 40 says, "Many will see and fear and will trust in the Lord."

> Then the king promoted Shadrach, Meshach, and Abednego in the province of Babylon.
>
> Daniel 3:30 ESV

Now read Daniel 3:30 in the margin. The faithful three were promoted, but only after pain. With pain comes growth, and only through growth will you be trusted with a greater position. This leads us to another very important lesson:[2]

Without pain, there is little growth, and without growth, there is no promotion. Only through testing will you be refined to shine.

Only fire can refine you. It may be painful, but if you stand the test, He can better use you.

Faithful friends, when the fire of testing comes, know He is using the fire to make you a stronger follower of Him. Be #readytoSHINE.

1 Hinnant, Greg. *Daniel Notes* (Lake Mary, Florida: Creation House Press, 2003), 93.
2 Hinnant, Greg. *Daniel Notes* (Lake Mary, Florida: Creation House Press, 2003), 76-94.
Chand, Samuel R. *Leadership Pain* (Nashville, Tennessee: Thomas Nelson, 2015).

Day Four – Chapter Four
Flourishing

When you pass through the waters, I will be with you; and through the rivers, they will not overflow you. When you walk through the fire, you will not be scorched, nor will the flame burn you. For I am the Lord your God.

Isaiah 43:2-3a

Nebuchadnezzar has witnessed some very exciting stuff from the "the God of gods and the Lord of kings" and the "Most High God." He has even witnessed three of His faithful servants literally walk through the flames and not be burned – which reminds me of a passage in Isaiah.

Read Isaiah 43:2-3 in the margin. When He calls you by name, what will happen in the flames? _____

You will not be burned if you are with Him. Nebuchadnezzar saw that. I truly believe many of the things transpiring in Daniel were there to convert Nebuchadnezzar to faith. For some reason God saw something in the king. He knew his heart. But if the miracle of the dream's revelation wasn't enough, was the miracle by fire? Let's find out.

Read Daniel 4:4-18

I have purposely skipped verses one through three. We will revisit those verses in the next lesson. For now, let's study just what Nebuchadnezzar revealed about his attitude and his dream. Take another look at verse four in the margin.

"I, Nebuchadnezzar, was at ease in my house and flourishing in my palace."

Daniel 4:4

This small verse yields a host of information. Nebuchadnezzar was at ease and flourishing. The word "ease" is also translated "rest" or "safe" in some translations of scripture. It is *shelah* (Strong's #7954), and it means "to be secure." Nebuchadnezzar was secure. He had no worry of other kingdom's attacking him, especially after Daniel's interpretation of Nebuchadnezzar's dream in chapter two. The word "flourishing" is *raanan* (Strong's #7487), and it really means "to be green." Isn't that interesting? It will be even more interesting in tomorrow's lesson, so keep that word in mind. It is figuratively translated "flourishing" due to the fact that green is associated with crops and plenty. So if Nebuchadnezzar felt "green" he meant to say he was "flourishing" and had "abundant" wealth and possessions. You could say he felt smugly secure and pridefully prosperous.

So, once again, the king has a dream. And once again, the king is troubled and calls in all the wise men of Babylon. Even though the king reveals his dream this time, the wise men can't help him. But then Daniel enters the king's presence. Let's see what the king said about the dream.

In verse 10, what did Nebuchadnezzar say about the tree's height? _____

Turn back to Daniel 2:31. How was the statue's height described? _____

The same word is used in the descriptions of both the tree and the statue. In Daniel 2:31, the statue is described as being "a single great statue" and in Daniel 4:10 the tree is described as being "great."

Where did the tree's height reach in verse 11? _____
Does this remind you of anything? _____

Compare this to Genesis 11:4. Where was the tower supposed to reach? _____
And what did the people want to do? _____

The tree's height reached to the "heavens" or the "sky" just like the tower of Babel. The people in Babel wanted to "make a name for themselves" and Nebuchadnezzar already thought he had. Have you come to a conclusion about the tree's identity? I thought so. I don't think Nebuchadnezzar was too ignorant about this fact either. I believe he had a suspicion that he, in fact, was the tree. Why do I say this?

Look again at verse 12. Describe the animals in relation to the tree. _____

Now turn back to Daniel 2:38. What did God say about Nebuchadnezzar? _____

I believe Nebuchadnezzar knew exactly who the tree symbolized. He had been described this way before. So why was he so troubled? Take a look at verse 14 in the margin.

Yikes. Clearly, if Nebuchadnezzar had an inkling (and I am quite certain he did) of the tree's identity, he would be fearful (Daniel 4:5). But hadn't Daniel's interpretation of the statue been that Nebuchadnezzar was the head of gold and only "after him" would arise another kingdom that would take control? Yes, that is correct. So what is going on here?

"Chop down the tree and cut off its branches, strip off its foliage and scatter its fruit; let the beasts flee from under it and the birds from its branches . . ."

Daniel 4:14

Read Daniel 4:19-27

Daniel is disturbed. I daresay I would be too if I had to tell the king the interpretation. But the king tells him "Belteshazzar, do not let the dream or its interpretation alarm you." Just stop here for a moment and picture this scene. The Bible is very factual; it is a blow-by-blow recount of what actually happened and does not reveal many emotions of the characters in the scene. Daniel had been in the service of the king for quite some time. Were they friends by this point? Although Nebuchadnezzar had taken Daniel from his homeland, he had also honored him. Based on this chapter, it is obvious the king greatly respected Daniel. I would wager a guess that Daniel and the king had grown to have some sort of positive relationship, especially given the fact that Daniel was "the ruler over the whole province of Babylon." Daniel and the king probably had to communicate daily. It would be quite surprising if feelings of friendship weren't present. Daniel knew Nebuchadnezzar was raised up to try to bring Judah back from completely falling away from God. Why do I say that?

What does Daniel 2:21 say about kings? _____

Daniel knew God had used Nebuchadnezzar, and Daniel also knew that God had used Nebuchadnezzar's dream to raise up the Jews both in position and also in respect (based on the degree given in chapter three). So let's get back to the dream of the tree. I can just imagine Nebuchadnezzar walking toward Daniel and placing a hand on his shoulder. I can even envision the king lowering his voice in order to assure Daniel that when he did interpret the dream, no harm would come to him. Imagine it with me. "Belteshazzar, do not let the dream or its interpretation alarm you." Don't you think Nebuchadnezzar knew the first thing that Daniel would say, "You are the tree!" Nebuchadnezzar assures Daniel that no matter the interpretation, all would be well. There would be no more, "Off with your heads!"

What emotion does it seem Daniel has in Daniel 4:19? _____

Daniel says he wishes the dream applied to Nebuchadnezzar's enemies! Even though Daniel is uncomfortable with the vision, he does not back down from revealing the dream. "It is you, O king!" There is a lesson here:

When confronted by the pagan world, we should not water down the message – but speak the whole truth.

The world wants everything it does to be acceptable. People want all of their actions justified. The spirit of tolerance in today's society makes speaking the truth a lot tougher. You can now be considered "intolerant" if you disagree. But Jesus didn't back down. He spoke in love, but He spoke the truth. So did Daniel. So should we.

Like I have said previously, I don't believe Daniel's "It is you, O king!" surprised the king one iota. What was befuddling him was what happened to the tree. What did it mean? Did this mean death? Not exactly. What would ultimately happen to Nebuchadnezzar?

Read Daniel 4:25. What did Nebuchadnezzar have to do? _____

God was bound and determined to humble the pride of the king so that he would acknowledge the Most High God. God wanted Nebuchadnezzar's heart. Now, with that in mind, I want you to see something very interesting.

Look at Daniel 4:13 in the margin. What is the angel called? _____

"I saw in the visions of my head as I lay in bed, and behold, a watcher, a holy one, came down from heaven."

Daniel 4:13 ESV

The angel in Daniel chapter four is called a "watcher." The word "watcher" is the Aramaic word *iyr* (Strong's #5894) and it is derived from a root corresponding to *uwr* (Strong's #5782), which means "to wake." Daniel chapter four is the only place an angel is described as a "watcher." But think about what the angel had come down to do! He was sent to "awaken" the king to the God of the universe and to humble his pride so that he could wake up to the fact that God was God. Do you see it? The angel was sent to awaken the king. That is why he is called a watcher in Daniel. Who said the Bible was boring? Some of your translations have the word "angelic" or "angel" right beside the word "watcher" but those words are not in the original text. The word used to name this being is "watcher." He was sent to wake Nebuchadnezzar up!

This watcher was told to cut down the tree, strip its branches of foliage and scatter its fruit. The watcher was told to destroy the tree – every aspect described. This is probably what had Nebuchadnezzar in a tizzy. No one wants to be destroyed. It doesn't sound like too much fun. Herein lies another lesson:

Sometimes God has to destroy us to wake us up.

This doesn't happen to everyone, but some of us need to be destroyed in order to purge out what needs to be purged in order to see God. If God had not "destroyed" Nebuchadnezzar, there was no hope of salvation. Nebuchadnezzar needed to be stripped of his pride in order to see the power that ruled him and his kingdom.

Read Daniel 4:25. How many periods of time? _____

God told Nebuchadnezzar that he would dwell with the beasts of the field, and eat grass like the cattle and be drenched with the dew of heaven for seven periods of time. This condition is known to us as lycanthropy, a form of schizophrenia. It is a condition where someone thinks he has transformed into an animal. The Babylonians thought this condition was a direct result of divine anger. And so it was![1] The prideful king would think himself a beast. This sentence was for a period of seven somethings. As we mentioned earlier in the study, seven is the number of perfection in scripture. We do not know how long these periods extended. It had to be more than seven days because Nebuchadnezzar's hair had to grow "like eagle's feathers and his nails like bird's claws" (Daniel 4:33). Some scholar's think Nebuchadnezzar's sickness lasted seven years. We can't say with certainty, but what we do know is that it was the perfect amount of time to perfect Nebuchadnezzar. We will look at this more tomorrow.

1 *One-Volume Illustrated Edition of Zondervan Bible Commentary* with General Editor F. F. Bruce (Zondervan, 2008), 889.

Day Five – Chapter Four
Humbled

"This is the interpretation, O king, and this is the decree of the Most High . . ."

Daniel 4:24

We left off yesterday looking at Nebuchadnezzar's impending destruction. We have yet to see what becomes of him, but first, we need to look at something very interesting.

Look at Daniel 4:24 in the margin. How did Daniel describe Nebuchadnezzar's sentence. It was God's _____

The word used here for decree is *gezerah* (Strong's #1510) and it has its root in *gazar* (Strong's #1504) which means "to cut down." Wrap your minds around that for a moment. The "decree" of God was "to cut down." This is a completely different word than the word used to describe Nebuchadnezzar's decrees in chapters two and three (Strong's #2942, #1882). So why did God speak this particular word that had its root in "to cut down?" I believe the importance is twofold. First, the decree was to cut Nebuchadnezzar down – the decree was to destroy him. Secondly, the meaning had to do with the covenants made in Old Testament times. When two parties would enter into a covenant, animals were cut in two and a path was made between the broken parts. Each party would walk down the path, indicating that they would keep the covenant or risk death. The covenant was binding. It was sure. It could not be broken.

God used this term to convey to Nebuchadnezzar that His words were final. The words He spoke would happen, it was only a matter of time before God would "cut" Nebuchadnezzar down. Yesterday we read Daniel's plea to Nebuchadnezzar. Let's re-visit it here.

Read Daniel 4:27. Daniel pleads with the king to turn from his ways, but does he say the verdict from God could be withdrawn? What word does he use?_____

Nebuchadnezzar's tranquility could only be prolonged, extended, or lengthened. Do you see it? The decree "to cut down" would come to pass. It could not be revoked. It was firm.

Read Daniel 4:28-37

How much time had passed (Daniel 4:29)? _____ Where was he? _____

Who built Babylon (Daniel 4:30)? _____ By what? _____ For what? _____

Ah, do you think Nebuchadnezzar's pride had risen to the heavens? I daresay it had. He was on his roof, looking out over his empire and pride swelled in his chest. The interesting thing to note here is that Nebuchadnezzar has gone down in history as one of the greatest kings to have ever walked the earth.

Nebuchadnezzar is noteworthy for a massive rebuilding program in Babylon itself. The city spanned the Euphrates and was surrounded by an 11-mile long outer wall that enclosed suburbs and Nebuchadnezzar's summer palace. The inner wall was wide enough to accommodate two chariots abreast. It could be entered through eight gates, the most famous of which was the northern Ishtar Gate, used in the annual New Year Festival and decorated with reliefs of dragons and bulls in enameled brick. The road to this gate was bordered by high walls decorated by lions in glazed brick behind which were defensive citadels. Inside the gate was the main palace built by Nebuchadnezzar with its huge throne room. A cellar with shafts in part of the palace may have served as the substructure to the famous "Hanging Gardens of Babylon," described by classical authors as one of the wonders of the ancient world. Babylon contained many temples, the most important of which was Esagila, the temple of the city's patron god, Marduk. Rebuilt by Nebuchadnezzar, the temple was lavishly decorated with gold. Just north of Esagila lay the huge stepped tower of Babylon, a ziggurat called Etemenanki and its sacred enclosure. Its seven stories perhaps towered some 300 feet above the city.[1]

Nebuchadnezzar was walking on his roof, looking out on all that has just been described and declares, "Is this not Babylon the great, which I myself have built as a royal residence by the might of my power and for the glory of my majesty?" The dream of the tree was not on his mind. Nebuchadnezzar had 12 months to repent but those months just furthered his delusion of how mighty he was. Even though the dream had faded from Nebuchadnezzar's mind, it had not faded from God's. Look at Daniel 4:31-32 in the margin. There is a lesson here:

"King Nebuchadnezzar, to you it is declared: sovereignty has been removed from you . . . until you recognize that the Most High is ruler over the realm of mankind and bestows it on whomever He wishes."

Daniel 4:31-32

God gives us time to repent – a grace period – but all grace periods come to an end.

When did this happen (Daniel 4:33)? _____

It happened at that very second, that very heartbeat, and that very breath. Nebuchadnezzar was sane one moment and then he was not sane the next. He became, in his mind, a beast. This leads us to a very important take away.

God can change your life in a moment. It only takes a moment.

Nebuchadnezzar was changed in a bad way. He was brought about as low as you could go – on his knees, eating grass like the ox. God can change you in a moment. If you continue down a wrong course, normally it is a slow burn of sinfulness but an abruptly quick demise. One moment you are fine, the next you are not. One moment you are driving, the next you are wrapped around a tree. One moment your lies are hidden, the next they are exposed. It just takes a moment.

This momentary change can also be for the better. If God has promised you something, it will come to pass – in a moment. One moment things are the same, the next they are changed. God is looking for faith in you during the span of time before that moment hits. Do you believe His promises even if they look impossible? It just takes a moment. For Sarah, one moment she was infertile, the next she was pregnant. For David, one moment he was a refugee, the next he was king. For Hananiah, Mishael, and Azariah, one moment they were in dire peril, the next moment they were saved.

It just takes God a moment to change your life for the good or for the bad. One moment. God is looking for faith during the grace period of a trial. During Nebuchadnezzar's twelve-month grace period, he displayed no faith in the one true God. But God saw something in old Neb, and God wanted his heart.

Read Daniel 4:15. What was left? _____ How was it protected?
_____

God told the watcher to leave the stump and its roots, meaning the tree was not dead. It was destroyed, all of its beauty was taken, but it remained alive. The roots continued to drink the "dew of heaven" even though Nebuchadnezzar lived among the beasts. Most scholars believe this took place in the palace grounds because in the end Nebuchadnezzar rises back to his throne. The tree stump was protected by a "band of iron and bronze." As we have seen from our statue in chapter two, bronze and iron represent the strongest of metals. Nebuchadnezzar's roots would remain, and he would be protected in the palace walls by strong forces. God did not want to annihilate old Neb; He wanted his heart. Nebuchadnezzar was probably isolated within the palace walls while Daniel and others took care of the king's affairs.[2]

Read Daniel 4:34. What did Nebuchadnezzar do? _____ Then what was restored? _____

What was reestablished in verse 36? _____ And what was added?
_____

Look at Job 14:7 in the margin. There is hope for a tree when it is cut down if the Lord is the one who has done the cutting! As soon as Nebuchadnezzar raised his eyes to heaven, his reason was restored. Not only was he restored, but his throne was also given back to him. Not only was his throne given back to him, but "surpassing greatness" was also added to him. That word "greatness" also translated "majesty" in some versions of scripture is *rabah* (Strong's #7235) and it means "increase." Nebuchadnezzar was not only reestablished, he was also "increased."

"For there is hope for a tree, when it is cut down, that it will sprout again, and its shoots will not fail."

Job 14:7

When you acknowledge that you are not on the throne and look to the One who is on the throne, you are restored and blessings are added to your life.

Nebuchadnezzar had acknowledged God before. Let's take a look back.

Read Daniel 2:47. "Surely _____ God is a God of gods and Lord of kings."

In Daniel 3:29, whose God was God? _____

Now look at Daniel 4:37. Who praises God now? _____ What does Nebuchadnezzar praise Him for? _____

Look back at verse 35. The inhabitants of the earth are _____.

Nebuchadnezzar has come to faith. It took God a little convincing didn't it? Nebuchadnezzar humbled himself – yet he increased. Being humble doesn't mean you don't know your own worth; it means you know your own worth in the sight of God. Even though we are "nothing," we can have "surpassing greatness."

Read 1 Peter 5:6. If you humble yourself, what will happen?_____

I wonder how much Daniel influenced Nebuchadnezzar over the years. How many times had Daniel talked to the king about the One true God? I bet it was a lot. I wonder how often Daniel spoke to Nebuchadnezzar after his transformation? I would wager it was quite a bit. Now think about this: this is the last we hear about Nebuchadnezzar. If he truly turned to God, we will see him in heaven. Daniel and Nebuchadnezzar – side by side – strolling down the streets of gold. You will have a chance to talk to him – the king of Babylon – the head of gold – the prideful one who was brought low. Which brings us to another lesson:

God can save the greatest and the most entrenched person in Babylon.

This will be important in the last days. Although another evil empire will rise, God wants us to know that even the most embedded person in that system can be saved. They can turn. We need to understand that and not deem those deep in Babylon unsalvageable. And here is what I find fascinating: Nebuchadnezzar, the greatest king of Babylon, has spoken throughout the ages, and will continue to speak to those living in Babylon in the last days. Take a look at the very first verses we skipped in chapter four. They are written for you in the margin.

To whom did the king speak? _____

What is His kingdom?_____

What is He able to do according to Daniel 4:37? _____

_____

Nebuchadnezzar the king to all the peoples, nations, and men of every language that live in all the earth: "May your peace abound! It has seemed good to me to declare the signs and wonders which the Most High God has done for me. How great are His signs and how mighty are His wonders! His kingdom is an everlasting kingdom and His dominion is from generation to generation."

Daniel 4:1-3

Nebuchadnezzar wrote to "all the peoples." He is writing to you, to me, and to all of those in future Babylon. He wrote to tell everyone throughout the ages that God is the "Most High God." That His kingdom is everlasting – meaning you cannot overtake Him – you cannot sit on the throne because the throne is already occupied. And He humbles those who walk in pride. In the last days there will be a lot of pride, a lot of people "building towers" to reach to heaven, a lot of people trying to get "the life" without Jesus. Nebuchadnezzar's story warns those throughout the ages – humble yourself now, before God humbles you Himself.

Turn to Daniel 8:25. What will this man do in his heart? _____

This verse foreshadows the Antichrist. The Antichrist will be full of pride. But like Nebuchadnezzar, he will be humbled. Unlike Nebuchadnezzar, he will not repent.

We will see the destruction of the gold kingdom tomorrow. Tomorrow, the silver kingdom will rule.

1 Butler, Trent C. et al.,eds. *Holman Illustrated Bible Dictionary* (Nashville, Tennessee: Holman Bible Publishers, 2003), 158-159.
2 Leupold, H.C. *Exposition of Daniel* (Grand Rapids, Michigan: Baker Book House Company, 1969), 201.

Week Five

"Then they brought the gold vessels that had been taken out of the temple, the house of God which was in Jerusalem . . . [and] drank from them."

Daniel 5:3

Day One – Chapter Five
From Pride to Insolence

We saw the last of Nebuchadnezzar in chapter four. The king reigned from 605 BC (when Daniel was taken into exile) until 562 BC – a period of 43 years. After Nebuchadnezzar's death his son Awel-marduk, also called Evil-Merodach, came to power. Let's turn to see where scripture mentions Nebuchadnezzar's son.[1]

Read 2 Kings 25:27-30. What year of Jehoiachin's exile did this happen? _____

What did Evil-Merodach do?_____

If you recall, Jehoiachin was the son of Jehoiakim and he only ruled Judah for three months. Nebuchadnezzar laid siege to Judah during Jehoiachin's short reign and he was taken into exile at eighteen years of age (2 Kings 24:8). Jehoiachin's exile was in 598 BC, at the same time Ezekiel was exiled. Evil-Merodach only ruled for two years in Babylon, from 562 BC to 560 BC, but sometime during his reign he released the former king of Judah. This would have made Jehoiachin approximately 55 at the time; Daniel would have been approximately 60. Even though it took a long time, Jehoiachin was able to live out his life in peace.

After Evil-Merodach, there were a few more individuals who came to power but their reigns were short: Neriglissar (Nebuchadnezzar's son-in-law) and Labashi-Marduk (Nebuchadnezzar's grandson) who ruled collectively from 560 BC to 556 BC. After them Nabonidus came to power in 556 BC and he stayed in power until 539 BC. We don't know for sure the relation of Nabonidus to Nebuchadnezzar, but one theory is that Nabonidus married Nebuchadnezzar's widow the queen (who comes into the picture in chapter five) since Nabonidus came to power only six years after Nebuchadnezzar's death. Nabonidus was an interesting character. He doesn't fit the description of a normal king. He moved from the city of Babylon to northern Arabia for the last 10 years of his reign. He left his son Belshazzar as regent in Babylon.[2] That is where our story begins – in 539 BC. Daniel would have been approximately 82 years old at this point in his life.

Read Daniel 5:1-8

Oh to be a fly on the wall! Again, I am looking forward to a big screen in heaven. I want to see this live and in person.

Belshazzar was King Nabonidus' son, and he was regent in Babylon. In verse two it says his "father" Nebuchadnezzar but the Aramaic word for "father" can also mean "ancestor." Like his ancestor Nebuchadnezzar, Belshazzar possessed a little pride. Belshazzar ordered God's vessels to be brought to him at the feast so that "the king and his nobles, his wives and his concubines might drink from them."

Do you remember our discussion about God's vessels? They were to be "set apart" and "holy." They represented Jesus' future sacrifice. Those who touched them also had to be "set apart" and "holy." Nebuchadnezzar had never been so crass as to use God's vessels himself. He simply put them in the temple of his gods. It was a statement of "our gods have conquered your God." It was bad, to be sure, but it wasn't the bold declaration of defiance Belshazzar was initiating. It was customary in Nebuchadnezzar's day to "respect" all gods. Even if other "gods" were conquered, they were treated with reverence. This is why Nebuchadnezzar never misused God's vessels. He may have taken them, he may have placed them in the temples of his gods, but he in no way desecrated them. He still showed them some amount of respect. This is made clear when he acknowledges Daniel's God in chapters two through four. Nebuchadnezzar even comes to faith in chapter four after being humbled from his pride.

Now let's talk about Belshazzar. Take note that he had never lifted his hand in conquest. He sat on the throne Nebuchadnezzar had firmly established. He was prideful for nothing. He wasn't even king! Have you ever met someone like this? Someone who claims they have conquered and yet they have done nothing at all? That is Belshazzar.

Belshazzar doesn't just order the vessels to be displayed; he orders them to be used. Nebuchadnezzar had been prideful, but he was never insolent.[3]

Skip ahead to what Daniel tells Belshazzar in Daniel 5:20-22. What did Belshazzar know?_____

Do you see it? Nebuchadnezzar had died approximately twenty-three years prior. Belshazzar knew what had happened to Nebuchadnezzar. He knew exactly what God Nebuchadnezzar had served at the end of his life. He knew about the miracle of the fiery furnace. He knew Nebuchadnezzar had been humbled of his pride. I am sure he had read Nebuchadnezzar's account of his insanity that we studied last week.

Who did Nebuchadnezzar honor in Daniel 4:37? _____

Belshazzar knew this, and yet he had decided the Most High God was not for him. He was deliberately bringing up God's vessels in order to thumb his nose at the God of Israel. He knew the truth, yet he rejected the truth.

What did Belshazzar do while drinking out of God's vessels in Daniel 5:4? _____

Belshazzar desecrated God's vessels that promised Jesus' sacrifice. Can you imagine? This was an all out in-your-face-anti-God-act. God had to do something about it. This leads us to a major lesson:

If you desecrate God's vessels, you are under His wrath.

We are His vessels too. This applies to us. We are "set apart" for Him. We are "holy" because His Son is "holy."

Read 1 Corinthians 3:16-17 in the margin. If any man destroys us, what will God do? _____

We are under God's watchful eye, just like those vessels. Wrath will come upon those who mistreat us. And He won't take long to do it.

In Daniel 5:5, how soon did the hand appear? _____

Do you not know that you are a temple of God and that the Spirit of God dwells in you? If any man destroys the temple of God, God will destroy him, for the temple of God is holy, and that is what you are.

1 Corinthians 3:16-17

The word or words you put in the above blank will depend on your translation of scripture. Some translate the Aramaic word *sha-ah* as "suddenly," or "in the same hour," or "immediately." The word *sha-ah* (Strong's #8160) really means "a look." So, the more accurate translation is "immediately," or "at that moment." God sent the hand immediately in order to judge the insolent king. Do you recall that cliché "the handwriting is on the wall?" Well, that phrase stems from Daniel chapter five. The handwriting was literally on the wall, and it meant a sure and fitting end.[4]

What happened to the king in Daniel 5:6? _____

How fast the insolent one is humbled! In verse seven it says the king "called aloud" or "cried out" for the wise men of Babylon to be gathered. The word used for "aloud" or "out" is an Aramaic word we have looked at before: *chayil*. It can be translated "army." Belshazzar cried an army. You could literally say he "screamed."

The wise men were summoned, but once again, the wise men were clueless because they didn't have the Spirit of God. It was God's hand that wrote the message and only a vessel of God could deliver its truth. Herein lies a lesson:

The wisdom of God is greater than the wisdom of man.[5]

The world thinks it is wise, but in front of a holy God, the world is foolish. Look at 1 Corinthians 3:19 in the margin. God sure caught Belshazzar, did He not? Belshazzar thought he was crafty, but God spoke with such strength the kings "knees began knocking together."

Before we end for today, I want you to put yourself in Belshazzar's place. He was like Nebuchadnezzar – at "ease and flourishing." He didn't have a care in the world. He was, after all, the ruler of Babylon. He thought all nations and kings and lords would obviously have to bow to him – even the Most High God. He took a sip of wine out of a golden vessel that had been used in the temple of God. Fingers appear beside him, writing on the plaster of the banquet hall.

> For the wisdom of this world is foolishness before God. For it is written, "He is the One who catches the wise in their craftiness."
>
> 1 Corinthians 3:19

MENE, MENE, TEKEL, UPHARSIN.

No one knew what it meant. We will learn the meaning in a few days, but let me give you the translation of the Aramaic that the king probably saw.

NUMBERED, NUMBERED, WEIGHED, AND DIVIDED.

If you saw that message, would your knees be knocking together? I am quite certain the king messed his pants, because "the joints of his loins were loosed" (KJV).

We will see what happened to the king's joints tomorrow.

1 Butler, Trent C. et al.,eds. *Holman Illustrated Bible Dictionary* (Nashville, Tennessee: Holman Bible Publishers, 2003), 159.
2 Butler, Trent C. et al.,eds. *Holman Illustrated Bible Dictionary* (Nashville, Tennessee: Holman Bible Publishers, 2003), 159.
Leupold, H.C. *Exposition of Daniel* (Grand Rapids, Michigan: Baker Book House Company, 1969), 209.
3 Leupold, H.C. *Exposition of Daniel* (Grand Rapids, Michigan: Baker Book House Company, 1969), 215.
4 Hinnant, Greg. *Daniel Notes* (Lake Mary, Florida: Creation House Press, 2003), 132.
5 Hinnant, Greg. *Daniel Notes* (Lake Mary, Florida: Creation House Press, 2003), 133.

Day Two – Chapter Five
The Sentence

> "There is a man in your kingdom in whom is a spirit of the holy gods . . ."
>
> Daniel 5:11

Yesterday we saw the king's knees knocking together and the wise men clueless. Do you see a pattern here? God confounds the wisdom of the world in order to exalt his holy vessels (us). This was 539 BC. Daniel was approximately 82 years old. As far as we know, he hadn't served in an official position since Nebuchadnezzar's death in 562 BC. Just like Rehoboam appointed new counselors (1 Kings 12), so too would each new reigning king. This means Daniel had been "retired" for 23 years. This leads us to an important lesson:

If you are in a season of inactivity, don't think God doesn't have future plans for you.

Daniel was off the mighty men of Babylon's radar, but he wasn't off of God's radar. There was more for this shining star to accomplish.

Read Daniel 5:9-17

It seems the queen heard Belshazzar screaming because she enters the banquet hall with wise words. This wasn't Belshazzar's wife, because his wives were already present (Daniel 5:2). This had to be the queen mother. This was probably Nebuchadnezzar's widow, who would command great respect among those assembled.[1] She singled out Daniel, telling Belshazzar that Daniel had the spirit of the holy gods. She emphasized that Daniel had illumination, insight, and wisdom. Look at Daniel 5:11 in the margin.

> "And King Nebuchadnezzar, your father, your father the king, appointed him chief . . ."
>
> Daniel 5:11b

I believe the queen mother was emphasizing not only Daniel's wisdom, but also the wisdom of Nebuchadnezzar for appointing him "chief." Do you concur? I would wager a bet the queen was a little disgusted by the display of insolence occurring in that banquet hall. If this was Nebuchadnezzar's widow, we might conclude that she could have had a change of heart too. I would wager King Nebuchadnezzar could be pretty persuasive. We can't know for sure, but this section of the story just stands out to me. The queen says to Belshazzar, "King Nebuchadnezzar, your father, your father the king, appointed him . . ." She was emphasizing the kingship of Nebuchadnezzar without being too disrespectful to Belshazzar. Remember, Belshazzar wasn't the official king of Babylon. He was a stand-in. Do you see the slight emphasis on kingship, and the wisdom of King Nebuchadnezzar for appointing Daniel "chief?"

Now look at the latter part of Daniel 5:12. How did the queen mother first identify Daniel? By his Hebrew or Aramaic name? _____. Who was told to be summoned? _____

This too, I find extremely interesting. I believe the words of this passage speak volumes as to the relationship of the queen mother to the former chief wise man. She knew him, not by his Aramaic name, but by his Hebrew name. She knew the events that had transpired more than 23 years prior, and perhaps she had grown close to Daniel. After all, Daniel sat at the king's court (Daniel 2:49). This was equivalent to saying that Daniel sat at the king's gate, which was where the king would conduct official business. Daniel was front and center. The queen knew him. The queen even identified him as "Daniel." Daniel had an identity to the queen. Daniel was someone she knew – well. She emphasized Nebuchadnezzar's kingship, and she emphasized Daniel's Hebrew name.

Speaking of names. Let's pause here to consider something. The queen could have also been using Daniel's Hebrew name because it referred to Israel's god. *El* is in Daniel's name, and *El* was the God of the Hebrews. If the queen had seen God for who he was, like her husband before her, she could have very well chosen to use the name **Daniel** to emphasize her underlying point – your father Nebuchadnezzar was no fool. He made this Daniel chief of the wise man because *El* was with him. Now, notice something else with me. Daniel's Aramaic name was Belteshazzar and the regent's name was Belshazzar. The only difference is the "te" in Daniel's name. If you recall Belteshazzar means "Bel will protect." Belshazzar's name means "Bel's prince."[2] Close in meaning and lettering, but Belshazzar is found deficient in character just as his name is "lacking" in letters.

Let's get back to the queen. She also said, "He will declare the interpretation." There was no "he might" or "he may be able" but he will. There was no doubt in the queen's mind. Daniel could interpret the handwriting on the wall. Period.

What else did the queen mother say about Daniel? Look at Daniel 5:12 in the margin. Versions differ a great deal on how they interpret the queen's words, but I want you to focus on the words I have in bold italics. That word is *q'tar* (Strong's #7001) and it literally means "knots."

Daniel could dissolve knots.

That is an interesting way to put it isn't it? Daniel could dissolve knots. Now, I want you to recall the king's knees knocking together. "Then the king's . . . hip joints went slack and his knees began knocking together." The word "joints" in that sentence is the same word used in Daniel 5:12. You could literally translate that phrase as the king's "hip knots" went slack. Belshazzar had a knot problem, and Daniel was good at "dissolving knots." Fascinating!

> "Forasmuch as an excellent spirit, and knowledge, and understanding, interpreting of dreams, and showing of hard sentences, and dissolving of **doubts**, were found in the same Daniel . . ."
>
> Daniel 5:12 KJV

Daniel is summoned to the king, and the king tells him that if he can dissolve the "knots" of the mystery of the handwriting on the wall, he would be clothed in purple (the color of the nobility), adorned with a necklace of gold (a mark of high rank) and would be promoted to the third ruler in the kingdom.[3]

Belshazzar wasn't the king, so what number in "rank" was he? _____

So, if Daniel could solve the knotted mystery, he would become the third most powerful man in Babylon. Daniel tells the king to keep his gifts and then without hesitation, goes on to absolutely, yet honestly, dissolve the knots as to why the hand appeared in the first place.

Read Daniel 5:18-25

Daniel is direct and to the point. He is respectful, yet he does not sugarcoat his words. He tells Belshazzar like it is. We have looked at this before, but let's revisit it here.

In Daniel 5:22 what does Daniel tell Belshazzar he did not do? _____

Belshazzar had not humbled his heart even though he knew about the conversion of the king and what had happened for Nebuchadnezzar to convert in the first place.

What had Belshazzar done in respect to the Lord (verse 23)?_____

What had God given Belshazzar? _____ But Belshazzar had not _____ Him.

Belshazzar had exalted himself. The Lord had given him his life, yet Belshazzar had not glorified Him. That was why the handwriting was on the wall. Here is a very important lesson for us:

We are held accountable for the things we know.

Belshazzar knew God's laws, yet he rejected them. He knew God was the Most High, yet he pretended He didn't exist. We need to take this to heart. If we know God's laws and deliberately disregard them, we are held accountable. God held Belshazzar to account, and He didn't delay in doing it. He sent the writing immediately upon Belshazzar's insolence.

Daniel doesn't offer any sympathy like he did to Nebuchadnezzar in Daniel 4:19. He didn't even hesitate when he gave the king his sentence. Daniel was greatly disturbed by what was happening in that banquet hall. Belshazzar was not warned like Nebuchadnezzar. Belshazzar was sentenced. God knew the regent's heart. God knew there was no converting this one.

God judged.

MENE, MENE, TEKEL, UPHARSIN.

NUMBERED, NUMBERED, WEIGHED, AND DIVIDED.

We will study the meaning tomorrow.

1 Leupold, H.C. *Exposition of Daniel* (Grand Rapids, Michigan: Baker Book House Company, 1969), 225.

2 Butler, Trent C. et al.,eds. *Holman Illustrated Bible Dictionary* (Nashville, Tennessee: Holman Bible Publishers, 2003), 184.

3 Leupold, H.C. *Exposition of Daniel* (Grand Rapids, Michigan: Baker Book House Company, 1969), 222.

Day Three – Chapter Five
MENE, MENE, TEKEL, UPHARSIN

"Now this is the inscription that was written out: 'Mene, Mene, Tekel, Upharsin.'"

Daniel 5:25

I love diving deep into God's word; there is no end to the diamonds you uncover. Today will look at the exact meaning of the handwriting on the wall.

Mene

Read Daniel 5:26. What has God done? _____

Belshazzar's kingdom had been numbered. It was now at an end. The repetition of *mene* could be a double emphasis to the sentence. As in, "Truly, truly I say to you." It was true. It was trustworthy. Belshazzar's kingdom was done.

The Aramaic word *mene* (Strong's #4484) corresponds to the Hebrew word *manah* (Strong's #4487) and it means "numbered." Let's see how the Hebrew equivalent is used in scripture. Look at Psalm 90:12 in the margin.

Belshazzar didn't understand that his days were numbered. He didn't look to the One who gave him "life-breath" (Daniel 5:23). He was not wise.

His days were numbered. And it was sure.

So teach us to number [manah] our days, that we may present to You a heart of wisdom.

Psalm 90:12

Tekel

Read Daniel 5:27. What had been "done" to Belshazzar? _____ What was he found? _____

"Oh that my grief were actually weighed [shaqal], and laid in the balances together with my calamity!"

Job 6:2

Belshazzar had been weighed on God's scales and he had been found deficient. Ouch. The Aramaic word *tekel* (Strong's #8625) corresponds to the Hebrew word *shaqal* (Strong's #8254). Let's see where this Hebrew word is used in scripture. Look at Job 6:2 in the margin.

Read Proverbs 16:2. What are the ways of man in his own eyes? _____ What does God do? _____

Unlike Job, Belshazzar had been placed on the scales and the scales did not balance. Belshazzar's days were not only numbered, they were also judged by their lack of balance.

101

Upharsin or Peres

Read Daniel 5:28. What was going to be done to Belshazzar's kingdom _____
And given to who? _____

> "Nevertheless, you are not to eat of these among those which chew the cud, or among those that divide [paras] the hoof in two . . . they are unclean for you."
>
> Deuteronomy 14:7

The kingdom was going to be divided. Notice when Daniel first pronounced the sentence in verse 25 he used the word *Upharsin* but when he translated the phrase, he used the word *peres*. The "u" in *upharsin* is the conjunction "and." *Pharsin* is the plural form of *peres.*[1] The Aramaic word *peres* (Strong's #6537) corresponds to the Hebrew word *paras* (Strong's #6536). This word means to break into pieces, but normally this breaking is without violence. Let's look to see how this Hebrew word is used in scripture. Look at Deuteronomy 14:7 in the margin.

Out of the 14 times *paras* is used in scripture, 11 of those times refer to the unclean animal. Belshazzar's days were numbered, he was judged by his lack of balance, and he was considered like the unclean animal – his kingdom would be divided. It would be given to the Medes and to the Persians.

There is something else we should consider before moving forward. There may be a double meaning to "MENE, MENE, TEKEL, UPHARSIN." *Parsin* or *Pharsin* is a plural form of Persian – as in the last word can also be translated "and Persians."[1] Belshazzar's days were numbered, he had been weighed in the scales and found wanting, and his kingdom was now divided – to the Persians.

There is something I haven't told you. While Belshazzar was having his feast and drinking out of God's vessels, the Medes and the Persians were camped outside of Babylon's walls. As in, it appears that Belshazzar was so confident in his defenses that he didn't even bat an eye when he was told an army was about to attack. If you take the story as a whole, his insolence becomes even more detestable.

Read Daniel 5:29-31

Turn to Daniel 1:21. What name is mentioned here?_____

Cyrus is a very interesting character. History tells us that he was the grandson of Astyages, king of Media. Astyages had a dream that Cyrus would succeed him as king before Astyages' death. So, logically, Astyages ordered his grandson's death (sarcasm here people). The officer who was charged to kill young Cyrus was a little more sane that Cyrus' grandfather. He took young Cyrus to live with a shepherd. The dream proved true. When Cyrus was older he organized the Persians and revolted against his grandfather. He defeated him and claimed the throne of Media in 559 BC. So Cyrus was a Mede, but he raised his army in Persia.[2] Persia became the dominate power after its conquest of Media, but Media was always the second-most prominent region of the empire and was held in great esteem.[3] Daniel is not the only place in scripture that the Medes and the Persians are referred to as a united empire.

Turn to Ester 1:19. Whose laws cannot be revoked? _____

Ester becomes queen of the Medo-Persian Empire in the story of Ester, which takes place approximately 59 years after the handwriting on the wall.[4]

Let's get back to Daniel's day. It is 539 BC. Belshazzar is feasting without a care in the world, but armies were stationed outside of Babylon's walls. The Medes and the Persians diverted the Euphrates River –which ran under the walls of Babylon – and literally walked right into town, and right into the banquet hall. Remember when I said that the word *peres* meant breaking into pieces without a fight? There was little resistance when the Medes and the Persians claimed Babylon. The great and mighty Babylon fell in one night.

Read Daniel 5:31. What name is mentioned here? _____

Now turn to Daniel 6:28. What two familiar names are mentioned here? _____

This is where history gets a little cloudy. Some scholars believe Cyrus and Darius are the same person. We have seen from our study of Daniel that a person in ancient times could have more than one name.[5]

Read 1 Chronicles 5:26. How many names are associated with one king? _____

We have also seen that Cyrus was the grandson of the king of the Medes, but he raised the Persian army to conquer them. He united two kingdoms. An ancient Babylonian text also says that Cyrus was the king of the Medes. According to Daniel 5:31, Darius was 62 when the handwriting was on the wall. We know from history that Cyrus was approximately 60 years old when Babylon was taken.[6] It seems that Cyrus and Darius may be one in the same person. On a side note, it seems logical that when Cyrus went to live with the shepherd, he underwent a name-change in order to remain concealed.

If you recall in Daniel 6:28 it says that Daniel "enjoyed success in the reign of Darius and in the reign of Cyrus the Persian." From this translation it seems that Darius and Cyrus are not the same person. Yet, this portion of scripture could be translated "during the reign of Darius the Mede, that is, the reign of Cyrus the Persian."[7]

Another possibility is that Darius was actually Cyrus' general named elsewhere as Gubaru or Ugbaru.[8] Gubaru would have been the one to capture Babylon and kill Belshazzar. He could very well have stayed to rule Babylon under the power and kingship of Cyrus. In either case, whether this Darius was Cyrus or Cyrus' general, he became the ruler of Babylon. *(Note: don't confuse the Darius of Daniel to the Darius found in Ezra. There is another famous Darius that came to power after Cyrus' son's death in 521 BC -- this is the Darius we read about in Ezra.)*[9]

We can't stop today before looking back at Daniel chapter two.

Read Daniel 2:32. What was the head made of? _____

Who was the head? _____ (Daniel 2:36-38)

What came after the gold in Daniel 2:32? _____

You have just witnessed the demise of the golden empire and the rise of the silver. Babylon fell, and the Medo-Persian Empire took control. The territory of the Medes and the Persians just expanded – by a great deal. Daniel saw this all transpire in the handwriting on the wall. I can't even imagine what he was thinking when the banquet hall was breeched and Belshazzar was slain.

How did the conquerors know to spare Daniel? We don't know, but they did, and they were impressed with what they saw.

MENE, MENE, TEKEL, UPHARSIN.

More to come tomorrow.

1 Leupold, H.C. *Exposition of Daniel* (Grand Rapids, Michigan: Baker Book House Company, 1969), 235.

2 Butler, Trent C. et al.,eds. *Holman Illustrated Bible Dictionary* (Nashville, Tennessee: Holman Bible Publishers, 2003), 377.

3 Butler, Trent C. et al.,eds. *Holman Illustrated Bible Dictionary* (Nashville, Tennessee: Holman Bible Publishers, 2003), 1095.

4 *One-Volume Illustrated Edition of Zondervan Bible Commentary* with General Editor F. F. Bruce (Zondervan, 2008), 472.

5 *One-Volume Illustrated Edition of Zondervan Bible Commentary* with General Editor F. F. Bruce (Zondervan, 2008), 878.

6 *One-Volume Illustrated Edition of Zondervan Bible Commentary* with General Editor F. F. Bruce (Zondervan, 2008), 878.

7 *English Standard Version Study Bible* (Wheaton, Illinois: Crossway, 2008), 1597.

8 *English Standard Version Study Bible* (Wheaton, Illinois: Crossway, 2008), 1597.

9 Butler, Trent C. et al.,eds. *Holman Illustrated Bible Dictionary* (Nashville, Tennessee: Holman Bible Publishers, 2003), 389.

Day Four – Chapter Six
Jealousy

Then this Daniel began distinguishing himself among the commissioners and satraps because he possessed an extraordinary spirit . . .

Daniel 6:3

Yesterday we saw the handwriting on the wall come to pass. Babylon fell, and Darius the Mede took control. What happens to Daniel? Let's find out.

Read Daniel 6:1-14

There is so much going on here I don't know where to start: pride; jealousy; integrity; envy; loyalty; humility; faithfulness; devotion; friendship; enmity. Those emotions are all present in these 14 verses.

Darius saw something in Daniel. He probably heard about the interpretation Daniel provided on the night of the invasion and recognized wisdom when he saw it. Darius seemed to be a wise man, because at the beginning of his rule, he recognizes he needs to establish order in his new role.

What position did Darius give to Daniel? _____(verse 2)

What did Daniel start to do? _____ (verse 3)

So what position did Darius plan to give to Daniel? _____(verse 3)

Then this Daniel began distinguishing himself . . . because he possessed an extraordinary spirit . . .

Daniel 6:3

I'm starting to see a pattern in Daniel's life, aren't you? Daniel became one of three commissioners, but even among the three, Daniel stood out – just like he had stood out to Nebuchadnezzar. What you put in the second blank above depends on your translation. Some say Daniel "distinguished himself" others say Daniel was "preferred above" and others use the word "surpassed." The word in the Aramaic is *netsach* (Strong's #5330) and it means "to become chief or be preferred." It corresponds to the Hebrew word *natsack* (Strong's 5329), which means "to glitter from afar." Daniel glittered. He shone. He walked in Babylon (now Medo-Persia) and emitted light. Why?

Read Daniel 6:3 in the margin. Why did Daniel glitter? _____

What was this spirit according to Daniel 4:9 and 5:11?_____

He possessed an extraordinary spirit because he walked with God. Which leads me to a conclusion:

When you faithfully walk with God – you glitter from afar.

You can't help but shine because God is the consuming fire (Hebrews 12:29), and He lives in light (1 Timothy 6:16), and He is light (1 John 1:5). When you are with Him you reflect Him (Exodus 34:35). You shine.

The commissioners and the satraps saw Daniel's sparkle, and they didn't like it one bit. They were out to get him. Which leads me to another conclusion:

When you glitter for God, you will be persecuted, no matter your position or your integrity. Leadership is an honor, but it also arouses our enemy's attention.

Just because you get promoted doesn't mean you will be protected from pain. Satan doesn't like you glittering, and if you are glittering from a higher hill, he will like it even less. Satan will send his minions, and at times those minions are close associates. Don't think for a moment that those who call themselves friends can't turn against you. Satan can spark a multitude of emotions in us, such as pride, envy, and hatred. He will come at you with full force. We just have to remember who our true enemy is, and not focus on those attacking us in person. Satan is the force behind the persecution. Those who persecute are under his delusion.

How many satraps were appointed according to Daniel 6:2? _____

Who conspired against Daniel in Daniel 6:4? _____

We can't say with certainty it was all the satraps, but you can bet your last nugget it was all the commissioners excluding Daniel – there were only a total of three! They had heard in the wind that the king noticed Daniel's glitter, and they didn't like it. They didn't want Daniel running the kingdom. Their jealousy flared. Their envy ignited. Their hatred burned. They thought they deserved that position – not Daniel. Does this sound familiar? Recall back in Daniel chapter three Hananiah, Mishael, and Azariah were under the same scrutiny. What happened to them? They were thrown into the flames of jealousy.

What did the conspirators call Daniel in Daniel 6:13? _____

Daniel wasn't even Babylonian! I believe jealousy played a big part in the minds of the commissioners and satraps, but so did hatred. They hated Daniel, not only for his position, but also for his heritage. So they all got together and tried to find some wrong in Daniel. Of course, they found nothing. Daniel was faithful, not only to God, but also to his duties. When Daniel was in control, there was no deceit or negligence. There was only one way to trap Daniel.

Read Daniel 6:5. What would Daniel not compromise on? _____

This is the very reason the commissioners and satraps found no fault in Daniel in regards to his job. Daniel used God's laws not only at "church" but also at work. He didn't embezzle, cheat, steal, or lie on his papers or his taxes. He was the same Daniel at church as he was in the office. Do you see it? In Daniel 6:4 it says Daniel was "faithful." But this verse is talking about his faithfulness at work, not about his faith in God. But his faithfulness at his duties has everything to do with his faith!

The Aramaic word for "faithful" is *aman* (Strong's #540), which corresponds to the Hebrew word *aman* (Strong's #539). It means, "to render firm or faithful, to trust or believe, to be permanent." Daniel was firm and faithful in every aspect of his life. He was permanent. He stood firm on God's laws. Listen:

As believers, we should be faithful to God's laws in all areas of our lives.

Our enemies should find nothing dishonest in our lives. We should be examples of integrity and honesty. Some Christians today live their life one way at church and another way at work. They claim to be Christian, yet if the IRS came to their door, their knees would knock together like Belshazzar's in Daniel chapter five.

"All the commissioners of the kingdom, the prefects and the satraps, the high officials and the governors have consulted together . . ."

Daniel 6:7

The other day, I had to have a refrigerator repairman come fix a leak in my refrigerator's water line. I also had him look at the icemaker because at times the ice tray doesn't properly retract and the water spills over the ice tray directly into the ice bucket, which freezes the other pieces of ice into huge chucks and causes ice not to be distributed. He fixed my leak and quoted me $400 for a new ice try. I said I would deal with the chunks. Then he quoted me a warranty on top of the repair that would only be $100 more. Then he said, "You can call after 30 days and claim the ice maker broke." I said, "The ice maker is already broken." He replied, "But they don't know that. I'm just trying to save you $300." No one would have known but me – and God. No thank you. My glitter would have been less glittery if I would have taken the bait. My glitter is too important to me and to my God. I can't claim I am following Him if I deliberately lie. Daniel knew this. Daniel was "faithful."

Read Daniel 6:7 in the margin and fill in the blanks. "_____ the commissioners of the kingdom, the _____ and the satraps , the high officials, and the _____ have consulted together."

Did all the commissioners consult?_____ Were any officials involved in this plot besides the commissioners and the satraps according to Daniel 6:4? _____

All the commissioners weren't involved because Daniel had no part in it. And Daniel 6:4 doesn't say anything about prefects, governors, or other high officials. These men were lying to Darius. I don't know why Darius granted their request, but if he had just come to power he may have thought that signing the decree would help establish his throne. This seems the most logical explanation given the fact that Darius' reaction to Daniel's disobedience was in no way like Nebuchadnezzar's response when Hananiah, Mishael, and Azariah refused to bow down. Darius didn't want worship; he wanted a peaceful realm, but his hasty decision caused a faithful friend to be trapped in a web of deceit. There is a lesson here:

Don't make an important decision based on the words of a few without serious contemplation and prayer.

Darius listened, but he didn't think. Perhaps the words of the commissioners and satraps were flattering, but flattery is insincere if given with a selfish, evil, or malicious purpose. The commissioners and satraps didn't care about this decree – they only wanted to destroy Daniel. Darius should have been a little more aware that their words could have an underlying purpose.[1]

What did they say about the laws of the Medes and the Persians in Daniel 6:8? _____

_____

You could literally translate that phrase as "does not pass away."[2] Look at Daniel 7:14 in the margin. Man's laws can be repealed, but God's laws cannot. Yet, those ruling the Median and the Persian kingdoms believed their laws were sacred, hence why they could not be revoked. This is also why Darius should have taken a little more care in his decision to issue a decree in the first place.

What do the men remind Darius about in Daniel 6:15?

_____

"His dominion is an everlasting dominion which will not pass away; and His kingdom is one which will not be destroyed."

Daniel 7:14b

The law came back to bite Darius in the backside because man is man. And even a man who is a king can be wrong.

Darius wasn't too happy with his rash decision or the men bringing Daniel to his attention. We will study the king's reaction and what happens tomorrow.

1 Hinnant, Greg. *Daniel Notes* (Lake Mary, Florida: Creation House Press, 2003), 158.
2 *New American Standard Bible* (Grand Rapids, Michigan: Zondervan, 1999), 1237.

Day Five – Chapter Six
Boldness and Humility

Now when Daniel knew that the document was signed, he entered his house (now in his roof chamber he had windows open toward Jerusalem); and he continued kneeling on his knees three time a day, praying and giving thanks before his God, as he had been doing previously.

Daniel 6:10

We looked at the jealousy of the commissioners and satraps in yesterday's lesson, but we failed to focus on Daniel. So let's go back a bit. Read Daniel 6:10 in the margin.

Where exactly was Daniel?_____

What did he have open? _____towards? _____

How many times a day did he pray? _____

I want you to pause here and consider what you would have done. The decree had been given. Anyone discovered praying to any god would be thrown into the lions' den. At this moment there are three options for Daniel: Option one: cease to pray – out of the question; Option two: continue praying but conceal it somehow; Option three: continue to pray in the same manner as before. Now consider this carefully, Daniel was on his roof, on his knees, with his windows open! He could have shut the windows. He could have remained standing. I mean, you can pray standing up, and you can pray on the ground level. You can pray walking down the street. But not Daniel. He chose option three: be obvious about your loyalties – pray in the same way you have been praying. And it was quite obvious he was praying. It was quite obvious he didn't give a rip about the decree. Herein lies a lesson:

Sometimes we have to be bold enough to be audacious.

Daniel could have prayed in another way, but he was in-your-face about his loyalties. Do you see it? I mean, as I'm reading this lesson I'm thinking to myself, "Daniel! Shut your windows!" Anyone? There is nothing wrong with shutting your windows, so why didn't Daniel? I believe there are two reasons for this.

Read 1 Kings 8:46-49. When Solomon dedicated the temple, what was part of his prayer?

_____

What did he tell the captives to say (verse 47)? _____

Where did Solomon intend for those praying to face?_____

Daniel was in exile and he was facing Jerusalem. Now, he could have faced Jerusalem with his windows closed, so there is more to this than Daniel obeying Solomon's words. But I want to pause here anyway. I want you flip forward to Daniel chapter nine. I want you to see something very interesting.

Read Daniel 9:4-7. Daniel was praying for who? _____

Was this what Solomon said to do? _____

Now look at Daniel 9:1. What year was this? _____

This could have been the very prayer he was praying on his knees when the commissioners and satraps went to accuse him to the king! I am getting chills. This prayer occurred in the first year of king Darius. We may have the exact prayer that got the faithful man of God in trouble. And you know what happened while Daniel was speaking to God?

Read Daniel 9:20-23. Who came to Daniel? _____ What did Gabriel call him?_____

Daniel was highly esteemed because he did not compromise his God. He stood firm and resolute. And when Daniel prayed, heaven moved. Do you remember when I said that our real enemy when persecution comes is Satan himself? The persecutors are his minions, being deluded by his deception. Here is the real reason the decree was sent out: Satan wanted to stop Daniel's prayers![1] He also wants to stop yours. But like Daniel, we need to be deliberate in our prayer life:

When the Saints fall to their knees – heaven moves.

We can't forget how important prayer is. When you pray, you are talking to the God of the universe and He cares about you! This, I believe is the second reason why Daniel did not change anything about what he did. He met God on his roof with his windows open – period. This was where he felt closest to God. If he closed his windows, Daniel would have probably felt less close to the Almighty and Daniel refused to compromise his relationship with the Father – not one bit. If you have a relationship with God, you won't either. Listen:

The faithful will not compromise their relationship to the One.

In the last days, I fear we will be confronted by a scenario much like the one in Daniel chapter six. When it comes to our faith, we need to have our windows wide open. Shutting them in any form or fashion would be denying our faith.

In Daniel 6:11 it says the men "came by agreement" or "gathered" or "assembled" to trap Daniel. Look at the NASB translation in the margin. The word "agreement" is the Aramaic word *regash* (Strong's #7284) which means "to gather tumultuously." It corresponds to the Hebrew word *ragash* (Strong's #7283), which means "to be tumultuous." Can you see it? These men weren't quiet about their treachery. They were

Then these men came by agreement and found Daniel making petition and supplication before his God.

Daniel 6:11

uproarious in their approach. They were exuberant in their exclamations. They were bustling down the courtyard knowing that they had trapped him.

Then they go to the king. They remind Darius about his decree and about the irrevocable laws of the Medes and the Persians. Then they implicated Daniel.

Read Daniel 6:13. What did they say about Daniel's attitude toward Darius? _____
_____The decree? _____

They accuse Daniel of having no respect for the king or the laws. Darius is not fooled. Unlike Nebuchadnezzar who flew into a rage when Hananiah, Mishael, and Azariah refused to yield, Darius became "distressed" or "displeased" according to Daniel 6:14. The word for displeased is the Aramaic word *beesh* (Strong's #888) and it corresponds to the Hebrew word *baash* (Strong's #887) which means "to smell bad." Darius smelled a skunk and set his heart to rescue Daniel, but alas, the men returned and reminded the king again that the laws of the Medes and the Persians could not be changed.

Darius was stuck. Daniel was in trouble. And the men were ecstatic.

Read Daniel 6:16-20

Darius had to give in. He had to respect the law. If he disregarded this law, others would fail to obey other laws, and that he could not allow. He tried to save Daniel, but there was no saving to be found. He ordered for Daniel to be thrown into the lions' den. Before we move any further into the study, keep in mind that Daniel was approximately 82. When you look at many pictures of Daniel in the lions' den, you see a young man, but Daniel was in his eighties! Darius is 62 at this time. Based on what we know, he respected Daniel a great deal. He tells Daniel before he is thrown into the lions' den, "Your God whom you constantly serve will Himself deliver you."

How did Daniel serve God? _____

Darius recognized that Daniel didn't serve God once a week or during morning devotions – but constantly. Darius also seems to be telling Daniel that he had done his best to rescue him, but now it was up to Daniel's God.

Imagine this on the big screen. Daniel is shoved into the den. This was probably a pit where Daniel was thrown in from above (based on Daniel 6:24). Darius was there, watching. Imagine his face. Imagine his concern. The stone is shoved into place with a loud "boom."

What does Darius do in verse 18? _____

Daniel had a friend in Darius. The man is beside himself. He humbles himself. He fasts. He is alone. He can't sleep. I can't say with certainty, but I would bet my last dollar that the king prays.

111

If he prayed, to whom do you think he prayed? _____

This is a far cry from Nebuchadnezzar. Daniel had told Nebuchadnezzar to humble himself or the Lord would humble him. Nebuchadnezzar ignored Daniel's plea and Nebuchadnezzar crawled among the beasts of the field until he acknowledged that God was the Most High. Darius, however, goes the other route. He humbled himself before God. He fasted. He tossed and turned. And at the first light of day, Darius was up and out of his chambers. Daniel 6:19 says that he went in "haste" to the lions' den. The word haste is the Aramaic word *behal* (Strong's #927), which means to "terrify or hasten." It corresponds to the Hebrew word *bahal* (Strong's #926), which means "to tremble."

Darius runs to the den. He is terrified of what he will find. He cries out: "Daniel, servant of the living God, has your God, whom you constantly serve, been able to deliver you from the lions?"

Darius is talking to a stone. His seal is on it – the one that made certain Daniel's fate was in the lions' den that night. No one could take away that stone without breaking the seal – or breaking the irrevocability of Median and Persian law. I wonder if that seal mocked Darius. He had done this. He had no one to blame but himself. Yes, the men had conspired, yes they had accused, but Darius had decreed. It was his fault Daniel was in the lions' den. But I want you to remember: there was another seal that wasn't supposed to be broken. Look at Matthew 27:65-66 in the margin.

> Pilate said to them, "You have a guard; go, make it as secure as you know how." And they went and made the grave secure, and along with the guard they set a seal on the stone.
>
> Matthew 27:65-66

But Darius hadn't met the God of the Hebrews yet; he had only met Daniel.

I wonder if Darius was thinking, "Can Daniel's God save him – from this?"

We know the ending, but Darius did not. He was terrified.

What had become of Daniel?

Darius holds his breath. He waits.

Will Daniel answer?

Did Daniel live?

Was Daniel's God real?

1 Hinnant, Greg. *Daniel Notes* (Lake Mary, Florida: Creation House Press, 2003), 157.

Week Six

So Daniel was taken up out of the den and no injury whatever was found on him, because he had trusted in his God.

Daniel 6:23b

Day One – Chapter Six
The Den of Lions

Darius is at the stone. He cries out to Daniel. Is Daniel still alive? Did his God save him?

Read Daniel 6:21-28

Daniel is safe. God's angel came and shut the mouths of the lions. I want you to consider Daniel's experience. He was thrown into the den. There were hungry lions down there, but an angel shuts their mouths. Did Daniel see the angel? Did he realize the lions were "peaceful?" What transpired in that den? When you see images of Daniel in the lions' den, many times we utter a: "aw look at those nice lions!" Those lions weren't nice. They were ferocious! Daniel wasn't patting them on the head saying, "Nice kitty."   If those lions were pussycats the angel wouldn't have come to shut their mouths.

What did the lions do to Daniel's accusers in Daniel 6:24? _____

When did they do this? As in, how soon after being thrown in? _____

No, the lions weren't friendly lions. Not at all. The next time you have an image of Daniel in the lions' den, I wouldn't put Daniel with the lions. I would put him on the opposite side of the room, lifting his hands to heaven and praising the God who had shut the lions' mouths.

Scripture says that the king was "very pleased" or "exceedingly glad" when he heard Daniel's voice. The word used here is the Aramaic word *teb* (Strong's #2868) and it means "to rejoice." Darius wasn't just standing there smiling – he was rejoicing! Darius was ecstatic Daniel was unharmed. He immediately calls for Daniel's release – and the sentencing of his accusers. The accusation against Daniel cost his conspirators not only their own lives, but also the lives of their families. It was customary to sentence false accusers to the same fate they sought for the victim, and Persian law extended that fate to the accusers families.[1] Seems barbaric to us, but this was normal in Daniel's day.

I want you to take note that the lions devoured Daniel's enemies before they reached the bottom of the den! The lions were hungry – like really hungry. Those thrown into the pit didn't even hit the ground. Imagine this scene. The lions were leaping through the air grabbing their victims mid-fall. What do you think Darius was thinking? How greatly did this impress him? It had to leave a lasting impact on Darius' life.

What did Darius do in Daniel 6:26? _____What did Darius command the people in this decree? _____

Who else had done something similar in Daniel 3:29? _____ What would happen if anyone spoke against God in Nebuchadnezzar's decree? _____

Darius was slightly less dramatic than old Neb, but consider this: a decree about Daniel's God went out to the kingdom of Babylon and to the kingdom of Medo-Persia. And God used His servants to spark that end. The Most High God was recognized as "the Most High God" because His faithful did not waver. Herein lies an important lesson:

God uses His faithful to be declared Faithful.

Now consider this: the king of Babylon converted to Daniel's God. Did Darius? It would seem a logical conclusion, but we don't know for sure. If Darius did start believing in God, Daniel's glitter influenced two rulers a great deal. This chapter of Daniel probably occurred during the first year of Darius' reign because it seems clear he was setting up his cabinet. Whether or not Darius and Cyrus are one in the same person, or different, I want you to see something.

Turn to Ezra 1:1-4. When did the decree to free the Jews happen? _____

I wonder if the lions' den miracle had something to do with the declaration to free the Jews. If Darius was Cyrus it seems logical that this would have instigated his loyalty to the Jews. Even if Darius was a different man put in charge of Babylon, Cyrus may have heard about Daniel, the lions' den, and the miracle that occurred there. We can't know for sure, but it is interesting to think about. Now look at Matthew 17:20 in the margin.

"If you have faith the size of a mustard seed, you will say to this mountain, 'Move from here to there,' and it will move; and nothing will be impossible to you."

Matthew 17:20b

114

How much faith do you need to move mountains? _____

Mountains in scripture represent kingdoms. Look at Isaiah 2:2 in the margin. It is not God's mountain the nations will flock to, but God's kingdom. So, Jesus is telling us in Matthew 17:20 that if we have the smallest amount of faith – the mustard seed is the smallest of seeds – we can influence kingdoms – we can move kingdoms – we can change the world. Daniel did just that. He changed Babylon, and he changed Medo-Persia. He moved mountains. Think about this:

Mountains move over for faith.

We can see this clearly illustrated in Daniel. You too can be a mustard seed in Babylon. And mountains will move for you if you keep your eye focused on the One who is truly King of the universe.

> Now it will come about that in the last days the mountain of the house of the Lord will be established as the chief of the mountains, and will be raised above the hills; and all the nations will stream to it.
>
> Isaiah 2:2

Read Daniel 6:23. Why was no injury found on Daniel? _____

Daniel trusted in God – how often according to Daniel 6:20? _____

Daniel served, trusted, obeyed, and praised God continuously. His life was the Lord's, as ours should be.

Darius rejoices over Daniel and then he rejoices over God. We can't move too quickly past Darius' prayer because it captures the theme of Daniel.

Read Daniel 6:26. How long does Daniel's God endure? _____ When will His kingdom be destroyed? _____

Now turn back to Daniel 4:34. His dominion is _____ His kingdom endures from _____

Turn back to Daniel 2:44-45. How long would God's kingdom endure? _____

Look forward to Daniel 7:13-14. His dominion is _____

If you had to pick one theme in Daniel it would be this: God's kingdom will endure forever. The kingdoms we have today are fleeting. In the end, God will set up a lasting kingdom that will never be destroyed.

Daniel's faith glittered to both Nebuchadnezzar and Darius. This is the last we see of Darius, but we could see him again one day if Daniel's glitter rubbed off.

Read Daniel 6:28. What happened to Daniel? _____

Daniel enjoyed success, but only after he demonstrated an unwavering faith in God Most High. Know this:

We will achieve success only with an unwavering commitment to God.

In the last days, this commitment will be put to the test. There will be times when our windows will have to be open even though the accuser stands outside. God cannot be compromised.   Our faith cannot be compromised. Our glitter cannot be compromised.

In today's society, black is white and white is black. If you speak the truth you are found intolerant. If you walk in your beliefs you are considered ignorant. But we need to understand that we "glitter from afar." You may not know who is watching, but you are being watched. Your influence can spread in ways you can't even fathom. You might even move a mountain or two without knowing it. You might influence a king.   And if you find yourself in the lions' den?

Trust in your God.

Have no doubt, He will save you. You life is never in question. He is in you, and He is the life.

1 *English Standard Version Study Bible* (Wheaton, Illinois: Crossway, 2008), 1598.

Day Two – Chapter Seven
The Winds and the Sea

Daniel said, "I was looking in my vision by night, and behold, the four winds of heaven were stirring up the great sea."

Daniel 7:2

Today we will begin to look at Daniel in another way. The first six chapters were events that happened outwardly in Daniel's life. The remaining chapters of Daniel are visions and prophecies that God gave to Daniel privately.

Read Daniel 7:1-3

This dream occurred during the first year of Belshazzar. Belshazzar ruled as regent of Babylon for about the last 10 years of his father's rule, which would place this dream occurring in approximately 553 BC. Daniel would have been approximately 71 years old. Nebuchadnezzar's first dream about the statue occurred when Daniel was approximately 19 years old. So this would be approximately 52 years later. Within 10 years, Babylon would fall.

In Daniel 7:1, what did Daniel do when he had the dream?_____

Don't pass this by too quickly. We are reading Daniel's own account over 2500 years later. This scripture has two very important lessons. First:

Don't think what you do can't have lasting impact.

You never know how much your work is going to affect those in the centuries to come. You have no idea who will hear about you or see what you did. I am sure Daniel felt just as "unimportant" as we do at times. Do you think he thought for a second that he was going to be another Jeremiah? I would wager a bet he did not. I would wager a bet he had no idea how important his stories and visions would be for our generation. The next lesson is this:

When you hear from God – write it down.

Like Daniel, when we hear from God, we need to write it down. Humans tend to doubt their own memories a day later. We tend to discount things and explain them away. When you write God's words down, you can refer back to them later so that your faith can be built up. I am not a journaler on a daily basis, but when I feel like I have heard from God in a personal manner – I write it down. When I have doubts I can go back and look at my own words. It is a confirmation to me, an account I can look back on and know what I am currently doing or believing isn't crazy. This is extremely important – write down God's words.

In verse two Daniel goes on to explain his dream. The first thing that he saw was the four winds of heaven stirring up the great sea. The four winds have occurred elsewhere in scripture.

Look up Matthew 24:31. What do the four winds represent? _____

Jesus uses this combination of words to indicate the totality of the earth. Let's see where else these words are used.

Read Jeremiah 49:36-37. What do the four winds bring? _____

Now read Revelation 7:1 in the margin. Based on the Jeremiah passage you just read, what would the angels be holding back? _____

> After this I saw four angels standing at the four corners of the earth, holding back the four winds of the earth, so that no wind would blow on the earth or on the sea or on any tree.
>
> Revelation 7:1

The winds in scripture can represent calamity. In other words, the winds can represent the judgment of God. That is why they are deemed the "four winds of heaven." In Revelation, the angels are holding back God's wrath in order to seal the bondservants of God before God's wrath falls in chapter eight. So, it is important to see that the four winds in Daniel chapter seven represent the totality of the earth and God's judgment.

> Then thou shalt see, and flow together, and thine heart shall fear, and be enlarged; because the abundance of the sea shall be converted unto thee, the forces of the Gentiles shall come unto thee.
>
> Isaiah 60:5 KJV

The four winds were stirring up the great sea. What is the great sea? The "sea" in scripture can represent any nation that is not Israel. In other words – any Gentile nation. Look at Isaiah 60:5 in the margin. The sea can also represent turbulent times (like the tossing of the sea).

Read Ezekiel 32:2. What nation are we talking about here?_____ To what is it compared? _____

In Daniel 7:3, what is rising out of the sea? _____

Daniel's dream is about beasts rising out of the sea. In Ezekiel 32:2, the beast is Egypt. The beasts Daniel will see are the kingdoms (like Egypt) rising to "super power" status. All of these kingdoms are Gentile. If you had to guess, why is this important to Daniel? Think about it from his perspective. Babylon was a Gentile nation that had conquered Israel. All the kingdoms that Daniel witnesses rising out of the sea will have a major effect on Israel. Now, before we get too deep, you need to know that the beasts of Daniel's dream correspond perfectly to the divisions of the statue in Nebuchadnezzar's dream. You have already studied these kingdoms. Each time a new power takes control, times are "turbulent" like the tossing of the sea.

Nebuchadnezzar dreamed of a glorious statue. It was made of precious metals and had "extraordinary splendor." Daniel, however, sees things a little differently. From his perspective (and God's), the kingdoms are beasts. They are the kingdoms that will have a lasting effect on God's people.

How are the winds described? The four winds of _____.

God is allowing these kingdoms to come to power. Even though He sees these kingdoms as "beasts," they are serving His purpose. Let's take the first kingdom – Babylon.

In Habakkuk 1:6, who is raising up the Chaldeans (Babylonians)? _____

Read Jeremiah 51:60-62. Would Babylon be judged? _____

God allowed the Babylonians to rise up in order to punish Judah for playing the harlot with other gods (Jeremiah 3:9-10), but God would ultimately judge Babylon. The gold kingdom (Babylon) would fall to the silver (Medo-Persia). We saw this happen in Daniel chapter five. Eventually, the region of Babylon (and Medo-Persia) will ultimately be destroyed.

How and by who (Daniel 2:35, 44-45)? _____

Jesus is coming. And He will destroy the kingdoms of the sea with one smashing blow in order to set up His kingdom forever. Now, I want you to look at something else with me. Read Isaiah 27:1 in the margin.

> In that day the Lord will punish Leviathan the fleeing serpent, with His fierce and great and mighty sword, even Leviathan the twisted serpent; and He will kill the dragon who lives in the sea.
>
> Isaiah 27:1

Read Revelation 12:9. Who is the dragon?_____
Where does he live?_____

Satan is among the nations (the seas) and he is out to get Israel, the people of God. But Jesus will ultimately defeat Satan (Revelation 20:10).

Read Revelation 12:17-13:1. Where was the dragon? _____ What was he bringing up from the sea? _____

The dragon is standing on the seashore while a beast is rising from the sea. Even though God is the one who allows the beast to rise, Satan is the one at the helm, stirring up the beast's hatred for the Jewish people. Just like Habakkuk was shocked that God was raising up the Babylonians – a nation crueler than Judah – at times we are shocked at the judgment God allows in the lives of believers and unbelievers alike. But God has an ultimate purpose for these judgments – repentance.

After their time in exile—after being "judged" by the Babylonians – what would God's people do according to Jeremiah 29:12? _____

God wants His people to turn back to Him! What He allows in our lives will ultimately bring more people to repentance. The beasts that are rising from the sea are rising under Satan's influence but only on God's command. We see this represented clearly in the book of Job. Satan had to get God's permission to touch Job (Job 1:12). Satan inflicted pain, but God allowed it. We may never understand some of the pain we endure in this life, but rest assured – it has a purpose. Some things that touch us are evil, but God will take that evil and transform it into good: a rape victim will become a rape counselor a battered women will become a legislator for women's rights, a terrorist victim will become a leader of a charity to fuel the fire of freedom. Was the evil directed from God? No. But He can take that evil and transform it to a cause worth fighting for, a cause that can have ultimate kingdom impact. Herein lies another important lesson:

God will use your tragedy to become your testimony.

What have you lived through while clinging fast to God? That, my faithful friends, is probably where your light can shine the brightest.

We will look at the beasts tomorrow.

Day Three – Chapter Seven
The Beasts

And four great beasts were coming up from the sea, different from one another.

Daniel 7:3

Today we will see the beasts (Gentile kingdoms) Daniel saw rising out of the sea (turbulent times). These are the same kingdoms we looked at in chapter two. Although Nebuchadnezzar sees the kingdoms as precious metals, Daniel sees the kingdoms as ugly beasts.

Read Daniel 7:4-8

Babylon – The Head of Gold

Read Daniel 2:37. What did Nebuchadnezzar's kingdom have? _____

In Daniel 2:38, what did Nebuchadnezzar rule over? _____

Nebuchadnezzar's kingdom was over man, beast, and bird. Interesting, given the description in Daniel 7:4.

What three creatures represented this kingdom? _____, _____, and _____

All three of the components mentioned in Daniel chapter two are present in Daniel chapter seven: a beast, a bird, and a man. The lion is the "king of the beasts" and an eagle is the "king of the birds."[1] If you recall from our study of Babylon, one road leading into Babylon was flanked by high walls and decorated with lions.[2] The lion has been associated with Babylon since the time of Nebuchadnezzar. The lion is strong, powerful, and regal (see Proverbs 30:30 in the margin). The beast in Daniel has eagle's wings because of its speed of conquest. Interestingly to note, winged lions guarded the palace gates of Babylon. Daniel would have been very familiar with them. He would have immediately recognized this image as that of Babylon.[3]

The lion, which is mightiest among beasts and does not turn back before any.

Proverbs 30:30 ESV

In Daniel 7:4, what happened to the four-footed beast? _____

What was given to it? _____ What do you think this represented? _____

We have already seen this occurring in Daniel chapter four. Nebuchadnezzar's power was taken away (wing's plucked out) and a human heart (or mind) was given to him when he humbled himself before God. The lion with eagle's wings is Babylon – the head of gold. Now let's look at the next beast.

Medo-Persia – Chest and Arms of Silver

How is the second kingdom depicted in Daniel 7:5? _____

Which would you say is more "regal" between the bear and the lion? _____

Turn to Daniel 2:39, does this match the silver kingdom's description? _____

Medo-Persia is depicted as the bear and deemed "inferior" to Babylon. The bear is a less regal and more lumbering than the lion. It is depicted as raised up on one side because Persia dominated Media in it strength, size, and longevity. It is unclear what the ribs represent but many scholars believe they symbolize Medo-Persia's greatest conquests: Lydia, Egypt, and Babylon.[4] The bear is commanded to "Arise, devour much meat." Compared to Babylon, that is exactly what this empire did – it conquered much more territory that its predecessor.

Greece – Belly and Thighs of Bronze

In Daniel 7:6, what was the third kingdom depicted as? _____
How many wings did it have? _____ Heads? _____

A leopard with four wings is much faster than a lion with two. Scripture is telling us this kingdom will conquer the other kingdoms with greater swiftness. Alexander the Great did just that. He conquered the territories of Babylon, Medo-Persia, and much more with a speed most consider unfathomable.[5] The leopard is depicted as having four heads because when Alexander died at a young age, his kingdom was divided into four pieces and given to his four generals.

Turkish-Ottoman Empire – Legs of Iron

In Daniel 7:7, how is the fourth kingdom described? _____, _____, and _____ What familiar metal do we see here? _____

Does any word look familiar to you from that description? The first word "dreadful" is the Aramaic word *d'chah* (Strong's #1763) and it means *to slink*. This is the same word used to describe the statue in Nebuchadnezzar's dream. It corresponds to the Hebrew word *zachal* (Strong's 2119), which means *to crawl*. Look at Daniel 2:31 in the margin. The statue made Nebuchadnezzar's skin crawl; the fourth beast made

"Thou, O king, sawest, and behold a great image. This great image, whose brightness was excellent, stood before thee; and the form thereof was terrible [d'chah]."

Daniel 2:31 KJV

Daniel's skin crawl. I would wager a bet that the fourth kingdom represented in the statue caused the entire statue to be *d'chah*. It is the fourth kingdom – the iron kingdom – the terrifying beast – with this characteristic.

What does it say about the fourth beast compared to its predecessors in Daniel 7:7?

_____

It was different from all the other kingdoms that had come before it. What did it do? It "devoured and crushed and trampled down the remainder with its feet." That is why it was different. It not only conquered, it devoured, it not only ruled, it crushed, it not only dominated, it trampled. Do you see the difference? The head of gold is said to have "glory" (Daniel 2:37), the inferior bear is commanded to "devour" but is not shown devouring (Daniel 7:5), the leopard is said to have "dominion" (Daniel 7:6), but the terrifying beast is said to devour, and crush, and trample. Look at what it says about the iron kingdom of Daniel chapter two in the margin.

> "Then there will be a fourth kingdom as strong as iron; inasmuch as iron crushes and shatters all things, so, like iron that breaks in pieces, it will crush and break all these in pieces."
>
> Daniel 2:40

Not only did this fourth kingdom take the territories of Babylon, Medo-Persia, and Greece, it also took the makeup of those societies and changed them. It devoured the people. It crushed the culture. It trampled the gods of the land. It broke apart traditions and beliefs. It shattered the systems that had come before it. We looked at the fourth kingdom in chapter two. We said many feel like the fourth kingdom is Rome, but Rome doesn't fit the equation. It didn't conquer the entire region known as Babylon, and Rome didn't altar the very essence of society. The Turkish-Ottoman Empire did. It conquered Babylon, Medo-Persia, Greece and much, much more. It fundamentally changed the way of life for those in the Middle East. Mohammad died in 632 but by the eighth century, Islamic territory stretched from India to Spain. The Crusades, often quoted as being an unnecessary holy war were actually in response to centuries of Islamic jihad in southern Europe. The fourth empire of Daniel conquered Spain and Portugal and went as far as France. If the Crusades hadn't halted this advance, Europe may very well have become Islamic.[6] Even though this empire was pushed out of Europe, it fundamentally transformed almost the entire Middle East to the religion of Islam.

Look ahead to Daniel 7:19. What are its claws made from? _____

What kingdom is the bronze kingdom? _____ Where in the order is it? _____

The terrifying beast has bronze claws. Bronze represents the kingdom of Greece and it came directly before the iron kingdom. As we have just discussed, after Muhammad's death in 632 AD, the Islamic nation conquered and converted its way into Europe until it reached a peak in approximately 1200 AD. Many of the innovations and ideas attributed to the Islamic nations were inherited from their Greek predecessors.[7] Thus the bronze claws of the fourth kingdom.

In World War I the Ottoman Empire sided with Germany and because of that the Allies broke up the Ottoman Empire by dividing its lands into different nations, creating boarders that weren't there before. The Ottomans and the Caliphate still existed in name, but they were under European occupation. At about the same time, the British wrote the Balfour Declaration which promised Jews a home in Palestine.[8] Jews started returning to their native land.

In 1924, the new leader of Turkey (where the seat of Ottoman power stemmed) abolished what was left of the Caliphate (or the Islamic Empire). Although the empire was broken up and the Caliphate dismantled, the people were still Islamic. Their theology taught them that Islam would take over the world (it still does). Globalization was affecting their culture. What were they to do? In the 1930s a man by the name of Hassan al-Benna rose to influence who would ultimately form the Muslim Brotherhood. He claimed Muslim problems were because of the west and the Jews and he brought about revitalization of the ideology of the first conquerors of the Middle East – jihad. Another leader arose within the Muslim Brotherhood – Haj Amin al-Husseini. He formed a tight bond with Hitler. It was al-Husseini's suggestion that Hitler demand the Jews wear the yellow star of David.[9] The fourth kingdom had come to kind of an end in 1924, but it wasn't conquered. No, the people were just divided into states such as Iraq, Syria, and Lebanon.

Turn back to Daniel 2:33. What were the legs made of? _____ How about the feet?_____ How many toes do two feet have? _____

Now turn to Daniel 7:7. How many horns does this fourth beast have? _____

The legs of iron represent the old Turkish Ottoman Empire that started in the days of Muhammad (600 AD) and continued until 1924.   But the spirit of the Caliphate still exists. In fact currently ISIS has declared a new age – the age of a second Caliphate.   The ten toes are starting to emerge. Although it is the same kingdom, it will have entirely different leaders in an entirely different era. The picture on the following page sums up what we have learned so far. We will look at the toes (or the 10 horns) tomorrow.

1 Hinnant, Greg. *Daniel Notes* (Lake Mary, Florida: Creation House Press, 2003), 181.
2 Butler, Trent C. et al.,eds. *Holman Illustrated Bible Dictionary* (Nashville, Tennessee: Holman Bible Publishers, 2003), 159.
3 Leupold, H.C. *Exposition of Daniel* (Grand Rapids, Michigan: Baker Book House Company, 1969), 288.
4 Hinnant, Greg. *Daniel Notes* (Lake Mary, Florida: Creation House Press, 2003), 182.
Leupold, H.C. *Exposition of Daniel* (Grand Rapids, Michigan: Baker Book House Company, 1969), 290-291.
5 Leupold, H.C. *Exposition of Daniel* (Grand Rapids, Michigan: Baker Book House Company, 1969), 294.
6 Beck, Glenn. *It is About Islam* (New York, New York: Mercury Radio Arts, Inc., 2015), 41, 107.
7 Beck, Glenn. *It is About Islam* (New York, New York: Mercury Radio Arts, Inc., 2015), 45-46.
8 Beck, Glenn. *It is About Islam* (New York, New York: Mercury Radio Arts, Inc., 2015), 53-54.
9 Beck, Glenn. *It is About Islam* (New York, New York: Mercury Radio Arts, Inc., 2015), 58.

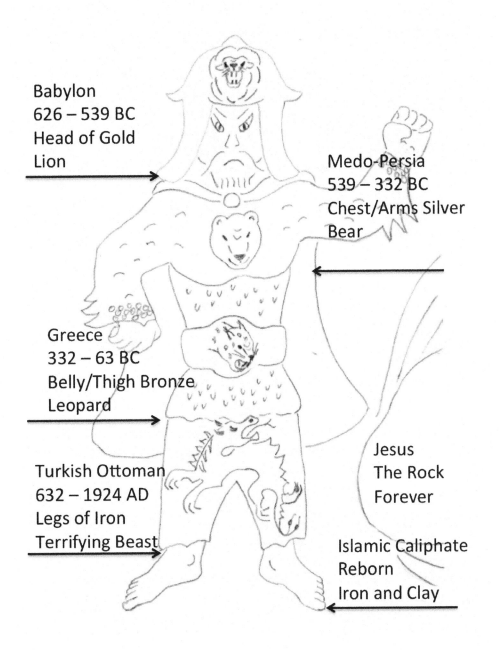

Babylon
626 – 539 BC
Head of Gold
Lion

Medo-Persia
539 – 332 BC
Chest/Arms Silver
Bear

Greece
332 – 63 BC
Belly/Thigh Bronze
Leopard

Turkish Ottoman
632 – 1924 AD
Legs of Iron
Terrifying Beast

Jesus
The Rock
Forever

Islamic Caliphate
Reborn
Iron and Clay

Most dates taken from *Rose Book of Bible Charts, Maps and Time Lines* (Torrance, California: Rose Publishing, 2005). Dates of the Turkish Ottoman Empire from the death of Muhammad until the end of WWI.

Day Four – Chapter Seven
The Horns

> "I kept looking, and that horn was waging war with the saints and overpowering them."
>
> Daniel 7:21

Yesterday we looked at the main components of the statue. Today we will look at the area of the statue that is most important to us. Daniel was looking forward into history, but we are looking back, and the end of his visions are pertinent to our generation. We are seeing the toes beginning to emerge. We are living in the "time of the end" (Daniel 12:4). We are going to skip ahead in Daniel chapter seven and return to the climax tomorrow.

Read Daniel 7:15-28

We left off yesterday saying that the iron kingdom was divided, but it was never conquered in the sense of a takeover. Britain and France ruled the newly divided Middle East for a time but eventually those boundaries became independent. Each state began governing their own affairs with their own leader. The Muslim Brotherhood started to help rid the Middle East of European occupancy. That movement has continued until today with increasing jihad. These people have never forgotten the "glory days" of the Caliphate and their theology tells them that one day the world will be in complete submission to Islam. As in, the Caliphate will be global and Sharia law (laws based on Allah's demands in the Quran) will rule.

When Daniel asks about the vision of the beasts, notice he doesn't ask specifically about the first three beasts. He is concerned about the fourth – the beast that made his skin crawl. Look at the following recaps of how this fourth beast is described:

As iron crushes and shatters all things, so, like iron that breaks in pieces, it will crush and break all these in pieces. Daniel 2:40b

Dreadful and terrifying and extremely strong; and it had large iron teeth. It devoured and crushed and trampled down the remainder with its feet. Daniel 7:7b

The fourth beast . . . exceedingly dreadful . . . devoured, crushed and trampled down the remainder with its feet. Daniel 7:19b

The ferocity of this beast is emphasized over and over again. Daniel seemed even more concerned about something he called "the little horn."

Read Daniel 7:8. What did this little horn have? _____

"And the meaning of the ten horns that were on its head and the other horn which came up, and before which three of them fell . . . and which was larger in appearance than its associates. I kept looking and that horn was waging war with the saints and overpowering them."

Daniel 7:20

Look at Daniel 7:20-21 in the margin. Even though this horn was "little" and came up after the other ten, what did it eventually become? _____
And what did it do? _____

The terrifying beast, or the iron kingdom, is depicted as having 10 horns or 10 toes. Another horn comes up after the ten and becomes larger than its predecessors. It eventually "pulls out" (Daniel 7:8) or "subdues" (Daniel 7:24) three of the previous horns. Daniel later elaborates on these horns.

What are the horns according to Daniel 7:24?
_____

In Daniel 11:43, what three powers of the Middle East might the little horn subdue? _____

_____

We don't know for sure, but it seems likely the kings of Egypt, Libya, and Sudan (ancient Ethiopia) will be the three kings the little horn will subdue.

Now, according to our previous study, we know that the iron kingdom of Daniel was the Caliphate or the Turkish Ottoman Empire of the past. This empire was completely dismantled after WWI and the Caliphate title was tossed aside in 1924. Today, we see it reforming. ISIS has declared a new Caliphate. Many are joining their cause. What scripture is telling us is that the Caliphate will eventually reform into a region that matches, if not supersedes the Empire of the past. It will be ruled by ten kings (represented by the ten toes and the ten horns). This may be ten separate areas, states, or groups of people that have a leader at their helm. Then another king will arise and take control of the Empire. He is someone you should be very familiar with. He is known by the title of Antichrist.

What three things will he do according to Daniel 7:25?
1) _____
2) _____
3) _____

He will speak out against the Most High, the One whom Nebuchadnezzar eventually acknowledged (Daniel 4:34). Revelation talks about this same empire and its leader. It expands on what is said in Daniel.

Read Revelation 13:6 in the margin. When the Antichrist opens his mouth to speak, he will blaspheme God's name, His dwelling place, and His saints. He will be Anti-God and Anti-Jesus. What will he eventually do?

And he opened his mouth in blasphemy against God, to blaspheme his name, and his tabernacle, and them that dwell in heaven.

Revelation 13:6 KJV

What will he do according to 2 Thessalonians 2:3-4? _____

Eventually, this little horn will claim to be God himself. This will lead his followers to issue a mark. If you do not take the mark, you are not declaring him "god." In the last days, the little horn of Daniel will demand our worship.

Read Revelation 13:16-17. If you do not take the mark, what will you be unable to do?
_____

You will be unable to buy or sell if you do not take his mark. According to Daniel 7:25, he will also "wear down the saints." Daniel 7:21 says that he will "wage war with the saints and overpower them." The Antichrist, the little horn of Daniel will come to power and subdue kings. He will blaspheme the Most High and persecute the saints. And here is the kicker – he will be successful. Let me say that again – he will be successful. Which leads me to my next point: the Antichrist will bring "fiery furnaces." He will bring "lions' dens." He will bring all-out persecution. Will you stand firm like Daniel, or will you bow down?

Do you see why the lessons we have learned in Daniel are so important? Daniel was living in Babylon. In the last days, so will we. We will be living in a time of persecution. We will have to make a choice like Daniel to "be resolved." We will have to make a choice like Hananiah, Mishael, and Azariah to not bow down. We will have to confront kings and speak the truth, no matter what harm or hurt will come to us. Daniel is a beacon of hope to the faithful. God is in control. No matter if the flames touch you, they cannot harm you. Yes, you might be killed, but no, you will live. God can bring you through the flames. He may deliver your life, like Hananiah, Mishael, and Azariah, or He may deliver you to life eternal. Either way – you have life.

In Daniel 7:25 it says he intends to "make alterations in times and in law." I want you to think about the little horn and his empire. It will be the Caliphate and it will be Islamic. Does it make sense that the little horn of Daniel will try to change the times and the law? Islam does not go by our calendar. Our calendar is the Gregorian calendar. It is based on a solar/lunar year. The Islamic calendar is based on a strictly lunar calendar. When they conquer a new territory, they force the conquered people to use their calendar. Their holy day is Friday, not Saturday or Sunday. They do not celebrate any Christian or Jewish holidays, only their own. They will try to change the times.[1]

They will also try to change the law to Sharia. Here is a quote from Glenn Beck's book, *It is About Islam.*

> *[Sharia] is a codification of the rules of the lifestyle (or deen) ordained by Allah, the perfect expression of his divine will and justice. Therefore it is the supreme law over everything and everyone, regardless of where that individual may live. There isn't a corner of life that sharia doesn't touch; it governs and dictates everything.*[2]

We see the Islamic world trying to impose Sharia on the world. In England a Muslim can use Sharia law in civil cases. There have been cases in the United States that have used Sharia.[3] They want everyone ultimately under Sharia. Islam isn't just a religion; it is an entire way of life. You cannot separate the religion of Islam from the political environment of Islam. Sharia law is the law because Allah ordained it. We see this unification of the political and the religious environment in Muslim countries today, but can we see this clarified in scripture? Yes, we can.

Turn to Revelation 17:1-6. How is the woman identified in verse one? _____

What are the kings of the world doing with her in verse two? _____
What are they drunk with? _____

What was the woman sitting on in verse three? _____ How many horns does this beast have? _____

What is the woman identified as in verse five? _____

What was she drunk with in verse six? _____

A harlot in scripture represents a false religion (Exodus 34:14-16). This harlot is sitting on a beast with 10 horns, meaning she is actually driving the beast. Let me say that another way – the false religion is controlling the political beast (or kingdom) that is ruled by the ten horns. This matches Islam. This matches Daniel chapter seven. The kings of the earth are drinking her wine. They are falling for her ideology; they are buying her lie. Yet, she is drunk with the blood of the saints. In the last days the nations will side with the harlot over the saints. They will agree to her demands They will take the mark. We are already doing that today, are we not? Many in the States are sympathetic to the Palestinian cause. Do you think giving the Palestinians land will end the conflict? Nothing but the annihilation of Israel will end the conflict. I don't know why we don't listen to the words of Islamic leaders. They radically declare that the Jewish nation needs to be wiped off the map. Yet we ignore what they are saying, not once, not twice, but over and over again. True Islam is not a peaceful religion. There is no such thing as a peaceful follower of Islam if they are following the prophet Muhammad. If you are a Christian, you try to emulate Christ. If you are a true Islamic believer, you try to emulate Muhammad. Muhammad was a jihadist. Muhammad beheaded his enemies. You can be a peaceful Muslim, you can be a reformed Muslim that uses a watered down form of Islam, but you cannot be a peaceful follower of Muhammad's Islam or you have left your religion.

The entirety of Islamic philosophy is too much to get into here. I want you to pick up some books and research it yourself.

Glenn Beck: *It is About Islam*
Joel Richardson: *Antichrist: Islam's Awaited Messiah*
Brigitte Gabriel: *Because They Hate*
Wahid Shoebat: *God's War on Terror*

We have already glanced at Revelation's beast, but for now, I want you to see what happens to the little horn.

Read Daniel 7:26. What happens? _____

Jesus wins, my faithful friends. Jesus wins! We will look at this tomorrow.

1 Shoebat, Walid, written with Joel Richardson. *God's War on Terror* (Top Executive Media, 2008), 86.
2 Beck, Glenn. *It is About Islam* (New York, New York: Mercury Radio Arts, Inc., 2015), 121.
3 Beck, Glenn. *It is About Islam* (New York, New York: Mercury Radio Arts, Inc., 2015), 130-132.

Day Five – Chapter Seven
The Kingdom

"I kept looking in the night visions, and behold, with the clouds of heaven one like a Son of Man was coming."

Daniel 7:13

Yesterday we looked at the horns of the beast. Today we look at the horn's destruction.

Read Daniel 7:9-14

We see an awesome picture of both the Father and the Son in this section of scripture. If someone tells you that Jesus isn't in the Old Testament, you might want to refer him or her to Daniel chapter seven.

Now before we look at the Father and the Son in detail, I want you to notice the beginning of verse nine. In some translations the beginning of this verse says: "I kept looking until thrones were set up." The King James Version translates this verse a little differently. It says: "I beheld till the thrones were cast down." That is an extremely different translation. The Aramaic word *remah* (Strong's #7412) means "to throw or to set." You can see where the confusion comes in. Were the thrones set up or were the thrones cast down? The Aramaic word *remah* corresponds to the Hebrew word *ramah*, which means to hurl. The verses directly before the *remah* verse are discussing the "horns" or the "rulers" of the beast. I believe the best translation is really "cast down." Daniel was waiting for and anticipating the destruction of the "thrones" of the beast. He kept looking until they were "cast down." Then the Ancient of Days was there. Most translations say the Ancient of Days "sat" but the Aramaic word *yethib* (Strong's #3488) also means "to dwell." It corresponds to the Hebrew word *yashab* and as a verb it means "to dwell, sit, abide, inhabit, remain." I believe Daniel saw the thrones cast down and then the Ancient of Days was just "there."

Read Psalm 90:2. God is from _____ to _____

Read Exodus 3:13-14. What does God call Himself here? _____

He is who He is because He always was. He is from everlasting. He is always present. Daniel was focused on the thrones of the beast, but when they were cast down – God was there – because He was always there. He is the Ancient of Days. His clothing and hair are white. Jesus is described like this in Revelation. Look at Revelation 1:14 in the margin. Both the Father and the Son are described like this in scripture because of their righteousness. In Revelation 19:8, white garments are used to signify righteousness. God the Father and God the Son are holy, they are true, and they are righteous. Their white hair and garments reflect this. Notice that their hair is described like "wool" in both Daniel and Revelation. And Jesus is the Lamb of God (John 1:29).

His head and His hair were white like white wool, like snow; and His eyes were like a flame of fire.

Revelation 1:14

The Ancient of Days' throne is said to be ablaze with flames and the throne's wheels were burning with fire. Take note that God's throne is on wheels. When God needs to move, He moves – quickly. Also a river of fire was coming from before Him. Fire is a big part of the image of the Ancient of Days. Look again at Revelation 1:14 on the previous page. Jesus' eyes were a flame of fire. Fire is an element present with both the Father and the Son.

What is our God according to Hebrews 12:29? _____

What are His Words according to Jeremiah 23:29? _____

What will destroy the world in the end according to 2 Peter 3:7, 10-12? _____

What will Jesus be at the end of days according to Zephaniah 3:8? _____
And what will He assemble? _____ And what will be poured out?
_____

According to Joel 3:2, what does Jesus do? _____

These are an amazing set of verses. Our God is a consuming fire, and His Word is a consuming fire because Jesus is the Word (John 1:1). If Jesus lives in us, we have His fire (His Spirit), which is represented as tongues of fire in Acts 2:3. The world will be destroyed by fire in the end, which is very well documented in Revelation. Before Jesus' second coming, God's wrath will be poured out on the earth (Revelation 8, 16). Scripture says we are not "destined for wrath" (1 Thessalonians 5:9), so we will be raptured to Heaven before God's wrath falls. A complete study of Revelation is too much to get into here, but if you want to learn about the timing of events please pick up my *Revelation in Black and White* study. So, when God's fire is poured out, the faithful who are still alive after the persecution of the Antichrist will no longer be on earth (but take note, we are here for the rise of the Antichrist and his persecutions). At that time, fire will pour down on the unfaithful. They are given time to repent. But in the end, everyone will have to choose between God and the Beast.

> And the Ancient of Days took His seat . . . a river of fire was flowing and coming out from before Him . . . and myriads upon myriads were standing before Him; the court sat, and the books were opened.
>
> Daniel 7:9-10

As it says in Joel 3:2, the armies of the world will be gathered in one place. They are gathering to fight each other, but in the end they will combine forces to fight the Savior. Let's see how Jesus makes His appearance.

How will Jesus appear according to Acts 1:9-11? _____

How does Jesus say He will appear according to Matthew 24:30? _____

How does Jesus appear in Daniel 7:13? _____

Daniel is watching a summary of Jesus' second coming! He comes on the "clouds of heaven." The fire coming out of the throne is representative of the wrath of God that has been falling to the earth prior to Jesus' appearance.

As it says in Zechariah, Jesus will be a witness against the nations in God's court. God is sitting in the judgment seat, but judgment has already been given to the Son. Look at John 5:22 in the margin.

Why is Jesus' witness taken without any cross-examination?

> "For not even the Father judges anyone, but He has given all judgment to the Son, so that all will honor the Son even as they honor the Father."
>
> John 5:22-23a

Read Revelation 3:14. What is Jesus called here? _____

There is no need for another witness, because He is faithful and true. He can witness and He can judge because He is saturated with righteousness.

Let me pause here and say that although Daniel is seeing this scene in rapid succession, there are a lot of underlying things happening if you study Revelation in-depth. Let me try to explain. The little horn boasts in the end times and persecutes the saints. At some point, God will say "enough."

Read Matthew 24:21-22. What will happen to the persecution? _____

God knows the exact number of His saints that will be killed in the last days. Until that time is complete, His wrath will not fall. But at some point He will "cut short" the persecution. When that final martyr arrives in heaven, the rapture will take place and God's fiery wrath will fall on the unfaithful still remaining on earth (represented by the fire in Daniel). There will be a grace period where God will allow those on earth time to repent. Once that grace period is over, Jesus will return to the earth "in the clouds of heaven." Even though the fiery wrath of God has already fallen, Jesus will wage war against the armies that come against Him.

Read Zechariah 14:12. What will happen to the armies? _____

Can anyone say "Raiders of the Lost Ark?" Flesh is melting off our Savior's enemies! Jesus will annihilate those who oppose the Ancient of Days. What will happen to the beast?

What happens to the beast in Daniel 7:11? _____

The beast is slain. When Jesus returns, there is no contest. Let's back up a minute. It says in Daniel that thousands were attending the Ancient of Days and myriads were standing before Him. These are those in Heaven, both the angelic host and the saints that have been raptured. They are all watching the destruction of the beast. What is interesting about Daniel 7:10 is the word "attending." It is the Aramaic word *shemash* (Strong's #8120) and it means "to serve," but it is from a root word that means "to be brilliant." When you are serving Him, you are brilliant.

The beast's fate is sealed and the hosts of heaven and the saints witness the beast's destruction. The next verse (verse 12) is a little confusing because it seems like the other beasts (the lion, the bear, and the leopard) are allowed to "continue." But this verse should be read in contrast to verse 11. As in, the final beast was destroyed and thrown into the fire. The other beasts did not meet that fate, but were allowed to continue until the destruction of the fourth.[1]

When Jesus comes on the clouds of heaven to set up His kingdom, Revelation states this kingdom will last 1,000 years. We call this kingdom the Millennial Kingdom of Christ. This is where all those who believe in Jesus will be able to live their life as Jesus intended for them to live it. The Millennium is a gift to us. We are eating, drinking, fellowshipping, serving, ruling, and celebrating Jesus' triumph over evil. Then after the 1,000 years are over, there is another judgment – this time for those who rejected Jesus' sacrifice.

Read Revelation 20:11-15. Where are the unbelievers thrown? _____

The final judgment for those that reject Christ is the lake of fire, but they are judged at the end of the Millennium. If you want to study more about the Millennium, please pick up my *Revelation in Black and White* study. Daniel gets a glimmer of the end times in his vision. He sees the Ancient of Days and the judgment of the beast. He sees our Savoir riding the clouds and given dominion over "men of every language" (Daniel 7:14). I want you to take a look at Daniel 7:27 in the margin.

Jesus rules the kingdom and we will be the kingdom. We will serve and obey Him for those thousand years. Then, after the judgment of the unbelievers, eternity will begin. Here, the old order – or our present way of doing things – will pass away (Revelation 21:4). God the Father will come to earth (Revelation 21:3) and we will never worry about death again (Revelation 21:4). We will live forever under the light of the Father and the Son (Revelation 21:23).

"Then the sovereignty, the dominion and the greatness of all the kingdoms under the whole heaven will be given to the people of the saints of the Highest One; His kingdom will be an everlasting kingdom, and all the dominions will serve and obey Him."

Daniel 7:27

1 Leupold, H.C. *Exposition of Daniel* (Grand Rapids, Michigan: Baker Book House Company, 1969), 307.

Week Seven

"The ram which you saw with the two horns represents the kings of Media and Persia. The shaggy goat represents the kingdom of Greece."

Daniel 8:20-21a

Day One – Chapter Eight
The Ram and the Goat

In Daniel chapter eight the language switches back to Hebrew. We first saw a change in Daniel 2:4 when the Chaldeans spoke to the king in Aramaic. So from Daniel 2:4 – Daniel 7:28 the language has been Aramaic. Now it makes another change back to Hebrew. Why is this? Most scholars believe that the switch signifies that the next chapters are more focused on the future trials of Israel (and also, but less directly to God's saints as a while). That is not to say these chapters are exclusively for Israel, but that they have more of an application to Israel than to other nations.[1]

Read Daniel 8:1-8

What year was the vision given? _____

And where was Daniel in the vision? _____

This was given in the third year of Belshazzar, or about 550 BC. This is still the kingdom of Babylon, although we have already seen its demise in Daniel chapter five. Belshazzar was still in power. This vision happened at approximately the same time that Cyrus united the Medes and the Persians into one empire.[2] Daniel is in Susa, which is the capital of the Persian Empire. This would have helped Daniel understand the ram's identity as that of Medo-Persia (Daniel 2:20). The two horns on the ram correspond to the Medes and the Persians becoming a united kingdom. One horn is larger because Persia came up last, but it took control of the weaker Median kingdom. It is standing in front of the canal in Susa, which Daniel would have recognized as the seat of the Persian Empire. This is the second kingdom of Nebuchadnezzar's statue and the bear from the previous vision in Daniel chapter seven.

In verse four, in which directions did the ram go? _____

This is exactly what Medo-Persia did. It went west, north, and south in its conquests but it didn't venture to the east because it originated from the east. It didn't turn it sights behind it, but only to the other three points of the compass.[3] This ram "did as he pleased and magnified himself" but trouble was on the way from a kingdom that stemmed from the west represented by a male goat.

What is strange about how this goat came in verse 5? _____

The goat didn't touch the ground. This portrays the speed with which Alexander the Great conquered the prevailing empires of his day. This is the four-winged leopard of Daniel chapter seven. He came swiftly and with power, just like it is portrayed in Daniel chapter eight. The large horn between its eyes is Alexander. He crushed the ram, or the Medo-Persian Empire, and trampled it down. Then, as soon as the horn had conquered, it was broken and in its place four horns grew. This is when Alexander died at a young age and his kingdom was divided between his four generals: Cassander in Macedonia; Lysimachus in Thrace and Asia Minor; Seleucus in Syria, Mesopotamia and Persia; and Ptolemy in Egypt.[4]

So far, not much of this information is new, but now we begin to focus on something that happened during the time of the four generals.

A small horn appears out of one of the horns. Just like the horn of the ram represented Alexander and the four horns that came after him represented his generals at the time of division, the little horn represents another leader growing out of one of the

Read Daniel 8:9-14

divisions of the Grecian Empire. We know this leader as King Antiochus 1V or Antiochus Epiphanes. He was the eighth leader of the Seleucid dynasty of Syria and ruled between 175 and 163 BC. Antiochus means "withstander" but Antiochus felt like his name didn't adequately define him. He gave himself the name Epiphanes which means "God is manifest." He minted a coin with his image with the inscription "King Antiochus . . . God made visible."[5] Obviously the man thought he was divine and had a little bit of an ego problem.

In verse nine it says he grew great toward the "south, toward the east, and toward the Beautiful Land." He made attempts to conquer Egypt (the south), which was under his nephew's control and was one of the divisions of the Grecian Empire. He also warred against the Medo-Persian territory of the east, which was another division of the Empire. Lastly, he tried to subdue Israel, or the Beautiful Land.[6]

The Jewish region was under Antiochus' control and one of his life's missions was to destroy the Jewish religion and culture in order to saturate Israel with Greek values and gods. Soon after coming to power he passed laws that forbade observing Jewish laws and he destroyed every copy of the scriptures he could find. At one point Antiochus defiled the temple by offering a pig on the altar to Zeus. This is what prompted the inevitable Jewish revolt.[7]

What does scripture say he did in Daniel 8:10?_____

What are the stars in Daniel according to Daniel 12:3?_____

Who did he claim equality with in Daniel 8:11? _____ What did he remove? _____

What did he cast down in Daniel 8:12? _____ Who is the truth (John 14:6) _____

Basically, Antiochus caused an all out war in Israel that caused many of God's people to be killed. He took away the daily sacrifices in the temple and offered unclean sacrifices to foreign gods in God's house. He even went so far as to set up another altar in God's temple which was probably the transgression that "causes horror" referred to in Daniel 8:13. You can see where this would not sit well with the Jews. There was a massive revolt. Although some of the Jews sided with Antiochus, many sided with the Maccabees who were loyal to God. If Antiochus' minions caught the faithful, they were executed. Thousands of Jews died under the reign of Antiochus.[8]

Not long after Antiochus IV desecrated the temple in Jerusalem, he sent a representative to the nearby Jewish village of Modin and ordered the priest Mattathias to offer sacrifice to a Greek god. Mattathias, a godly Jew, immediately refused. An apostate Jew then stepped forward to offer the sacrifice. Horrified and enraged by the idolatry, Mattathias killed the unfaithful Jew (and by some accounts, the Syrian representative also) and then fled to the Judean hills with his five sons. Other Jewish zealots (including the Hasidim) rallied to their side, and soon a full-scale rebellion was launched. Led first by Mattathias and later by his son Judah Maccabee (the "Hammer"), the Jews' guerilla warfare tactics won them several impressive victories over the Syrian armies. After three years of fighting, the Maccabees finally prevailed. In December 165 B.C. they retook Jerusalem and cleansed and rededicated the temple.[9]

This dedication or *Hanukkah* is celebrated every year by the Jewish people. It is also called the "Festival of Lights" and the "Feast of Dedication." In fact, it is mentioned in scripture. Look at John 10:22-23 in the margin.

At that time the Feast of the Dedication took place at Jerusalem; it was winter, and Jesus was walking in the temple . . .

John 10:22-23

Now we come to a slight mystery. Read Daniel 8:13-14 again. Daniel hears some holy ones (or angels) asking how long these horrors will continue (the killing of the faithful, the idolatrous altar in the temple, and the halting of the sacrifice). One of the holy ones answer: "For 2,300 evenings and mornings; then the holy place will be properly restored."

There are a few problems when trying to reconcile this number. Scripture could be saying 2,300 twenty-four hour days; it could also be saying 2,300 total evening and morning sacrifices, or 1,150 days because there are two daily sacrifices. The other problem comes in when you try to use a certain calendar. Is this the lunar calendar that has approximately 354 days and then throws in another month every two or three years to balance it back with the solar calendar? Or do we use the prophetic calendar of a 360-day year (30 day months like it appears was used in the calculations of Noah's Ark)? Add this into uncertain dates and you get a lot of guesses but not a lot of concrete conclusions.[10] But saying that, I have seen one interpretations that make sense. If you use the 1,150 days this could easily be the time frame when Antiochus first set up the altar to Zeus until the rededication of the temple by the Maccabees.[11] What we need to remember here is that these numbers are in the past. We will run into similar numbers in chapter nine, but they are future numbers that will come into play in the last days. The numbers in Daniel chapter eight are about Antiochus Epiphanes and his rebellion against God.

Before we stop for today. I need you to ask yourself why this vision was important. This is just a side note in a long line of kings that ruled in the Grecian Empire. Yes, Antiochus Epiphanes was a tyrant who desecrated God's temple and persecuted his people, but why are we highlighting him in scripture?

What is he called in Daniel 8:9? _____

Turn back to Daniel 7:8. What came up here? _____ Out of what kingdom? _____

Antiochus Epiphanes came up out of the Grecian Empire – or the bronze kingdom. The little horn that appears in Daniel 7:8 is the final ruler of the iron kingdom – or the Antichrist. Antiochus Epiphanes is highlighted in Daniel chapter eight in order to show us what the Antichrist will be like. It is someone from the past we can study that will be similar to the "little horn" of the future. Antiochus is a future ruler for Daniel, but one in which God knew we needed to study. Many attributes of Antiochus will be made manifest again in the Antichrist. We will see this manifestation tomorrow.

1 Leupold, H.C. *Exposition of Daniel* (Grand Rapids, Michigan: Baker Book House Company, 1969), 330.
2 *English Standard Version Study Bible* (Wheaton, Illinois: Crossway, 2008), 1602.
3 Leupold, H.C. *Exposition of Daniel* (Grand Rapids, Michigan: Baker Book House Company, 1969), 337-338.
4 *One-Volume Illustrated Edition of Zondervan Bible Commentary* with General Editor F. F. Bruce (Zondervan, 2008), 894.
5 Hinnant, Greg. *Daniel Notes* (Lake Mary, Florida: Creation House Press, 2003), 204.
6 Leupold, H.C. *Exposition of Daniel* (Grand Rapids, Michigan: Baker Book House Company, 1969), 345.
7 Hinnant, Greg. *Daniel Notes* (Lake Mary, Florida: Creation House Press, 2003), 205.
8 *English Standard Version Study Bible* (Wheaton, Illinois: Crossway, 2008), 1603.
9 Hinnant, Greg. *Daniel Notes* (Lake Mary, Florida: Creation House Press, 2003), *214.*
10 *One-Volume Illustrated Edition of Zondervan Bible Commentary* with General Editor F. F. Bruce (Zondervan, 2008), 894.
11 Moore, Beth. DVD Study *Here and Now ... There and Then: A lecture series on Revelation* (Houston, Texas: Living Proof Ministries, 2009), 168.

> "In the latter period of their rule, when the transgressors have run their course, a king will arise, insolent and skilled in intrigue."
>
> Daniel 8:23

We left off yesterday mentioning that the "small horn" of Antiochus Epiphanes foreshadows the "little horn" of Daniel 7:8 or the Antichrist. Today we will study the "man of lawlessness" (2 Thessalonians 2:3).

Read Daniel 8:15-22

This is the first section of scripture where we meet the angel Gabriel. Gabriel's name means "man of God" which is interesting to understand when Daniel describes him as "one who looked like a man." When you understand the Hebrew, you see something very interesting. There are a variety of words you can use for the word "man." *Adam* (Strong's #120) is one way to say "man" and it is used 552 times in scripture. Another word for man is *iysh* (Strong's 376) and it is used 1639 times. A third way to say man is the word *geber* and it is only used 68 times. Gabriel's name stems from the root word *geber* plus *el* which means God. *Geber* is not just an ordinary man – *geber* is a valiant warrior (Strong's 1397). What Daniel was saying was this: "Standing before me was one who looked like a valiant warrior . . ." And a voice from the banks of the Ulai, which was probably God's voice, said: "Gabriel (valiant warrior of God) . . . " Like I have said previously, in the Middle Eastern culture you became your name. Gabriel's name was who he appeared to be to Daniel. He was a "valiant warrior" of God. We will meet Gabriel one more time in the next chapter. Both times the angel Gabriel appears he tells Daniel things pertaining to the end times. The other two times he appears in scripture we should know very well.

Re-familiarize yourself with Luke 1:11-1:26. What two births did he announce? _____

Gabriel announced the "time of the end" to Daniel (Daniel 8:17). He also announced those who would herald the time of the end.

What did John the Baptist say would happen to the chaff in Luke 3:16-17? _____

And what is coming out of the throne in Daniel 7:10? _____

What did Jesus say would happen to the tares in Matthew 13:30? _____

What did Jesus say He was sent to cast to the earth in Luke 12:49? _____

In Daniel 8:17 Gabriel tells Daniel his visions pertain to the "time of the end." Jesus will ultimately fulfill these times by returning with fire and destroying the kingdoms of the earth. John the Baptist heralded Jesus' mission and pointed the way to the one that would bring the fire. Gabriel was involved in all of this. We can't say for sure Gabriel doesn't appear elsewhere to warn the saints of something, but he is not named in any other section of scripture. It seems he has been chosen by God to be His special messenger to the faithful about the coming kingdom.

Daniel falls to his knees and into a "deep sleep" or *radam.* This Hebrew word means "to stun or stupefy (with sleep or death)" (Strong's 7290). You could say that Daniel was overwhelmed. Then Gabriel touches him and Daniel is strengthened and stands up. Angels can strengthen us. You might go so far to say that they have God's touch. An angel strengthened Jesus in the Garden of Gethsemane. Take a look at Luke 22:43 in the margin. I wonder if it was Gabriel?

Now an angel from heaven appeared to Him, strengthening Him.

Luke 22:43

What does Gabriel tell Daniel in Daniel 8:19? How does he identify the final period? _____ And again he labels it the appointed _____

Gabriel tells Daniel that what he is about to reveal will occur during the final period of indignation, or the time of the end. Next he identifies the ram and the goat for Daniel.

In verse 23 what period does he specify? _____

Like we discussed yesterday, Antiochus Epiphanes foreshadows the leader or the "little horn" that will emerge from the iron kingdom of Daniel chapter seven. The following summary by the angel Gabriel is descriptive of the Antichrist that Antiochus Epiphanes foreshadows. We are going to take this one verse at a time. Look back at Daniel 8:23.

In the _____ of the rule when _____

That phrase "when the transgressors have run their course" says a lot. The Hebrew word *pashar* (Strong's 6586) means "to transgress or rebel, most often in order to gain independence" (2 Kings 8:20). The word for "run their course" or "come to the full" is the Hebrew word *tamam* (Strong's #8552), which means "to be complete, finished, and perfect." As in, the time Gabriel is talking about is the time when transgressions have been perfected. This would be when the 10 toes of the statue emerge, or the 10 horns of the terrifying beast. Although Antiochus Epiphanes came at a time when sin was full, it was not yet complete – or worldwide.[1] Let's see what scripture says about the end time and its "transgressions."

What do those in the last days mock according to 2 Peter 3:3-4? _____

Read 2 Timothy 3:1-7. List some of the characteristics of the last days? _____
_____

What do they never come to know? _____

Read Romans 1:18-32. What are we talking about in verse 18? _____

What happens when you turn from the truth according to verse 26-27?
_____

What will people become according to verse 29-31? _____

I do believe in today's age we are getting very close to being so full we are running over. Now, over the course of history, people could always look at these verses and say, "yes, that is happening in today's society" but they could not say that it was a worldwide phenomenon, or even that the world was saturated with these specific transgressions. We are entering a time when we will be unable to return from the brink of disaster. We have turned a corner in our society where there is no going back. Once laws are passed allowing some of these transgressions, there is no repealing the law without rebellion. Sin is like that. Once you consider one sin acceptable, the next is easier to swallow. As one of my friends always says, "What is tolerated in one generation becomes acceptable in the next." Our transgressions have almost reached perfection.

What had the nations done in 2 Chronicles 28:3? _____ What did the Lord do to them according to Daniel? _____

Yet we are doing the same thing. We abort our children and cast them into the flames without remorse. Look at Isaiah 5:20 in the margin. We disguise it cleverly with the name pro-choice, but isn't that substituting bitter for sweet? We call it gay pride but God calls it "degrading passions" (Romans 1:26) and an abomination (Leviticus 18:22). There is now an online dating service for married people. Its slogan is "Life is short. Have an affair." Isn't that calling evil good?

> Woe to those who call evil good, and good evil; who substitute darkness for light and light for darkness; who substitute bitter for sweet and sweet for bitter!
>
> Isaiah 5:20

We are messed up. We are so messed up that we can't even see it at times. We see what we want to see. We get what we want to have. Then we want something else. There is no waiting. There is no thought of whether it is right tor wrong. Like Nike says: "Just do it." People say there are a lot of "gray" areas in life's choices but I don't know if God sees it that way. There is freedom but there is also a right and a wrong. There is freedom within a choice but there is a correct way and a wrong way. There is a black and a white.

Seven churches are addressed by Jesus in Revelation. The book of Revelation is about the return of the King. Even though the seven churches existed in John's day, the seven church environments Jesus describes in Revelation exist right up until Jesus returns. We can learn a lot from these environments. Although we can't get into them in-depth here, pick up my *Revelation in Black and White* study. But for now, let's look at a few highlights.

Read Revelation 2:4. What had this church done? _____

Jesus should be our first love, and this church had checked Him at the door. This seems a little outlandish to some of us, but I have been inside one of these churches. I didn't think anything was amiss for a time. The preacher was decent, but after a while I noticed that Jesus wasn't in the sermons. The pastor spoke mostly of "God's love." I approached the pastor about it, asking him to do a sermon on what Jesus had done for us. Do you know what he said? "There are many different opinions about Jesus." What? I moved a short time later. A few years went by and I received an Easter bulletin in the mail from that pastor. He had circled Jesus' name. "See," he seemed to be saying," I do reference Jesus." Wow. But like Ephesus, many churches have left Jesus at the door. Jesus is offensive. He tells you to "go and sin no more" (John 8:11) and we don't like it. Jesus tells us to walk the narrow road (Matthew 7:13-14) and the narrow road is hard at times. Don't be like Ephesus. Don't check Jesus at the door.

Read Revelation 3:1. What was this church? _____

This church thought she was alive, but she was dead. Jesus is the way the truth and the life (John 14:6). This church thought she was alive in Christ but she was dead in sin. She had a head knowledge of Jesus, but not a changed heart. She thought she was getting to heaven, but she was on a straight track to the fire.

What does Jesus tell this church to do in Revelation 3:2?
_____

For this reason it says, "Awake, sleeper, and arise from the dead, and Christ will shine on you."

Ephesians 5:14

This is second coming language. In scripture, if you are "asleep" you are not with God. Look at Ephesians 5:14 in the margin. If you are asleep, you do not see Christ clearly. You are missing the mark. You are walking in darkness. The church of Sardis was in the dark. They were dead asleep. They didn't have the life because He is the life.

Now read 1 Thessalonians 5:2. How will the day of the Lord come? _____

The day of the Lord is the wrath of God that ends with the second coming of Christ – it comes with fire (Revelation, 2 Peter 3:7, Daniel 7:10).

Now read 1 Thessalonians 5:2-6.   The day of the Lord will come like a thief in the night to who?
_____ Are we in darkness? _____
What should we not do? _____ What should we do? _____

The "thief in the night" analogy has been used for centuries to tell the church we can't possibly know the time or the season of His coming. This is a false doctrine. Scripture clearly teaches that only if you are asleep will He come like the thief. If you are of the day (the light – Him – John 14:6) then you will not be surprised by His coming. You will be awake and sober.

You will see the Antichrist when he rises, because you will be in the light. We will look at the Antichrist tomorrow.

1 Hinnant, Greg. *Daniel Notes* (Lake Mary, Florida: Creation House Press, 2003), 207.

Day Three – Chapter Eight
The Antichrist

A king of fierce countenance, and understanding dark sentences, shall stand up. And his power shall be mighty, but not by his own power; and he shall destroy wonderfully, and shall prosper, and practice, and shall destroy the mighty and the holy people. And through his policy also he shall cause craft to prosper in his hand, and he shall magnify himself in his heart, and by peace shall destroy many: he shall also stand up against the Prince of princes, but he shall be broken without hand.

Daniel 8:23b-25 KJV

We left off yesterday with the environment of the latter days. We continue our tour of Daniel with the description of the Antichrist. Look at Daniel 8:23-25 in the margin. Let's take this apart piece by piece.

Fierce Countenance

The Hebrew word *az* (Strong's 5794) means "strong, vehement, and harsh." The Hebrew word *paneh* (Strong's 6440) means face. This means his face is harsh, his countenance is vehement and strong. Some versions of scripture translate this phrase as "insolent, stern, arrogant, or hard-faced." All of these convey the point scripture is trying to make.

Dark Sentences

This is one Hebrew word translated as two. It is the word *chiydah* (Strong's 2420) and it means "a trick." It is derived from the root *chuwd* (Strong's 2330), which means "to tie a knot or to propound a riddle." So *chiydah* is a puzzle or a riddle – but it is normally a dark one. Some versions of scripture translate this word as "skilled in intrigue, master trickster, understands sinister schemes, or is an expert in dark sayings." What scripture is trying to convey is that this man will be a deceiver. He will be a masterful speaker who will trick you with his words.

His Power Shall be Mighty

His strength or power will be great. The word translated "might" is the Hebrew *atsam* (Strong's 6105) and it means "to bind fast or to crunch the bones." That is how great his strength will be.

Not by his own Power

Although the Antichrist will be powerful, he will get that power from something else. We learn the identity of his strength in Revelation.

Read Revelation 12:17-13:1. Who is watching the beast rise? _____
And who is the dragon according to Revelation 12:9?_____

Satan will empower the Antichrist. Some scholars believe that he will even inhabit the Antichrist like he inhabited Judas (Luke 22:3).

Read Isaiah 14:12-14. Who does this sound like we are talking about? _____

Now read Isaiah 14:16. Now what does scripture call him? _____

Isaiah starts out talking about Satan and then describes him as a man. If you think for a minute, if the Antichrist receives worship, Satan would want that worship. He wants the worship God receives. He wants the world to bow to him. Read Revelation 13:15 in the margin. The Antichrist will demand the world's worship. He will be great, but not by his own power. Satan could very well inhabit the Antichrist.

He will Destroy Wonderfully

This seems like an odd phrase to us. The Hebrew word *pala* (Strong's #6381), translated here as "wonderfully," means "to separate or distinguish, to do or make a wondrous thing." It is used primarily of God to express something that is beyond the scope of human abilities to do. This goes hand in hand with the end of the sentence that says, "and shall destroy the mighty and the holy people." His destruction will be beyond the ability of humanity to accomplish. But we have already seen that his power is not his own. It belongs to the dragon and the dragon's influence will capture the Antichrist and those who follow him. Antiochus was not a legendary conqueror like the Antichrist will be.

He shall Prosper and Practice

Again, this is an unusural way to phrase what the Antichrist will do. That he will prosper or succeed is self explanatory, but what does "practice" mean? Some translations of scripture translate this phrase as "he will prosper and do his pleasure," or "all will go well with him and he will do as he pleases," or "he will succeed in all that he does." The Hebrew word *tsalach* (Strong's #6743) means to "push forward and to succeed and prosper." The Hebrew word *asah* (Strong's #6213) means "to do or make." You can see where some translations would say, "he will succeed or prosper in whatever he does." In a general sense, the word *asah* (to do or make) means to make objects. This includes making idols. What will ultimately happened when the Antichrist who will "*asah*" comes to power?

Look again at Revelation 13:15 in the margin. What is set up? _____ And what happens if you do not worship it? _____

> And it was given to him to give breath to the image of the beast, so that the image of the beast would even speak and cause as many as do not worship the image of the beast to be killed.
>
> Revelation 13:15

He Shall Destroy the Mighty and the Holy People

We have already talked about this, but let's look at some verses that emphasize this destruction. We have already looked at Revelation 13:15 which states that if you do not worship his image, you will be killed.

Read Ezekiel 38:8-9. When will this happen? _____ What will he be like? _____ Who is he coming against in verse 16? _____

Read Revelation 12:17. The woman is Israel. Who else does the dragon come against? _____

What does Jesus tell us in Matthew 24:9? _____

Through his Policy also he shall cause Craft to Prosper in his Hand

The word "policy" in the Hebrew is *sekel* (Strong's #7922) and it means intelligence. The word "craft" is *mirmah* (Strong's 4820) and it means fraud. In other words, he will be so intelligent that his fraud and deceit will be accepted. He will prosper even though he is a fraud.

He shall Magnify himself in his Heart

The word "magnify" in the Hebrew is *gadal* (Strong's 1431) and it means to "become strong, grow up, to be great, or to magnify oneself." This word can signify an increase of size. In other words, the Antichrist will enlarge himself in his own heart. He will become great in his own eyes. This is demonstrated very clearly in scripture.

Read 2 Thessalonians 2:3-4. What will he do? _____

By Peace shall Destroy Many

The word peace is the Hebrew word *shalvah* (Strong's 7962) and it means security, but there is a caveat: this word can mean either genuine security or false security.

Read Revelation 6:1-2. This is a picture of the Antichrist coming to power. What is he wearing? _____ What is he holding? _____ Does he have arrows? _____ What is he doing? _____

What does Satan disguise himself as in 2 Corinthians 11:14? _____

The Antichrist comes peacefully because he has a bow with no arrows. He is wearing a crown, which signifies his power and leadership, but because he has no arrows, he is coming under the doctrine of peace. He will disguise himself as an angel of light – as one who can solve the world's problems – peacefully. The world will be deceived into trusting him. Many will place their hope in him.

He shall also stand up against the Prince of princes

The Hebrew word for "stand up" is *amad* (Strong's 5975) and it means "to take one's stand." The word for "prince" is the Hebrew word *sar* (Strong's #8269) and it means the official leader or commander. It has been used as the leader of Israel's army (1 Samuel 17:55). But the Prince of princes can refer to no one but Jesus himself. Jesus is described similarly in the book of Revelation.

Read Revelation 19:16. What are His names? _____

When Jesus is returning in Revelation 19:19, what does the Antichrist (or beast) do? _____

The Antichrist who represents the beast will try to defeat Jesus when He returns on the clouds of heaven. Can you imagine the arrogance? And the people of the earth will stand there with him. What will happen?

He shall be Broken without Hand

The Antichrist will fall but it will not be by any mortal means. Let's take a look.

Read Revelation 19:20. What happened to the beast? _____

Read Ezekiel 38:22-23. What happens to the Antichrist? _____

Look at Habakkuk 3:12-13. What happened to the head of the house of the evil?
_____

> "The vision *[mareh]* of the evenings and mornings which has been told is true; but keep the vision *[chazown]* secret, for it pertains to many days in the future." Then I, Daniel, was exhausted and sick for days. Then I got up again and carried on the king's business, but I was astounded at the vision *[mareh]*, and there was none to explain it.
>
> Daniel 8:26-27

In Daniel 2:34, what did the stone do? _____

No man will be able to touch the Antichrist – His destruction will come from Jesus. Antiochus Epiphanes opposed God indirectly; the Antichrist will oppose God directly.

Look at the remaining verses of Daniel 8:26-27 in the margin. At first glance you get the sense that the vision of the "evenings and the mornings" is the same vision being sealed. But the first word used for "vision" is *mareh* (Strong's #4758) and it is used for a view – as in the act of seeing. This pertains to the vision Daniel beheld – the ram and the goat, the little horn, and the desecration of the temple (Daniel 8:3-14). Gabriel is telling Daniel that vision is true – it will happen – it will come to pass. The second word used for "vision" is *chazown* (Strong's #2377) and it refers more to the divine revelation or the entirety of a prophetic message. Although it still means "sight" it more specifically refers to a revelation or oracle. This seems to indicate that Gabriel is telling Daniel that his vision of the evenings and mornings is true, but also to seal up the revelation of Gabriel's words (those that deal with the Antichrist) because those words (or the revelation of those words) pertain to many days in the future. Daniel was astonished at the vision (*mareh*) that he actually saw – the ram and goat and the little horn and was distressed for many days.

There are a few questions we need to ask ourselves. First – why would God tell Daniel to "keep the vision secret?" Scripture isn't telling Daniel to keep the visions or revelations to himself because many people have read and learned from Daniel. What scripture is saying is that the revelation of Gabriel's words would not be understood until "many days in the future." As in, the world as a whole would not understand the end time system or the man that leads it (the Antichrist) until God unlocks the mystery. There is a lesson here:

Sometimes God gives revelations that will not be fully exposed until the proper time.

It can be frustrating to be the one with the revelation if your words will not be heard or received by the church as a whole. It had to be frustrating for Luther to try to communicate his "faith by grace" revelation when the church as a whole believed "faith through works." If God has given you a gift to be used in some way and you haven't seen anything come to fruition – know that God is waiting on the proper time. He will do as He promised, but you have to wait until the moment when it is supposed to be seen by the world. Remember, God can change your life in a moment. It just takes one moment.

Daniel ends the chapter by saying "there was none to explain it." It rings in my ears as a cry of loneliness. Daniel had such revelation that no one else could help him, and at times that is a very lonely place to be. If you are in a leadership position, at times it can be very lonely and isolating. Most leaders are surrounded by people, but many times they have few friends. Your decisions are scrutinized, gossip surrounds anything others find out of sorts, and you are sought after for help but it is assumed that you yourself do not need any assistance. Leadership is painful and isolating. Daniel felt this here. He was surrounded by Babylon, and the converted king he once served was gone. His friends may have died. And "there was none to explain it." Here is another lesson for us to understand:

At times God isolates you in order to give you more revelation.

In the next chapter we will see Daniel get even more detailed information about the last days. Sometimes God wants you alone, on your knees, in order to bless you later with His glory.

---

1 Hinnant, Greg. *Daniel Notes* (Lake Mary, Florida: Creation House Press, 2003), 207.

Day Four – Chapter Nine
Daniel's Petition

"This whole land will be a desolation and a horror, and these nations will serve the king of Babylon seventy years."

Jeremiah 25:11

Yesterday we left Daniel in distress because of the little horn. In this chapter, Daniel will receive more revelation from the angel Gabriel. Before we begin reading Daniel chapter nine, I want you to see what Daniel was reading when he started his prayer to God. Look at the two Jeremiah scriptures written for you in the margin.

Read Daniel 9:1-19

Jeremiah prophesied that after seventy years the Jewish people would return to Israel. This is what prompted Daniel's famous prayer in Daniel chapter nine.

For thus says the Lord, "When seventy years have been complete for Babylon, I will visit you and fulfill My good word to you, to bring you back to this place."

Jeremiah 29:10

What year was it according to the king? _____

In chapter six we saw Daniel get thrown into the lions' den because he would not stop praying to God. This happened at the beginning of Darius' reign when he was setting up his cabinet. This prayer happened in the same year. This very prayer is what Daniel's enemies could have seen him pray. We can't know for sure, but it is interesting to think about.

Read Ezra 1:1. What year did Cyrus order the exiles to return to Israel? _____

Remember, the first year of Cyrus is the same as the first year of Darius. Whether or not Cyrus and Darius are one in the same person, the time of their reign is the same. Obviously, Cyrus had not issued the order when Daniel petitioned God because the return was what Daniel was praying about. So, take notice of this:

When God's saints fall to their knees, heaven moves.

Daniel's prayer may have been what prompted the return of the exiles. If Cyrus and Darius were one in the same person, Daniel could have spoken to the king himself. The lions' den miracle may have been a catalyst to sway Cyrus to issue the decree. Or as the historian Josephus said in his work, when Cyrus read his name in Isaiah, this may have so impressed the king that he faithfully went along with God's chosen timeline.

Revisit the prophecy of Isaiah in the margin. Keep in mind it was written approximately 150 years before Cyrus was born.[1]

Look at Daniel 9:2. I want you to understand what Daniel was doing when he discovered the years of the Israelites exile.

"It is I who says of Cyrus, 'He is my shepherd! And he will perform all My desire,' And he declares of Jerusalem, 'She will be built.' And of the temple, 'Your foundation will be laid.'"

Isaiah 44:28

What was he doing?_____

I know you realize what I am about to say is true, but wrap it around your heart and leave here with a life-lesson: there are treasures in God's Word – deep ones. If you do not observe the books regularly, you miss out on a wealth of knowledge and profound direction for your life. If Daniel had not read Jeremiah, he may not have prayed, and if Daniel hadn't prayed, heaven may not have moved. We all know God can use anyone to change the course of the world, but God used Daniel. Did Daniel realize his significance? I would wager a bet he did not. I would wager a bet that Daniel questioned himself on a regular basis. After all, God can move mountains, but he hadn't moved Babylon for Daniel. The mountain of a pagan land was still in front of the man of high esteem, and after Babylon came Medo-Persia. Daniel was in the middle of a foreign land. He never returned home. Did Daniel question his standing? Did he realize his prayer would have such a profound effect? This is the prayer that moved mountains – literally. The mountain representing the Jewish people went home. I have mentioned before that mountains in scripture represent kingdoms (Revelation 17:9-10, Micah 4:1). And mountains move for faith. Daniel is living proof of that.

Daniel read the word, and the Word said the exile would be seventy years. At this point, Daniel was in the first year of Cyrus (and Darius). This is approximately 539-538 BC. Daniel is approximately 82 years old and would have been in Babylon approximately 67 years. Based on the Word, Daniel knew the exile was almost over. Daniel fell to his knees. Let's study the prayer that prompted heaven to move and the exiles to be returned to the land of Israel.

In Daniel 9:3, who did Daniel turn his attention to? _____. And what ways did Daniel seek God. 1)_____ and _____, 2) and with _____ 3) and with _____and _____.

How often do we humble ourselves for our nation like this? I would wager a bet none of us have. You can see why Daniel was a man highly esteemed by God. Daniel not only prayed, he also fasted. Daniel not only fasted, he also physically humbled himself by clothing himself with sackcloth and dousing himself with ashes. Do you see why Daniel had God's esteem? I sure do. Daniel went all out for the King.

Read Daniel 9:4-6. Sum up what Daniel thinks about God._____

What is Daniel's opinion of his people?_____

Daniel expresses the awesomeness and lovingkindness of God. He declares himself and his people (yes, he uses the pronoun "we" – he does not exclude himself from the mix) wicked and rebellious. Do you see the humility of Daniel? He lumps himself in with everyone else, as should we. We are all sinners. We have all turned away in some form or fashion. We have all hurt a holy God.

Read Daniel 9:7-8. What belongs to God? _____
To all Israel? _____

Read Daniel 9:9-10. What belongs to God? _____
What had all Israel done? _____

Read Daniel 9:12-14. What has God done? _____

Don't let this pass you by too quickly. God was good. Israel was bad. And God's Word came to pass. God had already warned Israel what would happen. They ignored the Word of God. And Daniel had just read the Word. And that Word said there would be seventy years of exile. Daniel understood that if God's Word said seventy years, God meant seventy years. But he was also not delusional. He knew Israel was still the same Israel God exiled. Yes, they might have learned some lessons. Yes, they might have grown closer to God, but wicked was still wicked and holy was still holy. This is what sent Daniel to his knees. I want you to read the verses in the margin and let them sink into your soul.

Daniel didn't point to the seventy years and say, "God, you said!" Daniel didn't point to any reformation on the part of the Israelites. Daniel didn't point to himself and speak of his own faithfulness. Daniel understood that the important thing was that God's name be honored. That His city be restored. That His people be returned. It had nothing to do with Israel and everything to do with God: to honor His name; to bring glory to His kingdom; and to prove to Cyrus and to the world that He was God.

"O my God, incline Your ear and hear! Open Your eyes and see our desolations and the city which is called by Your name; for we are not presenting our supplications before You on account of any merits of our own, but on account of Your great compassion. O Lord, hear! O Lord, forgive! O Lord, listen and take action! For Your own sake, O my God, do not delay, because Your city and Your people are called by Your name."

Daniel 9:18-19

It is all about God; it is not all about us. Mountains may move, but they move for God's name, not our own popularity. Rivers may be crossed, but it is for God's glory, not our own safety. Paths may be forged, but it is for His advancement, not for our cause. We are lucky He allows us to be a part of His plan. We should be honored that we can do anything at all to further His kingdom. We need to remember it is all for Him, not all for us.

But He uses us, He loves us, and He wants to lift us up. I will never understand why. Compared to the holy, we are dirt. But our God is loving and faithful. There will be times He will reach down and touch you and allow you to see the plans of a perfect God.

I want you to focus on a few things today and we will touch on more tomorrow.

Read Daniel 9:20-23

When did Gabriel come to Daniel in 9:20? _____

At about what time did he appear (verse 21)? _____
How did he find Daniel's condition? _____

When did God tell Gabriel to hightail it to Daniel (verse 23)? _____

Gabriel appeared while Daniel was still speaking, but Gabriel had been sent at the beginning of Daniel's prayer. I can just imagine God sitting on the edge of His throne as Daniel unrolls the Jeremiah scroll. I can imagine His hand raised in the air as Daniel falls to his knees. I can imagine as soon as the first words tumbled from Daniel's mouth the voice of the Almighty saying, "Gabriel! Go, and give Daniel insight with understanding!" I am getting goose bumps thinking about it. God knew the exact words that would fall from Daniel's lips. God knew Daniel would be in "extreme weariness." That means Daniel had been praying for some time (perhaps beginning with the morning sacrifice), and/or his prayer was so heartfelt that it physically exhausted him. God knew that Daniel would be pouring his entire heart and soul out to the throne of grace. God knew, and He was prepared to send Gabriel *as soon as Daniel started to pray.*

That is amazing.

When God's people fall to their knees, heaven moves.

Immediately.

When was the last time you fell to your knees for your nation?

When was the last time you found yourself in "extreme weariness" because of your heartfelt prayer?

Something to think about.

---

1 *The Complete Word Study – Old Testament*, King James Version with General Editor Warren Baker, D.R.E. Published in Chattanooga, Tennessee by AMG Publishers in 1994, page 1764.

Day Five – Chapter Nine
Noah, Job, and Daniel

"I have come to tell you, for you are highly esteemed; so give heed to the message and gain understanding of the vision."

Daniel 9:23b

Take a look Daniel 9:23 in the margin. These are some of the first words Gabriel said to Daniel. I know we have mentioned this before, but it needs to be highlighted again. Daniel was a man God held in "high esteem." Look at another verse that mentions Daniel.

Read Ezekiel 14:14. What three people are named specifically here? _____

After the deportation to Babylon, God told Ezekiel (who was taken after Daniel yet before the total destruction of Jerusalem by Nebuchadnezzar), that if Noah, Daniel, and Job were in the crowd, they could only deliver themselves. Wrap your mind around this. Noah was deemed righteous and was saved from the flood – but seven other people got on the ark with him. Scripture doesn't mention their righteousness – only Noah's (Genesis 6:8-9). Because of Noah's righteousness, his family was spared. Then the Lord said to Noah, "Enter the ark, you and all your household, for you alone I have seen to be righteous before Me in this time" (Genesis 7:1). And Job – God pointed Job out to Satan and said, "Have you considered My servant Job? For there is no one like him on the earth, a blameless and upright man, fearing God and turning away from evil" (Job 1:8). I want you to think about this for a moment with me. A lot of time had passed from when Adam was created until Ezekiel wrote those words in Ezekiel 14:14. A lot of heroes in the faith were written about in scripture, yet only three were named and set apart as "righteous." Adam had come and gone. Abraham had come and gone. Jacob had come and gone. Joseph had come and gone. David had come and gone. Josiah had come and gone. Lots of men God singled out had come and gone, yet only three were highlighted in Ezekiel 14:14: Noah, Job and Daniel. What made these three so special? We all know that we are only righteous through Jesus. The word "righteous" (Strong's 6666) in Ezekiel 14:14 is *tsedaqah*. It is derived from the word *tsadaq* (Strong's 6663), which is used of a man when he has "obtained deliverance from condemnation, and as being thus entitled to a certain inheritance." We were delivered and obtained an inheritance only through the blood of the Lamb, and all those heroes in the faith obtained that inheritance. So why again are only three highlighted in Ezekiel 14:14? Let's look at the uniqueness of these men one at a time.

Read Genesis 6:6, 6:9 and 7:1. What is unique about Noah's righteousness? What did God say about Noah's righteousness in these verses? He was righteous _____

I believe this was why Noah was such a shining star. Have you ever been surrounded by the not so Jesus-loving crowd? What have you noticed about being around those who do not love our Savior? Do you fall into their habits at times? Do your words mimic theirs at times? I remember times when my husband came home from the field after training with his men. Bad words tumbled from his mouth like a waterfall. He would catch himself and say, "Sorry, field mouth." In a day or two he would be completely back to his old self, but when you are surrounded by the world, the world tends to rub off on you. That was why Noah was so special. He was surrounded by the world, perhaps even skeptics in his own family! He did not give in. Do you know how hard this must have been? Noah didn't have any true friends. There was no one to talk to except his family and scripture doesn't call them righteous – not once. Did they ridicule him? Did they believe him? Did they laugh at him? We aren't sure, but Noah was isolated – in a big way. Yet, Noah did not back down. We can learn a lesson from Noah:

When we are surrounded by evil, we do not have to become it.

This will be an extremely important lesson in the last days. When those around us pick up their guns to fight the establishment, will we? When looters raid the grocery store for food, will we? When those in power confront us with evil, will we stand for the good? Noah did. Noah was surrounded by "wickedness" where "every intent" of mankind was evil (Genesis 6:5).

Now let's look at Job. Most scholars believe that Job is one of the oldest books in scripture – perhaps even older than Genesis. Many believe Job lived pre-Moses. He may have lived in the days right after the flood. We have looked at the verse where God pointed Job out to Satan. It declared Job "blameless and upright." It said he "feared God and turned away from evil" (Job 1:8). Now let's look at an interesting verse.

Read Job 1:10. What did Satan say God had done?
_____

We know the story. Satan then took away Job's wealth, his possessions, and his children. Job was left with nothing. Yet, what happened? Look at Job 1:21 in the margin. Job blessed God! After all his property was destroyed and after all ten of his children were killed – Job blessed God. Then Satan goes back to God in Job 2:5 and tells God that Job hadn't cursed God because his health was still intact. So God allows Satan to smite Job's entire body with boils. Notice that when I listed the things that were taken from Job, I never mentioned his wife. His wife lived. God never told Satan to withhold his hand from her, yet Satan didn't try to take her life. We find out why in Job chapter two.

He [Job] said, "Naked I came from my mother's womb, and naked I shall return there. The Lord gave and the Lord has taken away. Blessed be the name of the Lord."

Job 1:21

Read Job 2:9. What happened? _____

His wife turns against him. His wife. We know the rest of the story too. His so-called "friends" come to "comfort" him and they speak against him! Everyone thinks Job is to blame for his suffering. Tragedy strikes Job, and then isolation strikes Job – just like Noah. Job had to maintain his integrity despite those surrounding him telling him that he was in the wrong.

Then comes Daniel. He is taken from his homeland. He is sent to the crown jewel of Satan's domain. He is promoted, but he is isolated from his friends. He is walking in Babylon – alone. He is thrown into the lions' den by his peers. He is surrounded by darkness and he does not turn away from the light. Do you understand how hard this had to be? Do you get how much Daniel had to walk with God to walk in Babylon and not have any of it rub off? Surrounded by darkness, surrounded by tragedy, Noah, Job and Daniel did not turn from the light. In the last days, we will be surrounded by Babylon and by tragedy. We will be surrounded by those who think we are wrong. We will be isolated. But we can still be righteous in our generation – just like Noah, Job, and Daniel.

There is a lesson here.

When no one else agrees with us, it doesn't mean we are wrong.

Really take that to heart. Just because you are alone in your thoughts doesn't in any way indicate that you have deviated from God's path, or that you are wrong in your convictions. Sometimes the singularity of our stance indicates we are right where we need to be.

I believe that is why these men were highlighted so much. They did not waver, not at the beginning, or in the middle, or at the end. They stood firm. Through isolation, tragedy, and darkness, they did not blink. May we be like these men in the last days. May our faith never waver if no one believes us, if all of our children are killed in one blow, and if we are thrown into a den of lions. May we trust our God – no matter what.

Let's get back to the book of Daniel. Daniel had just prayed a prayer of great devotion because he had read in Jeremiah that the Israelites would be exiled for 70 years. The clock was ticking – the time was almost up. Daniel falls to his knees and God immediately sends Gabriel to answer Daniel's prayer.

Read Daniel 9:24

"O Lord, hear! O Lord, forgive! O Lord, listen and take action! For Your own sake, O my God, do not delay, because Your city and Your people are called by Your name."

Daniel 9:19

Now I want to pause here and have you really think about what Gabriel was saying. Daniel's prayer is in direct response to the scripture he read. His intention is to plead with God to carry out His Word. Daniel prays not specifically for the restoration of Jerusalem or for the Jewish people. He prays for God's name to be honored. Revisit Daniel 9:19 in the margin.

Daniel gets more than he bargained for, because God not only tells Daniel about the restoration of the Jewish people after the Babylonian exile – He tells Daniel about the restoration of all things back to God.

Take a look and speculate when these things will occur:

Finish transgression? _____
Make an end of sin? _____
Bring in everlasting righteousness? _____
Seal up – no more – vision and prophecy? _____
Anoint the most holy place? _____

The end of transgression and sin? Everlasting righteousness? These things can only occur when Jesus is walking the earth at His second coming. Then and only then will the holy place be anointed (Ezekiel 43) and vision and prophecy will be no more because we will be with Him!

How much time is carved out according to Daniel 9:24? _____ For who specifically? _____

Daniel was praying about a 70-year exile and he got a 70-week prophecy that would tell the story of the Jewish people from Daniel's time until the time of the end. We will look more closely at this time period in the next lesson. For now, I want you to leave with a very important thought.

When you ask sincerely for an answer to prayer, God may give you revelation that surpasses anything you ever dreamed you could know.

"Seventy weeks have been decreed for your people . . . and he will make a firm covenant with the many for one week . . ."

Daniel 9:24a, 27a

Week Eight

Day One – Chapter Nine
The Seventy Weeks

We left off with Gabriel's message about the time of the exile, and also the reconciliation of all things back to God. In other words, Gabriel gave Daniel the history of the Jewish people until the end of time. Let's look at the rest of Gabriel's words.

Read Daniel 9:24-27

What year was the prophecy revealed according to Daniel 9:1? _____

And where was Daniel when he received this prophecy? _____

The prophecy was given to Daniel in the first year of Darius, which would have been the first year of Cyrus, approximately 538 BC. Now let's look at the exact meaning of Gabriel's words. Look at Daniel 9:24 in the margin.

Seventy weeks have been decreed for who? _____ Who are? _____

The first thing we need to understand is that this prophecy has to do with the Jews. Seventy weeks have been decreed for the Jews. This is key to understanding the meaning of the prophecy. We have already looked at the rest of Daniel 9:24. All of those things mentioned in Daniel 9:24 come at the end, when Jesus once again walks the earth at His second coming. This is consistent with the theme of Daniel until now, but let's revisit it here.

In Daniel 2:35, a stone struck the statue. Who was the stone? _____ What did that stone set up in Daniel 2:44? _____ It will endure _____

In Daniel 7:13, who was coming? _____ What was given to him in Daniel 7:14? _____

The angel Gabriel is further describing what Daniel has already seen. Gabriel is now giving Daniel a timeline for the stone's appearance. When and how would the stone come? What we need to remember is that until this point, Daniel has only seen an image of Jesus' second coming. But Jesus was coming far sooner than that. He would come first as a suffering servant before He would come as the "stone." Daniel is now going to receive a prophecy about Jesus' first coming.

We also need to understand the meaning behind "seventy weeks." Other translations of scripture translate this phrase as "seventy times" or "seventy sevens." The text literally reads "seventy sevened." The word "sevened" is the word we translate as "weeks."

Read Genesis 29:25-28. What did Jacob have to complete?
_____

"Three **times** a year all your males are to appear before the Lord God, the God of Israel."

Exodus 34:23

There is our word again – translated as "week." It was customary for the marriage feast to last one week, or seven days. Now look at Exodus 34:23 in the margin. Our word is in bold, this time translated as "times." We know from scripture that Jewish males had to appear before the Lord during the week of Passover, the week of Pentecost, and the week of Sukkot – three times or three periods of seven days (three weeks). So Gabriel is telling Daniel that there are seventy different "weeks" that are decreed for the Jewish people. We take seventy and multiply that by seven (seven days in a week) and we get 490 periods of time. Most logically this is probably a period of 490 years (this verse can be contrasted to Daniel 10:2 where the Hebrew text literally reads "weeks of days."[1] There is no such distinction in Daniel chapter nine; hence this is not a period of days, but a period of years). Once we move further in the text you will see that "years" is in fact the correct period of time. So we are looking for a period of 490 years within Daniel 9:25-27. Let's see if we can find it.

What is the starting point of the 490 years? Look at Daniel 9:25. From _____
To do what? _____ Jerusalem.

The clock starts ticking at the issuing of a decree. Now, there were two decrees that were sent forth. We have already looked at one of them. Let's turn there again.

Turn to Ezra 1:1-3. When did this decree occur? _____ What were they going to rebuild? _____

This decree went out during the first year of King Cyrus. As in, it went out the same year Daniel beseeched the Lord of heaven in Daniel chapter nine. Remember, when the saints pray, heaven moves. I would wager a bet Daniel's prayer in chapter nine is what got Daniel in trouble with his rivals. I bet that prayer sent him to the lions' den. Darius (possibly the same man as Cyrus) sees God's hand in Daniel's rescue. He sends the exiles home. Daniel is there. He sees it all. His prayer in answered. But this decree is probably not the decree that starts our timeline of Daniel chapter nine. The return of the exiles in Ezra chapter one is the promise that the Jews would return in seventy years. This promise only restored the temple – it did not promise to rebuild Jerusalem entirely.

Look again at Daniel 9:25. What is promised at the end of the verse? _____

Jerusalem would be rebuilt "with plaza and moat, even in times of distress." That in no way describes the work of Ezra – it points to the work of Nehemiah.

Now read Nehemiah 2:3-5. What did Nehemiah say he wanted to rebuild? _____

Nehemiah was concerned about the entire city. He builds its wall under much persecution and distress. Nehemiah was sent to Jerusalem in 445 BC.[2] Our clock starts here. But this prophecy is interwoven with a second prophecy.

In Daniel 9:25, what else is prophesied besides Jerusalem's rebuilding? _____

Yes! Jesus, the Messiah – would come! There are two time frames depicted – seven weeks and sixty-two weeks. Together these add up to sixty-nine weeks, only one week shy of our seventy weeks.

To sum up, from 445 BC until the Messiah the prince would come there would be 69 weeks. What did the seven weeks within the prophecy point to? This is probably the time Jerusalem was completely "rebuilt." Although Nehemiah finished the wall, the entirety of Jerusalem still needed to be rebuilt. After Jerusalem was rebuilt another 62 weeks would pass until Messiah the prince would come. So a total of 69 weeks would put us forward in time by 483 years (69 x7). An important thing to note here is that the prophetic calendar is not our normal 365-day year, but a 360-day year (30 day months). We know this based on the calculation of Noah's ark. So, if we move forward from 445 BC based on just the calculation of 69x7 or 483 years, we will be off a good bit because of the additional 5 days to our calendar. So if we take 483 years and multiply that number by 360 days in a calendar year, we get 173,880 days. Now, take that number and divide by our "known" calendar year of 365 and we get to 478 years. Add this number to 445 BC and we reach 33 AD. This is when Jesus walked the earth and was close to being executed by the Jewish authorities.[3]

The Messiah would come after 69 weeks.

Now look at Daniel 9:26. What would happen to the Messiah after the 69 weeks? _____

Jesus would be "cut off." This was His death on the cross for our sins. The 69 weeks were looking forward for Daniel, but now we are on the other side of those weeks and we are looking back. The 69 weeks have already been fulfilled.

Tomorrow we will look at our future.

1 Hinnant, Greg. *Daniel Notes* (Lake Mary, Florida: Creation House Press, 2003), 245.
2 Hinnant, Greg. *Daniel Notes* (Lake Mary, Florida: Creation House Press, 2003), 245.
3 Moore, Beth. DVD study *Daniel: Lives of Integrity, Words of Prophecy* (Nashville, Tennessee: LifeWay Press, 2006), 175. This is by far one of the best Bible studies I have ever completed.

Day Two – Chapter Nine
The Future Time

"Then after the sixty-two weeks the Messiah will be cut off and have nothing, and the people of the prince who is to come will destroy the city and the sanctuary. And its end will come with a flood, even to the end there will be war; desolations are determined."

Daniel 9:26

Yesterday we went over "the past" time frame of Daniel chapter nine. There were seven weeks from the decree to "restore and rebuild Jerusalem" then another sixty-two weeks were added where "the Messiah would come."

Glance at Daniel 9:26 in the margin. What words begin the sentence? _____

There is a period of time after Messiah appears that He is "cut off" or crucified. This time period is not in the 70 weeks. It is after the 69 weeks (seven weeks plus sixty-two weeks = 69 weeks) specified in the previous verse have ended. I have seen many calculations of the exact day scholars pinpoint as the day the end of the 69 weeks occurred. There is some confusion to the time because history is hard to pinpoint in an exact way. We can estimate when Jesus was born, but we don't know with one hundred percent certainty. We can use the prophetic year to estimate when exactly the 69 weeks ended, but again, we can't say for certain that God was using this time frame. Also because the years of the kings' reign differed from Hebrew time to Babylonian time (the first year is really the second year according to Hebrew calculation) at times we are uncertain of the exact year the prophecy occurs in our time. What we can know for sure is that Jesus did walk the earth when this prophecy says the Messiah would come. But, for grins, here is one day that some scholars pinpoint as the day the Messiah would come which in turn could have ended the 69 weeks.

Read Luke 19:29-38. What were the crowds shouting? _____

The king had come! The Messiah was here! This would match the 483-year time frame (478 years on our calendar) of issuing the decree in Nehemiah (March or April of 445 BC) and the triumphant entry in approximately March 33 AD.[1]

But now, there is a pause in the forward action. After this day, the Messiah would be cut off. It also says He would "have nothing." If you think about this in the context of Daniel, what do you think this means? Remember the statue of Daniel chapter two. Remember the Ancient of Days in chapter seven. Write your answer here:

The Messiah would have no kingdom. The stone was not yet descending to the ground. The kingdom was yet to be established. He would have nothing – yet. Take another look at Daniel 9:26. It talks about a prince or a ruler who is coming.

Who do you think this prince might be based on our study of Daniel? _____

The Antichrist was coming. Daniel knew this prince was coming. He had seen the vision about the beasts, and he had seen the vision of the little horn. And if I know Daniel, I bet he wanted to know all he could. In his prayer he asked about the exiles, but his heart was still wondering about the "little horn." Daniel received what God knew his heart wanted to discover – more about the end.

Look back at Daniel 9:26. Who would destroy the city and the sanctuary? _____
When would this happen in regards to the Messiah? _____

Don't pass this by too quickly. It does not say the prince would destroy the city and the sanctuary, only that his people would. We are still looking in on the past. Jerusalem was destroyed in 70 AD by Rome. We have already looked at the Roman kingdom in Daniel chapter two and chapter seven. Rome was coming and it would destroy the city. The prince – the Antichrist – was not yet born – he is still future. But the people he would lead would take Jerusalem.

Now, if you recall, we said the Turkish Ottoman Empire would be the empire to rise up with the Antichrist at the helm. That is still true. What we need to understand is that the Roman Empire wasn't just European; it was also made up of many Middle Eastern nations. Titus was the Roman general that destroyed Jerusalem, but he didn't lead troops that consisted of Europeans. He led troops that consisted of Middle Eastern natives. They were "Roman troops" because Rome had conquered their territory, but they were far from European. Where were the troops from that conquered Jerusalem and tore down its temple? Most of them were from Syria and Turkey.[2] Remember, the nations surrounding Israel do not like her. It would have been their pleasure to wipe out the temple of the Jews. The Antichrist's people are those that destroyed the city and the sanctuary in 70 AD. And those troops were from Syria and Turkey. They were Middle Eastern.

Glance at the end of Daniel 9:26. What time frame are we now talking about? _____

Who is again mentioned at the beginning of Daniel 9:27 (refers back to someone in 9:26)?_____

The end is mentioned. This refers not only to the destruction of Jerusalem but also to the final time of the end. Many desolations will be in-between those two bookends, and at the beginning of the end our "prince" or our "he" will enter the scene. This is the man that has been whispered about throughout Daniel. He is the "little horn" that speaks blasphemies against the Most Holy God (Daniel 7:25). This is the man who will lead the people who destroyed Jerusalem. What will he do?

Look at Daniel 9:27 in the margin. We can learn a variety of things from this one verse. Let's break it down piece by piece. We have a 70-week prophecy to dissect and we have thus far accounted for 69 out of the 70 weeks. They are done, in the past, and fulfilled. The Messiah being "cut off" was the ending to those past weeks. We have had a gap in the prophecy for approximately 2000 years. How is this possible?

> "And he will make a firm covenant with the many for one week, but in the middle of the week, he will put a stop to sacrifice and grain offering; and on the wing of abominations will come one who makes desolate, even until a complete destruction, one that is decreed, is poured out on the one who makes desolate."
>
> Daniel 9:27

What group of people were the recipients of this 70-week prophecy? _____

In Luke 21:24, what did Jesus label the time we are now in, or the time Jerusalem would be trampled? _____

When did Paul say the hardening of Israel would be over according to Romans 11:25? _____

We are now in what Jesus calls "the times of the Gentiles." There will be a partial hardening of the Jewish people until the fullness of the Gentiles has come in. Jesus came to the Jewish people, yet He died for the world. The majority of His own people rejected His sacrifice. For approximately 40 years, the Jews continued to worship in the temple, but they didn't need to offer sacrifices anymore. They were free of the old law, purified by Christ, if they would only believe.

Read John 2:19-21. When was the true temple "destroyed?" _____

They rejected His sacrifice. Therefore, God let their temple that foreshadowed His Son's sacrifice be destroyed because of their rejection of the one, true, and only sacrifice that would forever cleanse them. The Jews were once again dispersed throughout the land. They had no home. They were persecuted. They were shunned. Until finally, in 1948, Israel was reborn. The clock of the final seven years still hasn't started ticking because the Antichrist hasn't risen, but here is what we need to understand: the times of the Gentiles are almost over – Israel has been reborn. The final seven-year clock hasn't started ticking but it can start ticking at any time. Know this:

The final seven-year period can start at any time because Israel has been reborn.

This is seen clearly in the last and final week. Israel has to be a nation in order for the final seven years to begin. Let's really look at Daniel 9:27.

What will the "prince" do? _____ With who? _____ For how long? _____

Here is our final week. The clock starts when a covenant is made with "the many." If we are talking about the Jewish people in this passage, "the many" refers to Israel. The Antichrist will confirm a treaty, or a covenant for a period of seven years. Notice that it says "confirm" (some translations say "make"). That Hebrew word is *gabar* (Strong's #1396) and it means "to be strong." In other words, he will strengthen a covenant. This could mean that he will strengthen something already there, or confirm a treaty already on the table. We have many treaties drafted that would declare peace between the Middle Eastern nations and the nation of Israel. This prince doesn't necessarily have to draft a treaty himself, he just has to "make it strong" or sign a treaty already on the table.   But then, what does it say this prince will do?

How long into the treaty before he does something else? _____

In the middle of the seven years, he will break the treaty. It says he will put an "end" to sacrifice and grain offering. This is very important. The Jews currently do not have a temple standing in Jerusalem. The Dome of the Rock, one of the most famous Islamic mosques, is standing on the temple mount where the Jewish temple once stood. The Jews want a temple, and they have actually begun preparations to build one. All they need is a treaty. I guarantee you that as a stipulation of peace, the treaty that will be confirmed will allow the Jews to begin reconstruction. The Antichrist will watch this temple being rebuilt and he won't like it. He will secretly know he will break the treaty. The Jews will not suspect. But scripture is clear. Let's see what the Antichrist does.

Read 2 Thessalonians 2:3-4 in the margin. What does the Antichrist (the man of lawlessness) do? _____
_____Where? _____

Most logically this will be in the middle of the final seven years when he breaks the treaty and stops sacrifice and grain offering.

Because what happens after that according to Daniel 9:27? _____

Desolations will come.   The Hebrew word *shamem* (Strong's 8074) means to "devastate or stupefy." It implies seeing something so awful that it "horrifies or appalls."   The Antichrist will make things horrible

Let no one in any way deceive you, for it will not come unless the apostasy comes first, and the man of lawlessness is revealed, the son of destruction, who opposes and exalts himself above every so-called god or object of worship, so that he takes his seat in the temple of God, displaying himself as being God.

2 Thessalonians 2:3-4

"And he will make a firm covenant with the many for one week, but in the middle of the week, he will put a stop to sacrifice and grain offering; and on the wing of abominations will come one who makes desolate, even until a complete destruction, one that is decreed, is poured out on the one who makes desolate."

Daniel 9:27

Look again at Daniel 9:27 in the margin. He will also put up an "abomination" on the "wing." What does this mean? The Hebrew word translated "abomination" is *shiqquwts* (Strong's 8251) and it means "disgusting or filthy." It can also mean an idol. The Antichrist may very well put up an idol of himself at God's temple – on the wing. The Hebrew word "wing" is *kanaph* (Strong's 3671) and it can mean "edge or extremity" like a wing is an edge or an extremity of a bird, but this word can literally mean "wing" as in the wing of a bird. This indicates one of two things. The Antichrist could put an idol up near or around the temple, but it could also refer to another place.

Read Exodus 25:18-22. What had wings in the temple?_____

The mercy seat covered the Ark of the Covenant and it sat in the innermost room of the temple. It was the most sacred room of the temple. Why? This is clearly seen in Leviticus.

Read Leviticus 16:2. Who appeared above the mercy seat?_____

God's presence lived above the mercy seat. The wings of the cherubim covered the mercy seat. What scripture could be telling us is that the Antichrist will set himself up in the most holy place of the temple. He may desecrate the mercy seat by setting up an idol of himself.

But Daniel 9:27 is clear – it has been decreed – there will be a complete destruction on the one who makes desolate.

The stone will come. The stone will destroy. The stone will become a mountain.

Jesus will have the final word.

1 Moore, Beth. DVD study *Daniel: Lives of Integrity, Words of Prophecy* (Nashville, Tennessee: LifeWay Press, 2006), 175.
2 Shoebat, Walid, written with Joel Richardson. *God's War on Terror* (Top Executive Media, 2008), 350-352.

Day Three – Chapter Ten
Preparation for Revelation

> And the message was true and one of great conflict.
>
> Daniel 10:1b

Daniel has a vision in the third year of King Cyrus – or the third year of King Darius. Look at Daniel 10:1 in the margin. Daniel emphasizes that the vision that he had was true. He also says that the vision was one of great conflict. This is perhaps why Daniel emphasized that the vision was true. As we will see, everything that transpires in chapter 10 is preparing you for the vision Daniel reveals in chapter 11 about the next kingdom that will rise up to conquer the territory of Babylon (currently ruled by Medo-Persia). The information Daniel receives about the next kingdom is extremely detailed, almost unbelievably so. Daniel assures us that this vision would come to pass.

Read Daniel 10:1-4

I want to camp on something for a brief time. I want you to really consider something with me.

How long was Daniel in mourning? _____ What did not enter his mouth? _____ What did he not drink? _____ What else did he not use? _____

Choice food was probably things such as meat (specified in the text), cheeses, oils, and desserts. Daniel was probably only eating vegetables, and perhaps some grains and fruits. Nothing was added to these foods. Daniel was eating to keep his body moving; he was not eating for pleasure. There wasn't a quick stop at a fast food restaurant or a late night bowl of ice cream. There was no robust glass of wine at dinner or a refreshing glass of milk before bed. Daniel drank water. Daniel didn't even anoint himself with oil. In today's language that meant he didn't splash on any aftershave after shaving, perfume himself, or even lather on deodorant. He may not have even taken a bath, because anointing would come after immersing oneself for cleansing.[1] This went on for three weeks.

I have had many friends tell me they are "cleansing" themselves by using certain food plans that are supposed to help wash toxins out of the body. They do so by eating specific foods and avoiding others. I have had others specify they are on a certain diet that doesn't allow them to do one thing or another. Sometimes we cleanse because we want to diet or diet because we want to cleanse. But all this is for our own benefit. None of these things are wrong, but they are for us. America has become a selfish nation, and we have become selfish servants of the cross. When is the last time we did something like Daniel and fasted because we were mourning over the state of our nation? When was the last time we have given up something we love for any length of time in order to knock on the doors of heaven? I want you to hear me with everything you are and everything you will be.

Revelation comes after sacrifice.

We can't expect God to move mountains in our life without showing Him how much the move means to us. We can't expect God to shake the earth if all we do is send up one or two quick prayers during the day. I'm not saying those prayers don't count, or that God won't move things if we fail to go to the extreme like Daniel, but I am saying that there are times in our lives – and we should recognize them – that we need to bang on the doors of heaven. And when that happens, we need to get serious about our prayers. We need to sacrifice, just like Daniel.

I need you to really think about that. What are you passionate about? What is going on in your nation today? In the world? Do you want to rescue those enslaved to human trafficking? Do you want officials elected to end abortion? Do you want to shut down ISIS? What have we really done about it? Sometimes we feel like we are helpless, but we aren't. We have prayer. We have the ear of the One sitting on the throne. Where have we sacrificed? Write your thoughts here.

Now, why was Daniel mourning? This is the third year of Darius, which means the decree to allow the Jews to return home had already been issued. If that is so, why was Daniel in mourning? We cannot say with certainty, but there is something we can point to that might have caused Daniel's distressed state.

Turn to Ezra 1:1-3. In what year of Cyrus' reign did the decree go out that the Jews could return home? _____

Now turn to Ezra 3:8. When did the temple construction begin? _____
What was laid in verse 10? _____ Does it take time to lay a foundation?
_____

What happened after this in Ezra 4:4? _____

The Jewish temple's construction started in the second year and the second month of Cyrus. Some months after that the foundation was laid, and there was a great shout and celebration in Israel. Then enemies came and discouraged building. Daniel is mourning in the third year of Cyrus. I would wager a bet that news had reached him about the ceased construction on the temple. Daniel was troubled and Daniel beseeched God for three weeks.

Then suddenly and without warning, Daniel gets a vision.

He sees a man, dressed in linen, with a belt of what appears to be gold. His body was like beryl and his face looked like lightning. His eyes were fire and his arms and feet were bronze. His voice was like the sound of a tumult.

Read Daniel 10:5-9

Who is this man? There are a few options. First, this could be a pre-incarnate vision of Jesus. Second, it could be an angel that reflects Jesus' attributes. Let's look at the properties of this man.

Dressed in Linen

Look at Leviticus 16:4 in the margin. What are linen garments considered? _____

The High Priest wore these garments. Jesus is our High Priest (Hebrews 5:1-10).

What else did linen represent according to Revelation 19:8?
_____

Linen in scripture represents righteousness and holiness.

> "He shall put on the holy linen tunic, and the linen undergarments shall be next to his body, and he shall be girded with the linen sash . . . (these are holy garments)."
>
> Leviticus 16:4a

Golden Belt

Notice again the Leviticus scripture in the margin. The apparel of the High Priest also talks about being girded with a linen sash.

Read Revelation 1:13. What is Jesus seen to have here? _____

Body like Beryl and Face like Lightning

Look at a very cool translation of Daniel 10:6 in the margin. Some versions translate beryl as topaz but the word just means a precious stone. So, in other words, this man sparkled, radiated light, and emitted a brilliance. His face also radiated light – like lightning most translations say. I like the translation in the margin that says his face looked like a thunder-flame. The Hebrew word *baraq* (Strong's 1300) means "lightning." So imagine looking at this man's face and experiencing brilliant flashes of light.

Read Ezekiel 1:27-28. Who are we describing and how is He described? _____

> And his body was like the beryl, and his face had the look of a thunder-flame, and his eyes were like burning lights, and his arms and feet like the color of polished brass, and the sound of his voice was like the sound of an army.
>
> Daniel 10:6 BBE

Eyes of Flaming Torches and Arms and Feet of Polished Brass

Everything about this man shone: his body, his face, his arms, his legs, and even his eyes. We have just looked at how God is described in Ezekiel – with fire and glowing metal. This man has the same characteristics.

Read Revelation 1:14-15. How are Jesus' eyes described? _____ His feet?
_____ What about Revelation 19:12? What do His eyes look like?
_____

Now look at some angels in Ezekiel 1:4-7. What was in the center or the midst of the beings?
_____

His Voice Sounded Like an Army

The word used to describe this man's voice is *hamon* (Strong's 1995) and it means "a noise, a tumult, or a crowd." It is most often translated as "multitude" but most of the time this word carries with it a loudness, or a rushing. In 1 Kings 18:41 this word is used to depict the roar of a downpour of rain. So, this man's voice was loud – like rushing water.

In Ezekiel 43:2, what was God's voice like? _____

In Revelation 1:15, what was Jesus' voice like? _____

All of these characteristics could be used to depict an angel because in scripture angels are described as having some of these attributes. When I first started writing this, I thought I would tend to lean toward this being an angel. But the more I dig, the more I think this is probably a pre-incarnate Christ because these attributes in scripture are never used in totality unless they are referring to Jesus. The cherubim of Ezekiel have a fiery bronze appearance but their attire is not described and their eyes aren't depicted like lightning.   There is an angel in Revelation with fiery feet and face like the sun, but again, his eyes aren't flaming, and his attire is not described. The only place we find this depiction with all of these attributes present is in Revelation where it describes how Jesus will look at His second coming. Daniel might have seen Jesus over that river and if you think about it, this makes sense given the visions Daniel has already received. He saw Jesus depicted as a stone in Daniel chapter two. He wrote of the Son of Man walking in the fiery furnace. He saw the Son of Man coming on the clouds of heaven in chapter seven. Now he sees Jesus in His glory.

Daniel is about the end times and the return of the King. This could be a vision of just that – the King as He will be in the end – the way He appears in Revelation chapter one. Look at Revelation 1:17 in the margin.   The vision of the return of the King caused John the apostle to fall down like a dead man. The same thing that happens to Daniel.

> When I saw Him, I fell at His feel like a dead man . . .
>
> Revelation 1:17a

What happened to Daniel in Daniel 10:9? _____

Daniel falls to the ground like he was in a "deep sleep." Those with Daniel flee, not because they saw anything, but because great dread fell upon them. If this is a vision of Jesus at His second coming, then their fear makes a lot of sense.

In Daniel 10:7, what did the people with Daniel do? _____

In Revelation 6:15, what do the people do before Jesus returns? _____

They hide themselves, just like Adam and Eve did in the garden. When the sinful confronts the holy the first emotion is fear – and then you hide.

Daniel had been faithful. He has sacrificed for his King, and his King rewards him with a sight only one other man in scripture gets to witness. John saw Jesus in His glory, but centuries before, Daniel saw Him too. Daniel was the first to see the vision of the coming King.

Revelation comes with sacrifice.

More to come tomorrow.

1 Hinnant, Greg. *Daniel Notes* (Lake Mary, Florida: Creation House Press, 2003), 251).

Day Four – Chapter Ten
The Fight Unseen

"O man of high esteem,
do not be afraid.
Peace be with you;
take courage and be
courageous!"

Daniel 10:19a

Yesterday, we witnessed a vision of a man that appears to be Jesus Himself. We saw Daniel falling to the ground in a deep sleep because of the awesomeness of the vision. Let's see what happens next.

Read Daniel 10:10-21

There is a lot going on here. An angel touches Daniel and basically gives him strength to rise. This is probably not the same man we have seen previously. For one thing, Daniel almost certainly would have described some of the earlier attributes depicting the man in the previous vision. Secondly, this angel tells Daniel he has "now been sent" seeming to indicate that he has just arrived.[1] This is an angel with the intention of describing the vision to Daniel. Like Gabriel did in chapter nine, this angel calls Daniel a man of "high esteem."

What does the angel say in Daniel 10:12. From the _____ day that you set your heart on _____ this and on _____ yourself before your God, your words were heard."

Like we said yesterday, revelation follows sacrifice. Daniel had mourned and fasted for three weeks, but on the first day that sacrifice was noticed by the throne. On the first day angels were sent to give a response. But something happened. We want to spend most of our time today talking about this. Read the scripture in the margin.

How long did this angel get held up? _____
In weeks? _____ How long was Daniel's fast? _____

Read Daniel 11:1. What was this angel's purpose? _____
_____

According to Jude 1:9, who is Michael? _____

So, the angel talking to Daniel had come to assist Darius in his first year. He was to be an "encouragement and a protection for him." This angel was defending Darius in the heavenlies, possibly protecting his unwavering support for the Jews. This angel calls

"But the prince of the kingdom of Persia was withstanding me for twenty one days; then behold, Michael, one of the chief princes, came to help me, for I had been left there with the kings of Persia . . . But I shall now return to fight against the prince of Persia; so I am going forth, and behold, the prince of Greece is about to come."

Daniel 10:13, 20b

171

other angels "princes." So, let's sum up what we know about these angels.

- God heard Daniel and sent for the angel speaking with Daniel on the first day of Daniel's fast.
- This angel was held back for three weeks by another angel – the angel of Persia.
- The angel speaking with Daniel had to wait for Michael's assistance before he could leave his post and reach Daniel.
- After he talks to Daniel he is going back to fight the angel of Persia.

Don't see answers to your prayers? It could be the angels that are sent to tell you the answers are delayed in the heavenly realms. Wrap your mind around this for a minute. The angel was delayed for three weeks while he was battling a fallen angel! He couldn't overpower this fallen angel until reinforcements came. Michael is a very interesting angel. Jude calls him an archangel. That word in the Greek means "chief angel." This is the exact wording used in Daniel. "Michael, one of the chief princes, came to help me." We can learn a little bit more about Michael.

Read Daniel 10:21. What pronoun is used to describe Michael here?_____

Read Daniel 12:1. What does it say Michael does here? _____

Michael is the prince of Israel. He is the angel that guards Daniel ("your" prince) and his people (the Jews). The prince Daniel's messenger fought is called the "Prince of Persia."

What year did Daniel receive the vision according to Daniel 10:1? _____
What kingdom did Cyrus rule? _____

Cyrus' kingdom seems to have had an angelic problem. There was an influencer, a restrainer, an angel that didn't want God's messages to get through to Daniel. Remember, although Cyrus allowed the Jews to return home and although Darius saw the miracle of the lions' den, this doesn't indicate that the Persian kingdom had come to faith. This kingdom is still one of the kingdoms in Nebuchadnezzar's statue; it is one of Daniel's beasts. It still controlled the Jews.

Think about this. Do answers to prayers get delayed because of cosmic conflict? It seems likely so. We have no idea what goes on above our heads. Maybe in heaven we will be able to understand the heavenly activity that has surrounded our prayers.

Look at Daniel 10:20. What other angel is introduced here? _____

The angel tells Daniel that the prince of Greece is about to come – meaning the kingdom of Greece would also have an angel standing guard over it – just like Persia. We have seen the rise and fall of Babylon. At the time of this vision, Medo-Persia was ruling the land. But there is another kingdom about to rise – the third section of the statue – and the leopard of Daniel's beast vision – Greece. This angel is telling Daniel that the kingdom of Greece is about to come and the vision Daniel records in the next chapter shows this very clearly. Even though Daniel is introduced to the kingdom of Greece, it wouldn't come to power for another 200 years.[2]

In Daniel 10:14, when was this vision to become a reality? _____

The vision was for a time far off, in the latter days, days yet in the future. Daniel wouldn't see these days, but the angel is sent to tell Daniel what would transpire in those latter years. I am sure the "little horn" was still on Daniel's mind. I am also sure that the status of the Jewish temple was still on his mind.

After this angel communicates what he needs to Daniel, he says he will be returning to battle the prince of Persia. He also says the "prince of Greece" is about to come, almost in anticipation of another cosmic struggle. Here is a lesson for today:

We have no idea what takes place above our heads in the heavenlies.

In Daniel, we see this cosmic struggle quite clearly. Throughout scripture we bear witness to angels that announce births (Matthew 1:21, Judges 13:5), appear in visions (Ezekiel 1, Isaiah 6), usher the faithful home (2 Kings 2:11), strengthen the faithful (Judges 6:12), and provide comfort (Genesis 21:17), but in Daniel we witness a cosmic struggle.

Look at Ephesians 6:12 in the margin. Our struggle is not against others, but against the spiritual forces of darkness and wickedness. The angels that ruled over the kingdoms of Persia and Greece hungered for spiritual darkness to rule the land. They promoted wickedness to a sinister degree. This is reality. There are forces at work that try to get us to steer down a dark path. That doesn't mean we aren't accountable for our actions, but that does mean we have to be aware of the forces that try to sway our decisions. Are we lured by beauty? Do we give in to temptation? Do we justify our actions even though they are wrong? Those dark forces are a constant above our heads and they influence the world around us, which means they influence us. Can we recognize them? Do we prepare our weapons daily? Are we sharpening our sword (the Word – Ephesians 6:17)? Do we stand for truth, even when it hurts us?

> For our struggle is not against flesh and blood, but against the rulers, against the powers, against the world forces of this darkness, against the spiritual forces of wickedness in the heavenly places.
>
> Ephesians 6:12

Read Revelation 12:7-9. What familiar name do we see here? _____ Who is thrown down in this cosmic battle? _____ Where is he thrown? _____

Read Revelation 12:13. After being thrown to earth, what does Satan do? _____

Read Revelation 12:17. What was Satan's emotion? _____ Who else does he make war with? _____

There will be a cosmic battle in the heavenlies at the time of the end, and this battle will be the final one. Satan and his minions will be thrown down. When they are thrown down, Satan will be enraged.

He will try to persecute Israel (the woman) and he will make war with the saints. Will we recognize the spiritual darkness surrounding us when Satan walks the lands? Or will we fall for his false beauty? We might think this is an absurd question, but the reality is, many will fall away (Matthew 24:10).

Like Daniel, we are in Babylon with all its luxuries. Unlike Daniel, most of us don't sacrifice anything more than a few dollars in an offering bucket. Many of us have never fasted for God, only for ourselves. When food is taken away, will we fall away? When medical needs are taken away, will we yield? And think about this: in the last days Satan and his minions will be thrown down. They will be "enraged" (Revelation 12:17). Do you think spiritual warfare will be at a high point?

I sure do.

Prepare your armor, my faithful friends. Prepare your armor.

1 Moore, Beth. DVD study *Daniel: Lives of Integrity, Words of Prophecy* (Nashville, Tennessee: LifeWay Press, 2006), 199.
2 *Rose Book of Bible Charts, Maps and Time Lines* (Torrance, California: Rose Publishing, 2005), 65.

Day Five – Chapter Eleven
The Coming Conflict

"And now I will tell you the truth. Behold, three more kings are going to arise in Persia. Then a fourth . . . will arouse the whole empire against the realm of Greece."

Daniel 11:2

We are now entering the explanation of the vision, and why Daniel said, "Anguish has come upon me, and I have retained no strength" (Daniel 10:16). Let's see what this angel will now tell Daniel about "what is inscribed in the writing of the truth" (Daniel 10:21). Chapter eleven is jam packed with information about things that have already transpired. Instead of making you go back and forth from your Bible to the explanation, I am going to write out the verses for you here. Today, there will be a lot of reading, but I think you will see why. We will begin with Daniel 11:2.

2"And now I will tell you the truth. Behold, three more kings are going to arise in Persia. Then a fourth will gain far more riches than all of them; as soon as he becomes strong through his riches, he will arouse the whole empire against the realm of Greece."

After Cyrus (and/or Darius), there will be three other kings that arise in Persia. After these a fourth will come that will be exceedingly rich. History shows that after Cyrus came:

Cambyses (530-522 BC)
Smerdis (522 BC)
Darius I HYSTAPES (522-486 BC)
Xerxes, known also as Ahasuerus (486-464 BC)[1]

Early in Xerxes reign he came into conflict with Greece but was defeated. So why does scripture pause at this particular king? Because we know him.

Turn to Ester 1:1-8. How long was Ahasuerus party? _____
Name some of the things that were present there? _____

Who did Ahasuerus eventually marry in Ester 2:16-17?_____

This is the king that "showed the riches of his royal glory and the splendor and pomp of his greatness for many days." You can say that again. The initial party lasted for 180 days! Then he threw a "thank-you" party for his servants for another seven days. Rich? You can say that again! This king is singled out because he would become the one who issued a decree to slaughter the Jews, but then ultimately saved them through the wisdom and courage of his new bride Ester. There were other kings that came after Ahasuerus, but scripture doesn't consider them noteworthy to mention.[2] It jumps forward to another king that would arise.

3"And a mighty king will arise, and he will rule with great authority and do as he pleases. 4But as soon as he has arisen, his kingdom will be broken up and parceled out toward the four points of the compass, though not to his own descendants, nor according to his authority which he wielded, for his sovereignty will be uprooted and given to others besides them."

We know this mighty king from the vision of the ram and the goat – Alexander the Great. He arose and conquered the Middle East with surprising speed. We have already looked at this when we studied chapter seven. Here it says "but as soon as he has arisen" which implies he was still strong when he was broken – or dies – and his kingdom went to "the four points of the compass."[3] When Alexander died at a very young age – while still strong – his kingdom was given to his four generals (not to his own descendants). The four generals are as follows:

1. Cassander in Macedonia
2. Lysimachus in Thrace and Asia Minor
3. **Seleucus in Syria, Mesopotamia and Persia (Syria and Babylonia)– King of the North**
4. **Ptolemy in Egypt – King of the South**

[5]*"Then the king of the South will grow strong, along with one of his princes who will gain ascendancy over him and obtain dominion; his domain will be a great dominion indeed."*

Ptolemy of Egypt was the king of the South; Seleucus was the king of the North. For a short time Seleucus had to flee his kingdom because another general took power. He went to Ptolemy and became "one of his princes" but he was actually stronger and when his rival was defeated in battle, Seleucus went back to his kingdom of the north. So, in the end, even though Seleucus fled to Egypt he became stronger than Ptolemy.[4]

[6]*"After some years they will form an alliance, and the daughter of the king of the South will come to the king of the North to carry out a peaceful arrangement. But she will not retain her position of power, nor will he remain with his power, but she will be given up, along with those who brought her in and the one who sired her as well as he who supported her in those times."*

The Ptolemaic and the Seleucid dynasties were constantly at odds with each other. In about 250 BC the Ptolemaic line attempted to make peace with the Seleucid line. Ptolemy Philadelphus (King of the South) sent his daughter Berenice to become the wife of Antiochus II (King of the North). In order to wed Berenice, Antiochus had to cast aside Laodice, his current wife. Not a good idea. Although Antiochus's plan was to unite the two empires through the children of Berenice, it didn't go as planned. When Ptolemy Philadelphus died two years later, Antiochus II abandoned Berenice for Laodice but Laodice wasn't too happy about her former treatment. Laodice murdered her husband, Berenice and Berenice's child.[5]

[7]*"But one of the descendants of her line will arise in his place, and he will come against their army and enter the fortress of the king of the North, and he will deal with them and display great strength.* [8]*Also their gods with their metal images and their precious vessels of silver and gold he will take into captivity to Egypt, and he on his part will refrain from attacking the king of the North for some years.* [9]*Then the latter will enter the realm of the king of the South, but will return to his own land."*

One of the descendants of Bernice's line – her brother Ptolemy III– arose in place of his father. He was enraged about his sister's murder and sent his army to attack the northern kingdom. He took Antioch, the capital, and plundered its temples. After this Ptolemy III made a peace treaty with the new king of the north – Seleucus II Callinicus, and went back to Egypt. Seleucus II conducted an affront against Egypt but he had no success (will return to his own land).[6]

¹⁰"His sons will mobilize and assemble a multitude of great forces; and one of them will keep on coming and overflow and pass through, that he may again wage war up to his very fortress. **¹¹**The king of the South will be enraged and go forth and fight with the king of the North. Then the latter will raise a great multitude, but that multitude will be given into the hand of the former. **¹²**When the multitude is carried away, his heart will be lifted up, and he will cause tens of thousands to fall; yet he will not prevail. **¹³**For the king of the North will again raise a greater multitude than the former, and after an interval of some years he will press on with a great army and much equipment."

After Seleucus II died, his sons Seleucus III and Antiochus III continued picking at Egypt (sons will mobilize and assemble a multitude of great forces). After Seleucus III was murdered, his brother made the kingdom strong (and one of them will keep on coming) and made his advance far south (wage war up to his very fortress). The king of the south rose up and defeated Antiochus III even though Antiochus' army outnumbered the Egyptian army (that multitude will be given into the hand of the former). Antiochus wasn't deterred. He raised even a greater army (will again raise a greater multitude) and returned to battle Egypt.[7]

¹⁴"Now in those times many will rise up against the king of the South; the violent ones among your people will also lift themselves up in order to fulfill the vision, but they will fall down. **¹⁵**Then the king of the North will come, cast up a siege ramp and capture a well-fortified city; and the forces of the South will not stand their ground, not even their choicest troops, for there will be no strength to make a stand. **¹⁶**But he who comes against him will do as he pleases, and no one will be able to withstand him; he will also stay for a time in the Beautiful Land, with destruction in his hand."

Ptolemy IV had just died and many rose against the new Egyptian king – Ptolemy V Epiphanes. Even the Jews living in Egypt rose up (your people) thinking Antiochus III would be a better leader, but their revolt was crushed (they will fall down). Antiochus III fought against the Egyptian general at the battle of Panium (a well-fortified city) and the Egyptians were defeated. Antiochus took control of Palestine (the Beautiful Land).[8]

¹⁷"He will set his face to come with the power of his whole kingdom, bringing with him a proposal of peace which he will put into effect; he will also give him the daughter of women to ruin it. But she will not take a stand for him or be on his side."

After the battle there came an alliance (proposal of peace) between the two kingdoms and Antiochus III gave his daughter in marriage to Ptolemy V Epiphanes. Antiochus III wanted his daughter to be his ally and have her offspring rule Egypt in order to give him greater power (give him the daughter of women to ruin it) but his daughter sided with her new husband (but she will not take a stand for him or be on his side).[9]

¹⁸"Then he will turn his face to the coastlands and capture many. But a commander will put a stop to his scorn against him; moreover, he will repay him for his scorn. **¹⁹**So he will turn his face toward the fortresses of his own land, but he will stumble and fall and be found no more."

Antiochus then turned his sights to the coastlands (Asia Minor and the islands of Ionia). The Romans also wanted this territory and crushed Antiochus III's advance. Antiochus III then had to pay a large annual tribute to Rome (repay him for his scorn). When Antiochus III returned home, he was killed (found no more).[10]

²⁰"Then in his place one will arise who will send an oppressor through the Jewel of his kingdom; yet within a few days he will be shattered, though not in anger nor in battle."

Seleucus IV took over the northern kingdom and sent a tax collector named Heliodorus to the "Jewel of his kingdom" or the Holy Land in order to repay Rome. Heliodorus went to extract payment from the treasuries of the temple in Jerusalem. He ended up aborting the task after having a dream warning him away. Then Seleucus IV was killed (not in anger nor in battle) by being poisoned by Heliodonus.[11]

My brain is hurting. Is yours? I believe we have had enough history for the day, but I want you to pause and think about something. Look at how exact your God is? Look at how much detail He gave to Daniel about a time hundreds of years in the future. There is a lesson for us here:

God knows the future. Even yours.

Read Jeremiah 29:11. What does God have for you? _____ for _____ and not for _____ To give you a what? _____

Take this to heart, faithful friends. God has you. He HAS you. He knows what is coming and He will prepare you. He will be with you every step of the way. And ultimately, no matter what that future holds in the here and now, His ultimate purpose goes far beyond the struggles of this life.

Read John 14:1-3. What should we not let our hearts do? _____

What is Jesus preparing for us? _____ What does He promise? _____

The stone is coming. It will crush all the kingdoms of the earth. And the kingdom will be set up. We will be in it. That is a future with a hope!

1 *English Standard Version Study Bible* (Wheaton, Illinois: Crossway, 2008), 1610.
2 Leupold, H.C. *Exposition of Daniel* (Grand Rapids, Michigan: Baker Book House Company, 1969), 477.
3 Leupold, H.C. *Exposition of Daniel* (Grand Rapids, Michigan: Baker Book House Company, 1969), 478.
4 *English Standard Version Study Bible* (Wheaton, Illinois: Crossway, 2008), 1610.
5 *English Standard Version Study Bible* (Wheaton, Illinois: Crossway, 2008), 1610.
 Leupold, H.C. *Exposition of Daniel* (Grand Rapids, Michigan: Baker Book House Company, 1969), 481-482.
6 *English Standard Version Study Bible* (Wheaton, Illinois: Crossway, 2008), 1614.
Leupold, H.C. *Exposition of Daniel* (Grand Rapids, Michigan: Baker Book House Company, 1969), 484.
7 *English Standard Version Study Bible* (Wheaton, Illinois: Crossway, 2008), 1614.
 Leupold, H.C. *Exposition of Daniel* (Grand Rapids, Michigan: Baker Book House Company, 1969), 487.
8 *English Standard Version Study Bible* (Wheaton, Illinois: Crossway, 2008), 1614.
9 *English Standard Version Study Bible* (Wheaton, Illinois: Crossway, 2008), 1614.
 Leupold, H.C. *Exposition of Daniel* (Grand Rapids, Michigan: Baker Book House Company, 1969), 487.
10 *English Standard Version Study Bible* (Wheaton, Illinois: Crossway, 2008), 1614.
Leupold, H.C. *Exposition of Daniel* (Grand Rapids, Michigan: Baker Book House Company, 1969), 491.
11 *English Standard Version Study Bible* (Wheaton, Illinois: Crossway, 2008), 1615.

Week Nine

"And now I will tell you the truth. Behold, three more kings are going to arise in Persia. Then a fourth . . . will arouse the whole empire against the realm of Greece."

Daniel 11:2

Day One – Chapter Eleven
The Small Horn of the Past

God is very detailed. Daniel chapter eleven proves it. He knows our futures more than we know ourselves. We have learned a lot about the coming kings of Greece. We left off with Daniel 11:20. We will begin our tour of Daniel chapter eleven again today. This time we will focus on a very important king that will arise in Greece. Let us revisit what we already know about him.

Read Daniel 8:9. What is this man called here? _____

In Daniel 8:11, what did he do? _____ What did he remove?
_____

What will this king fling to the ground according to Daniel 8:12? _____

The small horn of the Grecian Empire foreshadows the "little horn" of Daniel 7:8 – or the Antichrist – the king that will arise in the latter days out of the reborn Turkish Ottoman Empire.

I want you to think about how gracious God is to give us this vision. Think about it. For Daniel, this "small horn" was in his future, but this "small horn" is in our past. We now have an opportunity to study the "small horn" in order to prepare ourselves for the "little horn" of our future. God is showing us what the "little horn" will look like, and what he will do.

So, now, let's step back in time and see just how the "small horn" is described, and what we need to look for in the "little horn" of our future.

[21]*"In his place a despicable person will arise, on whom the honor of kingship has not been conferred, but he will come in a time of tranquility and seize the kingdom by intrigue."*

If you recall, we left off yesterday with the king of the North - Seleucus IV – being killed by his tax collector Heliodorus. In Seleucus' place arose a "despicable person" named Antiochus IV Epiphanes who ruled from 175 BC to 164 BC He is our "small horn" of chapter eight. Although Seleucus' sons were the rightful heirs to the throne, one was imprisoned in Rome and the second was a minor. Antiochus IV was the boy's uncle who killed the assassin Heliodorus and was suspected of killing the boy heir. He also paid people to support him. So he took the kingship even though "the honor of kingship had not been conferred" and "by intrigue."[1]

Let's remind ourselves how the "little horn" of our future will arise.

Turn to Daniel 7:7-8. How many horns did the last beast have? _____
Then what happened? _____

Read Daniel 7:24. What will this little horn be compared to the others? _____

We don't know the manner of how the Antichrist will rise, but he will be different, and he will come up after the kingdom is already established. Let's get back to Antiochus IV Epiphanes.

[22]*"The overflowing forces will be flooded away before him and shattered, and also the prince of the covenant.* [23]*After an alliance is made with him he will practice deception, and he will go up and gain power with a small force of people.* [24]*In a time of tranquility he will enter the richest parts of the realm, and he will accomplish what his fathers never did, nor his ancestors; he will distribute plunder, booty and possessions among them, and he will devise his schemes against strongholds, but only for a time."*

Ptolemy VI Philometer of Egypt (prince of the covenant) came against Antiochus IV but he was captured. Later Ptolemy made an alliance with Antiochus in order to gain his throne back, because his brother, Ptolemy VIII, had taken power. Then he sides with his brother and once again turns on Antiochus IV. Antiochus then attacks the "richest parts of the realm" (even Judah) and plunders its treasures and distributes booty to his soldiers, which helped him gain even more power and influence. This distribution of riches wasn't a traditional thing to do.[2]

[25]*"He will stir up his strength and courage against the king of the South with a large army; so the king of the South will mobilize an extremely large and mighty army for war; but he will not stand, for schemes will be devised against him.* [26]*Those who eat his choice food will destroy him, and his army will overflow, but many will fall down slain.* [27]*As for both kings, their hearts will be intent on evil, and they will speak lies to each other at the same table; but it will not succeed, for the end is still to come at the appointed time.* [28]*Then he will return to his land with much plunder; but his heart will be set against the holy covenant, and he will take action and then return to his own land."*

This is probably still telling the original story of Antiochus IV and Ptolemy VI with greater detail. Ptolemy amassed a large army to attack Antiochus by his own people who "eat his choice food.'" But when Ptolemy attacked, he was captured. Then the alliance was formed but both the king of the North and the newly defeated king of the South (Ptolemy VI) were "intent on evil" and they spoke "lies to each other" at the same table. Basically, to both, the alliance was a matter of convenience. Ptolemy wanted out of jail and he wanted his throne returned. Antiochus wanted more power and control of more territory. Eventually Ptolemy returned to Egypt and helped rule with his brother. Antiochus then returns to his own land after plundering Egypt but stops off in Palestine where he crushes an uprising, kills 80,000 Jews, and plunders the temple.[3] The Jews began a revolt.

> "And through his shrewdness he will cause deceit to succeed by his influence; and he will magnify himself in his heart . . ."
>
> Daniel 8:25

The kings of the past spoke flattery to each other, but their hearts were intent on evil. What does the Antichrist of the future do? Look at Daniel 8:25 in the margin.

[29] *"At the appointed time he will return and come into the South, but this last time it will not turn out the way it did before.* [30] *For ships of Kittim will come against him; therefore he will be disheartened and will return and become enraged at the holy covenant and take action; so he will come back and show regard for those who forsake the holy covenant."*

Antiochus once again attacked Egypt but was met by Rome who had joined forces with the Ptolemies. The "ships of Kittim" indicate a Roman fleet. History bears witness that a Roman commander approached Antiochus and told him to leave the land of Egypt. When Antiochus hesitated the Roman drew a circle around him and said to make his decision before he left the circle or he would face the wrath of Rome. Antiochus then became "disheartened" and returned to the North, stopping off in Palestine and taking action against the "holy covenant."[4]

What will Satan and the Antichrist do in the future?

Read Revelation 12:17? What is Satan's emotion here? _____ Who does he come after? _____

[31] *"Forces from him will arise, desecrate the sanctuary fortress, and do away with the regular sacrifice. And they will set up the abomination of desolation.* [32] *By smooth words he will turn to godlessness those who act wickedly toward the covenant, but the people who know their God will display strength and take action."*

This clash between good verses evil is called the Maccabean revolt and it resulted in Antiochus' evacuation of Palestine and the festival known as Hanukkah. Forces from Antiochus entered Judea intending to crush the religion of the Jews. Antiochus IV Epiphanes stopped the regular burnt offering, set up an idol to Zeus (the abomination of desolation), and offered up pigs on the alter – desecrating the sanctuary. Antiochus' flattery was able to persuade some Jews to join him but those that stood in the truth of God's Word took action. We have already learned about the Maccabean revolt when we looked at Daniel chapter eight.[5] What will the Antichrist do?

Read Daniel 9:27. What will he put a stop to? _____

What will he set up according to Matthew 24:15? _____

Here Jesus is talking about a future time of trouble before the end comes. Antiochus IV Epiphanes had already come and gone when Jesus spoke those words. He was looking forward to the "little horn" of Daniel – the ruler that the "small horn" or Antiochus IV Epiphanes foreshadowed.

[33]"Those who have insight among the people will give understanding to the many; yet they will fall by sword and by flame, by captivity and by plunder for many days. [34]Now when they fall they will be granted a little help, and many will join with them in hypocrisy. [35]Some of those who have insight will fall, in order to refine, purge and make them pure until the end time; because it is still to come at the appointed time."

Those that have insight – or those that are wise will give others understanding, perhaps even encourage others to stand firm for their religious beliefs. Yet, even many would fall and be subject to the horrors of the time. The "little help" is probably referring to the Maccabees and their leadership. "Many will join with them in hypocrisy" seems like an odd phrase but this may refer to those that joined the Maccabees in order to save their lives, not out of firm religious convictions.[6]

What will happen in the last days?

Read Daniel 12:3. Who will shine? _____

There will be those who understand what is occurring in the last days, and like those in the past, they will shine their Savior – no matter the cost. And just like the past – many will fall – even those who are wise.

Read Daniel 8:24. Who will the Antichrist destroy? _____

Read Revelation 6:9. What will happen to many in the last days? _____

It is important to learn from the past. It is important to have our eyes wide open. As Jesus says, "He who has ears to hear, let him hear" (Mathew 11:15). Can we be strong like Daniel?

1 *English Standard Version Study Bible* (Wheaton, Illinois: Crossway, 2008), 1615.
One-Volume Illustrated Edition of Zondervan Bible Commentary with General Editor F. F. Bruce (Zondervan, 2008), 901.
2 *English Standard Version Study Bible* (Wheaton, Illinois: Crossway, 2008), 1615.
Leupold, H.C. *Exposition of Daniel* (Grand Rapids, Michigan: Baker Book House Company, 1969), 496.
3 *English Standard Version Study Bible* (Wheaton, Illinois: Crossway, 2008), 1615.
4 *English Standard Version Study Bible* (Wheaton, Illinois: Crossway, 2008), 1614.
Leupold, H.C. *Exposition of Daniel* (Grand Rapids, Michigan: Baker Book House Company, 1969), 501.
5 *English Standard Version Study Bible* (Wheaton, Illinois: Crossway, 2008), 1616.
Leupold, H.C. *Exposition of Daniel* (Grand Rapids, Michigan: Baker Book House Company, 1969), 503.
6 *English Standard Version Study Bible* (Wheaton, Illinois: Crossway, 2008), 1616.

Day Two – Chapter Eleven
The Little Horn of the Future

"At the end time the king of the South will collide with him, and the king of the North will storm against him with chariots, with horsemen and with many ships; and he will enter countries, overflow them and pass through."

Daniel 11:40

We have just looked at the "small horn" of the past, known to us as Antiochus IV Epiphanes. Now scripture takes a sharp turn and starts talking about the "little horn" of the future. How do we know this? Look at Daniel 11:40 in the margin.

Antiochus Epiphanes was the king of the _____.

Well, now we have a new king of the North, meaning we are not talking about the same king anymore. The king of the North actually comes against this next king, which we know as the "little horn" or the Antichrist. The switch comes in verse thirty-six.

36"Then the king will do as he pleases, and he will exalt and magnify himself above every god and will speak monstrous things against the God of gods; and he will prosper until the indignation is finished, for that which is decreed will be done."

We have looked at the arrogance of the "little horn" in multiple places in this study, but it would be foolish not to revisit it here.

What will the Antichrist do according to 2 Thessalonians 2:4? _____

What things will the beast (the political reign of the Antichrist) do according to Revelation 13:6? _____

What will this political empire do according to Revelation 13:16-17? _____

According to Daniel and Revelation, the Antichrist will succeed until the indignation is finished. When is it finished? Look at the Revelation quote in the margin.

Indignation will be finished when no one else repents and the final wrath of God falls. What is unleashed at the end, and when will the final time come? The end will occur when Jesus returns to wipe out the enemy at a battle we are very familiar with – Armageddon.

Men were scorched with fierce heat; and they blasphemed the name of God who has the power over these plagues, and they did not repent so as to give Him glory . . . and they blasphemed the God of heaven because of their pains and their sores; and they did not repent of their deeds.

Revelation 16:9, 11

37"He will show no regard for the gods of his fathers or for the desire of women, nor will he show regard for any other god; for he will magnify himself above them all. 38But instead he will honor a god of fortresses, a god whom his fathers did not know; he will honor him with gold, silver, costly stones and treasures."

We have already seen that the Antichrist will magnify himself above all gods, declaring himself to be God (2 Thessalonians 2:4). This mirrors but goes far beyond what Antiochus did in the past. Although Antiochus put a "God made visible" motto on a coin, he still worshiped other gods and set up idols. The Antichrist will declare himself god. He will show no regard for the gods of his fathers. What does this mean?

Read Exodus 3:15. Who is the god of your fathers? _____

The Hebrew word for "father" can also mean ancestor. And the phrase "god of their fathers" has been used multiple times in scripture to refer to the one true God (see also Genesis 43:23). The Antichrist will not acknowledge the one true God.[1] Now what does the "desire of women" mean? It seems from this scripture that his refusal to acknowledge the "desire of women" is because he fails to acknowledge "the gods of his fathers." This can be taken in a few ways.

If the Antichrist does not acknowledge the Father, he will also not acknowledge the Son. Look at 1 John 2:22 in the margin. Back in Daniel's day, the ultimate blessing a woman could receive was to birth the Messiah. Many scholars believe that this could be the interpretation. Others believe the "desire of women" could be referring to the false gods that women worshiped back in Daniel's day (like Tammuz in Ezekiel 8:14).[2] But if the "god of fathers" is the one true God, this doesn't exactly fit the context.

> Who is the liar but the one who denies that Jesus is the Christ? This is the antichrist, the one who denies the Father and the Son.
>
> 1 John 2:22

So let's think about this in context. If the Antichrist is Islamic, he will obviously deny the "god of his fathers." He will hail the god named Allah, the enemy of Jews, Christians – and women. In Islam women's rights are trampled on. At best women are treated as second-class citizens, at worst they are used as sex slaves. If he will not acknowledge God, that in turn will allow him to trample on any desires women might have of freedom – something that Jesus granted.

The Antichrist will magnify or set himself up above all gods, but he will also declare allegiance with the god of fortresses. Fortresses can also be translated "strength." This phrase insinuates a strong force or military strength. The Antichrist will worship a god of war. As Daniel is writing this, Islam did not exist. The god the Antichrist would follow was a "god his father's did not know."

How can the text say he will magnify himself above "all" gods, but then say he will honor a god of fortresses? Again, think about this in context. We too worship a God that is both a Father and a Son. Satan wants to imitate everything God does in order to better fool the masses. Allah can have a Messiah too – just like our God. That is exactly what Islam believes. They are looking for a Messiah who will usher in the age of Islam and global domination.[3]

[39]"He will take action against the strongest of fortresses with the help of a foreign god; he will give great honor to those who acknowledge him and will cause them to rule over the many, and will parcel out land for a price."

This foreign god (Allah) that Daniel did not know would help the Antichrist go against the strongest of fortresses – or nations. The Antichrist will give honor to those that acknowledge him. He will also parcel out land for a price. What land do you think he would parcel out?

Read Joel 3:2. Whose land has been divided up? _____ And what land do you think this refers to?_____

[40]"At the end time the king of the South will collide with him, and the king of the North will storm against him with chariots, with horsemen and with many ships; and he will enter countries, overflow them and pass through."

This is the verse we referred to at the beginning. This is one of the reasons we know that a new king is being referred to – one that will come in the end times. This will be further clarified as we move into chapter 12. So who is this scripture referring to when it says the king of the North and the king of the South? We can't be certain. The king of the North could still be pointing to a king in the region of Syria or Babylonia but it could also refer to any land North of the Middle East. It could be Russia, or even China. But if you read the next section of scripture, the king of the South might look familiar.

Who will the king stretch out his hand against in the next passage? _____

The king of the South could still refer to Egypt, and Egypt will not escape his hand – neither will the Libyans and the Ethiopians. We might have already seen a reference to this in a previous chapter.

Read Daniel 7:20. How many horns fell when the Antichrist (the little horn) rose to power? _____ And how many nations will he gain control over according to the paragraph below? _____

[41]"He will also enter the Beautiful Land, and many countries will fall; but these will be rescued out of his hand: Edom, Moab and the foremost of the sons of Ammon. [42]Then he will stretch out his hand against other countries, and the land of Egypt will not escape. [43]But he will gain control over the hidden treasures of gold and silver and over all the precious things of Egypt; and Libyans and Ethiopians will follow at his heels."

The Beautiful Land refers to Israel. According to Daniel chapter nine the Antichrist will stop sacrifice and offering in the middle of the final seven years. According to 2 Thessalonians he will set himself up in the temple of God and display himself as God. Yes, he will enter the Beautiful Land.

What does Jesus tell Israel to do in Matthew 24:15-16? _____ When? _____

Jesus tells His people to flee when they see the abomination standing in the temple. This would logically be at the middle of the final seven years when he stops sacrifice and offering. He tells them to flee to the mountains. There is a mountainous region near Jerusalem that many scholars believe the Jews will flee to – Petra, Jordon. It is a deserted city that is carved in sandstone cliffs. Jordon of the past was Edom, Moab, and Ammon.

Look back at Daniel 11:41, what land will escape the Antichrist's hand? _____

[44] *"But rumors from the East and from the North will disturb him, and he will go forth with great wrath to destroy and annihilate many.* [45] *He will pitch the tents of his royal pavilion between the seas and the beautiful Holy Mountain; yet he will come to his end, and no one will help him."*

The Antichrist will come to power under false peace (make a treaty according to Daniel 9:27 and Revelation 6:2).

Over what does the Antichrist and his kingdom have power according to Revelation 13:7?
_____

So, in some form or fashion, the Antichrist will have power over the entire world. His hand will touch all nations. That does not mean he will have control over them all, but that does mean his influence and trickery will reach the entire globe. We now live in a global society. What happens in the Middle East affects us here. We are not immune to things happening in the rest of the world. Our currency, our energy, and our possessions are all part of a global system. We do know that eventually, some nations will not like the Antichrist. They will try to stop him. This is the "rumors from the East and from the North" that disturb him. He will go forth to destroy, but some will stand against him. Who are these rulers from the East and the North? We can't say for certain. But know, these leaders may not be for our God. Let me explain.

In Revelation, armies assemble from around the globe. First, the armies of the Antichrist (Revelation 9:1-12) then the armies of the world (Revelation 9:13-21). In the end, a rider on a white horse will come from the sky, and what will these leaders do?

Read Revelation 19:19. What were they doing? _____

Although nations oppose the Antichrist, in the end, they will assemble to fight the Son of Man on a white horse.

Who does Jesus say He will assemble according to Joel 3:2?_____

According to Zephaniah 3:8?_____ Why? _____

Jesus will do some threshing when the kings of the earth are gathered.

Now, let's get back to the final sentence in Daniel chapter eleven. "He will pitch the tents of his royal pavilion between the seas and the beautiful Holy Mountain; yet he will come to his end, and no one will help him." The King James Version translates this better by saying: "And he shall plant the tabernacles of his palace between the seas in the glorious holy mountain; yet he shall come to his end, and none shall help him." Jerusalem was a land between the seas, the Holy Mountain is the temple mount in Jerusalem.

Where does Jesus touch down according to Zechariah 14:4? _____

The Mount of Olives is across the Kidron Valley from the Temple Mount. As in, you can see the temple mount from the Mount of Olives. Jesus will touch down there. I guarantee you when that happens the Antichrist will not be having a good day. He will "come to his end."

> "And through his shrewdness He will cause deceit to succeed by his influence; and he will magnify himself in his heart, and he will destroy many while they are at ease. He will even oppose the Prince of princes but he will be broken without human agency."
>
> Daniel 8:25

Read Daniel 8:25 in the margin. Who will the Antichrist oppose? _____ How will he be broken? _____

Jesus wins, faithful friends! Jesus wins!

1 Shoebat, Walid, written with Joel Richardson. *God's War on Terror* (Top Executive Media, 2008. 100)
2 Hinnant, Greg. *Daniel Notes* (Lake Mary, Florida: Creation House Press, 2003), 272.
3 Shoebat, Walid, written with Joel Richardson. *God's War on Terror* (Top Executive Media, 2008.
Joel Richardson's *Antichrist Islam's Awaited Messiah* published in 2006.
Beck, Glenn. *It is About Islam* (New York, New York: Mercury Radio Arts, Inc., 2015).

Day Three – Chapter Twelve
Shine Like Stars

"Those who have insight will shine brightly like the brightness of the expanse of heaven, and those who lead the many to righteousness, like the stars forever and ever."

Daniel 12:3

Remember, God didn't put chapter breaks in scripture – man did. The narrative we have been studying for quite some time is still moving forward. What started in chapter ten with "in the third year of Cyrus" will not end until the end of chapter twelve. The angel Daniel first met in chapter ten is still speaking with Daniel. Chapters eleven and twelve are the continuation of the angel's words. Do not forget that. We are not in a different narrative. We are finishing what we started back in chapter ten. With that being said, let's move forward.

Read Daniel 12:1-4

We have already mentioned verse one, but let's look at this verse a little more closely. Verse one begins with "Now at that time." We need to ask ourselves, "At what time?" What were we just reading about? When the Antichrist stops in Jerusalem, when war is happening, when countries are falling, when the Antichrist honors a god of war, when he declares himself God, when he disregards the desires of women, and when he magnifies himself above all else – that is the time we are discussing – the time of the end – I would argue that this is referring to the second half of the final seven years – when all hell breaks loose.

What does Daniel 12:1 say will happen at this time? _____ And because of that what will come? _____ And then who will be rescued? _____

Just like Daniel saw the summation of Jesus' second coming in chapter seven, so too Daniel is given a summary of what will happen during that final three and a half year time frame. Michael will stand up. We know that Michael is the prince or the angel that guards or protects Israel. What does it mean that he "stands up?" The Hebrew word *amad* (Strong's 5975) can mean cease, as in Michael stands still. *Amad* is what a soldier does when he is standing guard; it is to be immovable. When the moon stopped in the sky at Joshua's command, this was the word used. Look at Joshua 10:13 in the margin.

So the sun stood still, and the moon stopped *[amad]*, until the nation avenged themselves of their enemies.

Joshua 10:13

Why would Michael who stands guard over Israel stand up or stand still? Keep in mind, scripture tells you what happens after Michael stands up: "there will be a time of distress such as never occurred since there was a nation." Bad things happen after Michael stands up. It seems to indicate that Michael is indeed standing still – as in he is not doing anything to hinder this distress. There is only one explanation.

Who and what are we talking about in 2 Thessalonians 2:3-4? _____

What do you think restrains him now from attacking Israel according to 2 Thessalonians 2:5-6? _____

Who is taken out of the way in 2 Thessalonians 2:7? _____

In 2 Thessalonians 2:8, who is revealed once the restrainer is removed? _____
Until what happens? _____

Michael is the one who stands guard over Israel. In the middle of the final seven years, he will stand up and cease from protecting the nation. At that time the man of lawlessness, the Antichrist, will be revealed. He will break the treaty, stop sacrifice and offering, and declare himself god in the Jewish Temple. The Jews will flee, and the Antichrist will pursue and persecute the saints.

What does Daniel 12:1 say will happen at the time of great distress? _____

People will be rescued – those who have their names written in the book. What book are we talking about?

In Revelation 21:1-2 what are we talking about? _____

Who can enter this city according to Revelation 21:27? _____

The book of life is the book that holds the names of everyone who believes in Jesus. It is the book filled with saints, both Old Testament and New. During the distress of the end times, during the Antichrist's persecution, there will be a rescue. Jesus talks about it in Matthew 24.

Read Matthew 24:21-22. What are we talking about here? _____
Does this match the angel's words in Daniel 12:1? _____

What will God do according to Matthew 24:22? _____

There will be a time that God will say "Enough!" There will be a rapture, where we are taken from the earth before the punishment of the beast is inflicted. Do you remember the fire coming out of the throne in Daniel chapter seven? That is the trumpet and bowl judgments of Revelation 8-9. We are rescued right before the fire falls that dooms the political system of the Antichrist. Revisit Daniel 12:2 in the margin.

"Many of those who sleep in the dust of the ground will awake, these to everlasting life, but the others to disgrace and everlasting contempt."

Daniel 12:2

Some will awake to everlasting life; others will wake to everlasting contempt. Although this is a single verse, it is separated by a thousand years. In scripture regarding prophecy, this is common. Let me prove it to you. In Luke, Jesus reads scripture in the temple. Let's see what passage He picked.

In Luke 4:18 Jesus starts to read Isaiah 61. What did He end with in verse 19? _____

Now turn to Isaiah 61. Jesus didn't finish the original sentence found in Isaiah. What was the ending of this sentence according to verse 2? _____

At Jesus' first coming He was preaching good news to the poor, He had come to release the captives from sin, He was there to give sight to the blind – both literally and figuratively – and He was there to proclaim the favorable year of the Lord. He was in no way there to walk in vengeance – yet. That day would come at His second coming – thousands of years later. So don't think scripture is always in a timeline we can readily understand without digging deeper.

Let's get back to Daniel. Some dead will awake to life, others to death. In Revelation the resurrections are defined in greater detail. At the rapture, those with His life will wake. We see the rapture represented in Revelation chapter seven, but take note, the rapture is not until after the midpoint, after the Antichrist's persecution, and after the martyred saints cry out to God. If you want more detailed information about the rapture, please pick up my *Revelation in Black and White* study. But there will be a day when Jesus calls the saved home and they will rise to the heavenlies to prepare for the "day of vengeance of out God." Ultimately those saints will return with the King to set up His kingdom on earth (Revelation 19, Isaiah 65). After we rule the earth for 1,000 years, the dead (those who rejected Christ) will rise to be given their eternal punishment. Daniel is seeing a summary of this in Daniel chapter 12.

Next we get to a verse that should brighten your day. Look at Daniel 12:3 in the margin. The word for "insight" is the Hebrew word *sakal* (Strong's 7919) and it means "to look at, to give attention to." You are currently giving attention to Daniel. You are looking at his words intently and digging in. If you take Daniel's lessons to heart, you will shine brightly. But there is even more to this verse than that. The word "shine" in Daniel 12:3 has an even a deeper meaning. It is the Hebrew word *zahar* (Strong's 2094) and it means "to gleam, and to enlighten." It insinuates that when you *zahar* you are enlightening others by teaching, warning, and admonishing. If you have insight into the end, won't you warn others? Will you not enlighten those around you about what is to come? That is exactly what Daniel 12:3 is saying. If you have insight you will shine by teaching others and when you do that you will literally shine in the heavenlies.

"Those who have insight will shine brightly like the brightness of the expanse of heaven, and those who lead the many to righteousness, like the stars forever and ever."

Daniel 12:3

Then the angel tells Daniel to "conceal these words and seal up the book until the end of time." What does this mean? Daniel has clearly written down the prophecy and it has been studied for centuries. Daniel has been written about and talked about for years. Scripture indicates that until the time of the end, the words of Daniel would not be understood. They would be concealed. Only at the end time would the words of Daniel slowly be revealed. If you think about when Daniel lived, everything about the Grecian kings was in the future. Only as the years passed and kings rose and fell was the entirety of the message understood. Just so, with each passing year, with the lessons learned from Antiochus and with the revelation that the Turkish Ottoman Empire is the reunited empire of Daniel chapter two, does more of Daniel become clear. I firmly believe our generation will see these events take place. We will bear witness to prophecies coming to life. We live in an exciting time. It is a time we can *zahar* others and shine Him.

Look at Daniel 12:4 in the margin. The angel tells Daniel the environment of the time of the end: many will go back and forth, and knowledge will increase. The Hebrew for "go back and forth" is *shuwt* (Strong's 7751) and it means "to push forth, to lash (the sea with oars), to row" so by implication it means "to travel." The Hebrew word for increase is *rabah* (Strong's 7235) and it means "to multiply." So at the end of time people will travel, row, lash about and knowledge will be multiplied. In today's society, we can see where this would be the description. We can travel the world easily; knowledge is available at the touch of our smartphones. This knowledge and lashing can be used to study the scriptures, different commentaries, and other sources of worldwide information to understand what is happening in Daniel.[1] Yes, the understanding of Daniel's prophecies are coming to light with each and every day.

The angel isn't done with Daniel yet. More to come tomorrow.

"But as for you, Daniel, conceal these words and seal up the book until the end of time; many will go back and forth, and knowledge will increase."

Daniel 12:4

---

1 Leupold, H.C. *Exposition of Daniel* (Grand Rapids, Michigan: Baker Book House Company, 1969), 534.

Day Four – Chapter Twelve
The Wise Verses the Wicked

He said, "Go your way, Daniel, for these words are concealed and sealed up until the end of time."

Daniel 12:9

We will be closing the book of Daniel soon. These twelve short chapters have been jammed packed with information. I hate to see Daniel come to an end. The prophet has given us many lessons, has he not? An amazing witness, that Daniel. May we learn from him as we walk into the "end of time."

Read Daniel 12:5-10

We have met a variety of angels in Daniel. Here, we see two more appear. The man in linen is still there, hovering over the river, but now Daniel's attention is drawn by two additional angels that appear on either side of the river. These new angels turn their attention to the man in linen.

We have already indicated that the man in linen is probably a pre-incarnate Jesus. Let's pause here to do a little more digging. We looked at his attributes back in chapter 10, but here his location seems to be emphasized. He is still hovering over the river. Daniel is at the Tigris River when he receives the vision, but the word used in chapter 12 for "river" (Strong's #2975) is not the same Hebrew word used in chapter 10 (Strong's #5104). Daniel chapter 12 uses the Hebrew word *yaor*, and although it still means "river," it is mostly used in scripture to reference the Nile River. This word is first used in Genesis 41:2-3 when Pharaoh dreams of the cows coming out of the Nile. *Yaor* is the word used throughout the plagues of Egypt when the Nile is struck. This word is not used exclusively for the Nile but out of the 64 times it is used in the King James Version, at least 57 of those times it refers to bodies of water in Egypt, and this doesn't count the four times it is used in Daniel chapter 12.

Why the emphasis on the Nile if Daniel is at the Tigris? Remember, the book of Daniel is foreshadowing the return of the King. We have just seen the man in linen match the description of Jesus in Revelation, or Jesus at His second coming. Jesus is hovering over the river – but the Nile River seems to be a side note in Daniel chapter 12. Let's look at a second coming passage in Zechariah that talks about the Jewish remnant coming to faith when Jesus returns in His glory.

Read Zechariah 10:10-12. Where will He bring the Jews back from?_____
_____ What will be dried up?
_____

The Nile will be dried up at Jesus' second coming and He will call His people back from Egypt. Now let's look at another second coming passage.

Read Isaiah 19:1. What will Jesus be riding on? _____

Read Matthew 24:30 in the margin. What will Jesus be coming with?_____

Read Isaiah 19:5-7. What will be dried up? _____

"And then the sign of the Son of Man will appear in the sky, and then all the tribes of the earth will mourn, and they will see the Son of Man coming on the clouds of the sky with power and great glory."

Matthew 24:30

Jesus will return with the clouds. He will dry up the Nile. He will be seen over Egypt at His second coming. His feet will stand on the Mount of Olives (Zechariah 14:4), but before then He will be seen riding a cloud over Egypt, calling His people home. That is why the word *yaor* is used in Daniel chapter 12. It once again refers to the second coming. Amazing!

The two angels that have just appeared ask the one who is clothed in linen, "How long will it be until the end of these wonders?" The man in linen raises his right hand, and then he raises his left hand toward heaven. Just like we raise our right hand today to swear that our statement is true, this was also the case in ancient times. The raising of both hands emphasizes the trustworthiness of the statement – as in the words spoken would come to pass.[1]

The man in linen answers by saying that it would be for a "time, times, and half a time; and as soon as they finish shattering the power of the holy people, all these events would be completed." We know the angels are asking about the end of the wonders, but where is Jesus pointed back to in order to bring us to the end?

Look back at Daniel 12:1. What time are we talking about? _____

We have pinpointed that Michael will stand up in the middle of the final seven years, when the Antichrist takes his seat in the temple of God and declares himself god. This is when the all out persecution of Jews and Christians will begin according to Revelation chapter 12. We see this clarified in scripture.

Turn back to Daniel 7:25. What time frame are we talking about? _____
And who will be given into his hand for that time? _____

Now turn to Revelation 12:14 (the women represents Israel). What time frame is depicted? _____ And what happens during that time frame according to Revelation 12:17? _____

This is the second half of the final seven-year period carved out in Daniel chapter nine. A time is one year, a times is two years, and half a time is half of a year for a total of three and a half years. The man in linen emphasizes the Antichrist's persecution when he says, "as soon as they finish shattering the power of the holy people."

Daniel doesn't understand and asks, "My lord, what will be the outcome of these events?"

The man in linen doesn't answer Daniel specifically, but instead tells Daniel to "Go your way, for these words are concealed and sealed up until the end time." The man isn't pushing Daniel aside, but telling Daniel that the words describing the end wouldn't be understood until the time of the end.

Now look at Daniel 12:10 in the margin.

> "Many shall be purified, and made white, and tried; but the wicked shall do wickedly and none of the wicked shall understand; but the wise shall understand."
>
> Daniel 12:10 KJV

During the final time, times, and half a time, or three and a half years, many will be purified, made white, and tried. Let's take these one at a time. "Purified" is the Hebrew word *barar* (Strong's #1305) and it means "to clarify, or brighten." When you clarify something you take out the impurities; you take confusion and make things more clear. You brighten something! The saints will be clarified and brightened during the last days – they will see Him more clearly and hence shine Him more. They will turn their back on sin and stand up for truth. "Made white" is the Hebrew word *laban* (Strong's #3835) and it means "to be or become white." The saints will become whiter – more righteous (Revelation 19:8). "Tried" is the Hebrew word *tsaraph* (Strong's #6884) and it means "to fuse (metal), to refine." Again, the saints will remove their impurities and grow closer to the One who is about to return to claim the earth.

We have seen purification in Daniel. When Hananiah, Azariah, and Mishael stood before the flames and did not bow down, their faith was purified. When Daniel refused to yield and was thrown into the lions' den, he was refined. Those saints in the last days that walk through Babylon and refuse to bow down like the faithful four will have their faith clarified, refined, and made white. They will be bright. They will shine the Savior.

But the wicked are another story. They will have a chance to repent, but they will not. They will just act more wickedly. They won't understand what is happening around them, but those who have insight, those who are wise, will understand. We have already seen that "the fear of the Lord is the beginning of knowledge" (Proverbs 1:7), so only those who are with Him will be able to look around and clearly see what is happening.

In today's world, when you speak the truth, you are seen as intolerant, foolish, or offensive. When you stand for Christian values, you are declared ignorant. We look at the world and see darkness, but they don't see it that way. They feel enlightened, yet we see corruption. We want to help, but if we do we are found to be unaccepting of the situation.

It is only going to get worse. It will get so bad that Christians will be persecuted in a way they have never been persecuted before.

Read Matthew 10:21-22. Who will hate us? _____ Who will betray us? _____

Ready your armor, faithful friends. Ready your armor.

1 Leupold, H.C. *Exposition of Daniel* (Grand Rapids, Michigan: Baker Book House Company, 1969), 539-540.

Day Five – Chapter Twelve
Blessed

Yesterday we left off with the wise understanding but the wicked unable to comprehend. The last days will cause a rift between relatives, friends and brothers. If you are in the light you will understand; if you are in the darkness you will be clueless. But the man in linen is not finished revealing all he can about the end times. Today is going to be a long day, because these final three verses in Daniel pack a punch. So hang in there and put on your thinking hats.

Read Daniel 12:11-13

What is happening here? We have just said that Jesus returns after three and a half years, or a time, a times, and half a time. To refresh, a time is one year, a times is two years, and half a time is half of a year. If we use the prophetic calendar with 12 months of 30 days or 360 total days we get:

360 days (a time) + 720 days (times) + 180 days (half a time) = 1,260 days
If we double this number we should get the approximate time of the final seven years = 2,520 days

We know the Antichrist takes his seat in the temple of God in the middle of the final seven years, which would be approximately at the 1,260 day mark, or the three and one half year division. But if we go strictly by a prophetic calendar, we have a problem. Daniel says that from the time the abomination is set up – in the middle of the week – until the time of the end – there will be 1,290 days.

We can't go by a strictly prophetic calendar when we talk about the end times. Israel is not on a prophetic calendar – they use a solar/lunar calendar. They start their months based on the new moon. Their months last either 29 or 30 days, corresponding to the 29.5 day lunar cycle. Because of this, their years can be either 353, 354, or 355 days. However, if they just used a lunar calendar soon their summer would be winter and their winter would be summer, because the earth revolves around the sun every 12.4 lunar months. In order for their months to mirror the solar cycle they add in another month of 30 days every two or three years (bringing some years up to 383, 384, or 385 days). So, in any given seven-year period, there are two or three years where there is an extra month added. Let me say that another way. In every seven year period there are never less than two months added, and there are never more than three months added. So, if we base our calculations on a Jewish calendar, every seven-year period has either 87 months or 86 months.

12 months x 7 years = 84 months + 3 additional months = 87 total months
12 months x 7 years = 84 months + 2 additional months = 86 total months

Let me give you another factor that matters to the calculation of the days in Daniel. Jews celebrate seven Jewish feasts. Two of those feasts are extremely important to our final seven-year time line. Before I tell you about them, I want to give you just a small example of the detail God went to in fulfilling the first four feasts (Leviticus 23), so that you can better understand why the final three are so important.

The first feast is the feast of Passover. This was the day our Savior died for our sins. The Jews killed two lambs every day. History shows the morning sacrifice was at nine in the morning, the exact time Jesus was hung on the cross (Mark 15:25). The evening sacrifice was at three in the afternoon, the exact time Jesus died on the cross (Matthew 27:45-51). Jesus became our "Passover Lamb." Just as the lamb's blood in the Exodus covered the people as the angel of death passed by, Jesus' blood covers us and saves us for life eternal.

The next feast is the "Feast of Unleavened Bread." On this feast, Jesus was buried, the sinless (unleavened) Son of God.

The third feast is the "Feast of First Fruits." It is on this day that our Savior was resurrected, the "first fruits" of the dead. "But now Christ has been raised from the dead, the first fruits of those who are asleep" (1 Corinthians 15:20).

The fourth feast is the feast of Pentecost. Christians tend to believe this is solely a Christian holiday, yet the Jews have been celebrating Pentecost for thousands of years. Jewish tradition states that Pentecost was the day Moses received the Ten Commandments from God. Jesus fulfilled the law of Moses in life (Matthew 5:17) and also satisfied the law with His death (1 Corinthians 15:56-57). Notice, when the disciples received the Spirit there was a huge crowd in Jerusalem. Why? God had told the Jewish people to celebrate the feast of Pentecost!

For more information on the feasts, please study *The Feasts of the Lord*, by Mark Biltz.[1] Although the detail of the first four feasts would be too much for us to study here, we will briefly look at a few of the remaining feasts because they will be fulfilled during Jesus' second coming.

The first annual fall feast (occurring in September or October on our calendar) is Rosh Hashanah. The significance of this feast for Jesus' second coming is evident due to its trumpet blasts and symbolic gates of heaven. Rosh Hashanah is also known as the Feast of Trumpets and the Day of the Awakening Blast.

Rosh Hashanah is also called the "last trump" for on these feast days the shofar is blown one hundred times and the last blast is known as the "last trump." With that in mind, check out the verse in the margin. The Jews would recognize that Paul's language here was referring to the "last trump" or Rosh Hashanah.

The Rapture will be on Rosh Hashanah. We still won't know the day or the hour because the feast lasts for two days!

Now let's look at the next fall feast. It comes 10 days after Rosh Hashanah. Yom Kippur means "Day of Atonement." This was the only day each year the High Priest of the Jewish nation was allowed into the Holy of Holies where the ark sat. This was the day when the High Priest

"Behold, I tell you a mystery; we will not all sleep, but we will all be changed, in a moment, in the twinkling of an eye, at the last trumpet; for the trumpet will sound, and the dead will be raised imperishable, and we will be changed."

1 Corinthians 15:51-52

sprinkled the mercy seat with blood, representing Jesus' sacrifice. Because God's presence was above the mercy seat, this was the day where the High Priest met God "face to face." And when will the rest of the world see God face to face? At Jesus' second coming!

All Jews wear white on Yom Kippur, symbolizing their atonement from sin. This ritual does not exclude the High Priest, who is performing the bloody sacrifices. His white robes would be splattered with the blood of bulls and goats. Let's see if we can find this visual of the second coming in scripture.

Read Revelation 15:5. What is seen opened? _____

Read Revelation 19:11-14. What is Jesus' robe dipped in in verse 13? _____

What color do the armies wear in verse 14? _____

This is Yom Kippur! The tabernacle of the testimony is open – where the ark resides – and the only day it is open is on Yom Kippur. Jesus is wearing robes dipped in blood – how the High Priest would look on Yom Kippur – and He is our High Priest (Hebrews 4:14). The saints are wearing white robes – just like the Jews do on Yom Kippur. The end of Daniel's time line is Yom Kippur. Jesus' second coming will fulfill this feast, just like the first four were fulfilled at His first coming.

Yom Kippur is also known as the "closing of the book" or the day when judgment is over. And when is judgment over? When Jesus returns and walks the earth.

After these things I looked, and behold, a door standing open in heaven . . .

Revelation 4:1

The rapture on Rosh Hashanah will occur sometime after the mid-point of the final seven years (see my *Revelation in Black and White* study), but the final battle, the day Jesus will descend and decimate the Antichrist or the "little horn" of Daniel will be on Yom Kippur.

On a final note, Rosh Hashanah is also known as the "opening of the gates of heaven." Although Daniel doesn't give us a picture of the beginning of the final seven years, Revelation does. Read Revelation 4:1 in the margin.

The feast of Rosh Hashanah opens the doors of heaven, which starts the seven-year time frame, and the feast of Yom Kippur is the Day of Judgment that finishes the seven-year time frame. If you think about it, if the return of the King happens in the fall (September or October) and you have to go back seven years to get to the beginning, it will start during the fall (September or October). Although Rosh Hashanah will open the gates of heaven and begin the time frame of the final seven years, this is not the same Rosh Hashanah as the rapture – that occurs after the midpoint. But if events happen on the feast days, they begin seven years earlier on those same feast days.

Why is this important? Do you remember our discussion about the 1,260 days and the 1,290 days? Why does Daniel say that from the time the abomination is set up (which is in the "middle" of the week according to Daniel 9:27) until the end of the line is 1290 days? If we go by a strictly prophetic calendar, the midpoint is 1,260 days with another 1,260 days following the midpoint. Let's review:

- Seven years according to a prophetic calendar would be 2,520 days (1,260 day midpoint).

- If we use this timeline, the Antichrist takes his seat in the temple of God near the midpoint (1,260 days).

- If we go strictly by a prophetic calendar (2,520 days in the final seven years) it would not correspond to the Jewish calendar or the feasts that have to be fulfilled. The Jews start their months based on the new moon. Their months last either 29 or 30 days, corresponding to the 29.5 day lunar cycle. They add in another month of 30 days every two or three years. So, for every seven-year cycle, there are either 86 months or 87 months, depending on whether there are two or three months added.

- Daniel says that from the time the abomination is set up – in the midst of the final seven years – until the time of the end there will be 1,290 days.

- There will be 45 days after that (at 1,335 days) and those who reach it are considered "blessed."

Here is another thing to consider. In Daniel 12:11 it states the 1,290 days come after the sacrifice is abolished and the abomination is set up. Back in Daniel 9:27, it says that in the "middle" of the week the Antichrist will put a stop to sacrifice and offering, which is this same point. The Hebrew word "middle" is *chetsiy* (Strong's #2677) and can be translated "part, half, or middle." This does not necessarily refer to the exact midpoint, but sometime close to half, or the middle of the final seven years. This same word is used in Psalm 102:24 (see margin). So, the days before this "point" do not necessarily have to equal the days after this "point."

> I say, "O my God, do not take me away in the midst [chetsiy] of my days, Your years are throughout all generations."
>
> Psalm 102:24

So if Rosh Hashanah opens the seven-year time line, and Yom Kippur closes the seven-year time line (this is a seven year period plus an additional 10 days to bring us to Yom Kippur), during the seven years that have 86 months (only 2 extra months added), there are roughly 2,550 days.[2]

2,550 days = 1,260 days until the stop of sacrifice + 1,290 days until the end

This matches Daniel, with a final three and a half years of exactly 1,290 days. Now let's look at the 87 month scenario from Rosh Hashanah to the seventh Yom Kippur (7 years plus 10 days). Because there is an extra month, there will be an additional 30 days, which brings our days to roughly 2,580 days.

2,580 days = 1,290 days until the stop of sacrifice + 1,290 days until the end

Both scenarios work with Daniel because in every seven-year period, you can divide the timeline to have 1,290 days during the second half. If Daniel's timeline is during an 86-month period, there are 1,260 days in the first "half" of the timeline, corresponding to the prophetic calendar. If Daniel's timeline is an 87-month period there are 1,290 days in the first "half" dividing the time line equally. (If you want to see a more detailed discussion about this time frame with examples and exact days, please see the Appendix). You could argue the 87-moon cycle may be a better fit because it divides the days exactly in half. In summary, the Antichrist will stop the regular sacrifice and set up an abomination, but after that there will be 1,290 days according to Daniel 12:11. This matches the time frame of Rosh Hashanah starting the seven-year period and the seventh Yom Kippur ending the seven-year period.

Let's relook at what Daniel says about the timing of the end.

1)   The Antichrist will speak out against the Most High, try to change the times and the law, and wear down the saints for a time, times, and half a time (Daniel 7:25).
2)   The end of "these wonders" (the end of the Antichrist) will be a time, times, and half a time (Daniel 12:7).

This, again, is our three and a half year time frame. No matter if it is 86 or 87 months, the second half of the period can still be defined as three and a half years (because even if a year has an extra month, it is still one full year).

Now let's see where Revelation mentions the timetable of the end times.

1) The two witnesses will prophesy for 1,260 days (Revelation 11:3).
2) Israel will be protected (nourished) from the Antichrist persecution for 1,260 days (Revelation 12:6).
3) The nations will trample on the holy city for 42 months (Revelation 11:2).
4) The Beast will have authority to act for 42 months (Revelation 13:5).

Now, these events will begin at the midpoint or near the middle of the final seven years. So why does Revelation declare 1260 days (42 months of 30 days) and not 1290 days? Let's take this a point at a time.

Read Revelation 11:7-11. What happens to the two-witnesses? _____
How long are they "looked upon?" _____

The two witnesses will prophesy for 1,260 days but then they will be killed and their bodies will be gazed upon for three and a half days. The people surrounding them will pass out gifts to one another. This is actually done today. When enemies are killed in radical Islamic nations, their bodies are displayed and people rejoice over their deaths. Candies and gifts are even handed out in celebration. Seeing that the two witnesses will prophesy in Jerusalem (Revelation 11:8), and the Antichrist will reign from there, this scenario comes into sharp focus. So, even though the two witnesses prophesy for 1,260 days, there needs to be additional time remaining for their bodies to be displayed in order to account for the extra three and a half days.

Israel will also be protected or nourished from the Antichrist's persecution for 1,260 days. Let's take a look at this more closely.

According to Revelation 12:6, Israel will be protected from the dragon for 1,260 days in the wilderness. The sign of that flight will be the abomination of desolation standing in the holy place. So why doesn't Revelation say they are protected for 1,290 days?

Revelation also says that the nations will trample the holy city underfoot for 42 months. This is also the 1260-day time frame and not the 1290-day time frame. Why is this? Notice that the Antichrist has authority to act for only 42 months. This is the same amount of time that the nations are allowed to trample the holy city and the same amount of time that Israel is protected. Yet, in the Jewish calendar, there are 43 months both before and after the "midpoint" (43 in a 86-month cycle and 43.5 in an 87-month cycle). That means there is a period of at least one month or 30 days when the Antichrist has no authority and the nations aren't trampling the holy city. That means during these 30 days, Israel will not need protecting. So what is happening during this time?

I have a theory. Revelation details events that occur during the final seven years. The "seals" start at the beginning, the "trumpets" start after the middle, and the "bowls" are at the very end. But there is something sandwiched between the end of the trumpets and the beginning of the bowls that is often overlooked. Look at Revelation 10:3-4 in the margin. If you open books on Revelation you see detailed information on the seal, trumpet, and bowl "judgments," but you do not see any discussion about the thunders – with good reason. We don't know what they are and we don't know what they do. We only know when they occur – at the end of the time line, before the final Day of Judgment where the bowls fall and Jesus returns.

Here is what I believe. The Antichrist will have authority for 42 months of the final seven years, which corresponds with the nations trampling the holy city. Then the thunders will sound, halting the Antichrist's authority. At this time the Jews will be safe, away from the persecution, which matches the 1,260 days of their protection, leaving the thunders

And he [an angel] cried out with a loud voice, as when a lion roars; and when he had cried out, the seven peals of thunder uttered their voices. When the seven peals of thunder had spoken, I was about to write; and I heard a voice from heaven saying, "Seal up the things which the seven peals of thunder have spoken and do not write them."

Revelation 10:3-4

able to sound for 30 days.

Let's look at this on a timeline that may make a little more sense.

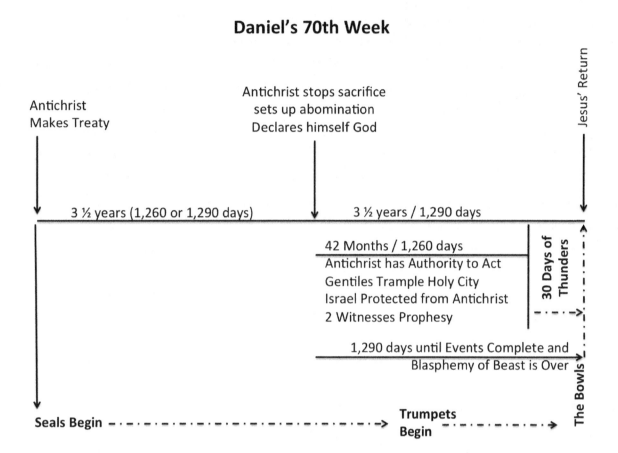

Daniel's 70th Week

This would explain the discrepancy between the 1,260 days of Revelation and the 1,290 days of Daniel. God will give authority to the Beast for 1,260 days, but He will have the final word!

Look again at Daniel 12:11-12 in the margin. We have accounted for the 1,290 days being the final three and one half years of the tribulation. But what about the extra 45 days that lead to the 1,335 days? Well, there is much to do in that time. What does Jesus do when He returns and sits on His throne?

"From the time that the regular sacrifice is abolished and the abomination of desolation is set up, there will be 1,290 days. How blessed is he who keeps waiting and attains to the 1,335 days!"

Daniel 12:11-12

Read Matthew 25:31-46. Who will be gathered to Him in verse 32? _____

What will He do to the sheep? _____ The goats? _____

What does He call the sheep in verse 34? _____

What does He call those who enter into the Millennial Kingdom in Revelation 20:6? _____

What does He call those who make it to the 1,335 days in Daniel 12:12? _____

The goats will be weeded out of the kingdom in those 45 days. The sheep will enter the kingdom and join those that returned with Him. Those who are allowed to enter the Millennium are "blessed and holy" because they are with Him and will inherit eternal life.

"How blessed is he who keeps waiting and attains to the 1,335 days!"

Daniel has taught us a lot, but I believe there is one more lesson he can teach us. Look at the last verse of Daniel in the margin.

Daniel would enter into rest and then rise with the righteous at the end of the age and attain an "allotted portion."

> "But as for you, go your way to the end; then you will enter into rest and rise again for your allotted portion at the end of the age."
>
> Daniel 12:13

Read Ecclesiastes 12:7. What will return to God? _____

What did Jesus commit to God in Luke 23:46? _____

Read 1 Thessalonians 4:15-16. If our spirit is with the Lord at death, what will Jesus raise up?
_____

And at that point, what will be done according to Luke 14:14? _____

Read Matthew 25:23. What will the faithful be in charge of? _____

What will some of those things be according to Luke 19:17?_____

Read Revelation 20:6 in the margin. The faithful will reign with Him. We will be given authority over cities. We will be His priests. Our new life in the Millennium is based on governance. There will still be life there – abundant life.

Daniel would rest in sleep until Jesus raises his body to be joined with his spirit. At that time Daniel will receive his allotted portion – he will be rewarded for a job well done. I am quite certain Daniel will be allotted many cities, perhaps even an entire continent. His faith shines throughout the ages, does it not? Why don't we close the book of Daniel with one more lessen:

> "Blessed and holy is the one who has a part in the first resurrection; over these the second death has no power, but they will be priests of God and of Christ and will reign with Him for a thousand years."
>
> Revelation 20:6

When we are with Him, the end is not death, but eternal life.

This is not the end of the man we have come to admire. We will learn more from him when we join him in the Millennial Reign of Christ. We will walk the streets with him, ask him questions, and get to know him. Nebuchadnezzar may be there too, laughing about his stubbornness to acknowledge the Most High God. And let us not forget Hananiah, Azariah, and Mishael. They will walk the streets of gold as well. We can ask them what they thought in the flames, and what others thought after they came out of the fire. We can ask them about their leader. I bet this is what they would say:

"Daniel? He was a faithful servant of God. A man of high esteem. A man that never wavered in his faith. A roll model for us, and more especially, a role model for all. He never doubted his God, because he knew his God was faithful. Even when he didn't understand, he trusted. Even when he was persecuted, he did not yield. Daniel? He shone like the brightest star."

Amen to that. May your faith stand firm in the fire. May your conviction leave your windows wide open. May your life shine in the heavenlies like the faithful four.

Until the shofar sounds,

Nic

1 Blitz, Mark. A DVD study entitled *Feasts of the Lord*. (El Shaddai Ministries, 2008). See also www.elshaddaiministries.us
2 www.endtimepilgrim.org

APPENDIX - More Details on Daniel's 70th Week

If Rosh Hashanah opens the seven-year time line, and Yom Kippur closes the seven-year time line (this is a seven year period plus and additional 10 days to bring us to Yom Kippur), during the seven-years periods that have 86 months (only 2 extra months added), there are roughly 2,550 days.[1]

2,550 days = 1,260 days until the stop of sacrifice + 1,290 days until the end

This matches Daniel, with the final three and a half years of exactly 1,290 days. But notice I said "roughly" 2,550 days. Here is what I mean. Like I have noted previously, Israel's calendar year doesn't have a set number of days every year. They have 353, 354, or 355 days depending on the moon cycle (they also add another 30 days some years which adds to those numbers). So in any given 86-month cycle there are between 2549 and 2551 days from Rosh Hashanah to the seventh Yom Kippur.

Years Starting with Rosh Hashanah that Have 86 Months				
2016	2019	2022	2024	2025
Year One 2016 – 2017 Oct 3 – Sep 20 **353 Days**	**Year One*** 2019 – 2020 Sep 30 – Sep 18 **355 Days**	**Year One** 2022 – 2023 Sep 26 – Sep 15 **355 Days**	**Year One** 2024 – 2025 Oct 3 – Sep 22 **355 Days**	**Year One** 2025 – 2026 Sep 23 – Sep 11 **354 Days**
Year Two 2017 – 2018 Sep 21 – Sep 9 **354 Days**	**Year Two** 2020 – 2021 Sep 19 – Sep 6 **353 Days**	**Year Two*** 2023 – 2024 Sep 16 – Oct 2 **383 Days**	**Year Two** 2025 – 2026 Sep 23 – Sep 11 **354 Days**	**Year Two** 2026 – 2027 Sep 12 – Oct 1 **385 Days**
Year Three 2018 – 2019 Sep 10 – Sep 29 **385 Days**	**Year Three** 2021 – 2022 Sep 7 – Sep 25 **384 Days**	**Year Three** 2024 – 2025 Oct 3 – Sep 22 **355 Days**	**Year Three** 2026 – 2027 Sep 12 – Oct 1 **385 Days**	**Year Three*** 2027 – 2028 Oct 2 – Sep 20 **355 Days**
Year Four* 2019 – 2020 Sep 30 – Sep 18 **355 Days**	**Year Four** 2022 – 2023 Sep 26 – Sep 15 **355 Days**	**Year Four** 2025 – 2026 Sep 23 – Sep 11 **354 Days**	**Year Four*** 2027 – 2028 Oct 2 – Sep 20 **355 Days**	**Year Four** 2028 – 2029 Sep 21 – Sep 9 **354 Days**
Year Five 2020 – 2021 Sep 19 – Sep 6 **353 Days**	**Year Five*** 2023 – 2024 Sep 16 – Oct 2 **383 Days**	**Year Five** 2026 – 2027 Sep 12 – Oct 1 **385 Days**	**Year Five** 2028 – 2029 Sep 21 – Sep 9 **354 Days**	**Year Five** 2029 – 2030 Sep 10 – Sep 27 **383 Days**
Year Six 2021 – 2022 Sep 7 – Sep 25 **384 Days**	**Year Six** 2024 – 2025 Oct 3 – Sep 22 **355 Days**	**Year Six*** 2027 – 2028 Oct 2 – Sep 20 **355 Days**	**Year Six** 2029 – 2030 Sep 10 – Sep 27 **383 Days**	**Year Six** 2030 – 2031 Sep 28 – Sep 17 **355 Days**
Year Seven 2022 – 2023 Sep 26 – Sep 15 **355 Days**	**Year Seven** 2025 – 2026 Sep 23 – Sep 11 **354 Days**	**Year Seven** 2028 – 2029 Sep 21 – Sep 9 **354 Days**	**Year Seven** 2030 – 2031 Sep 28 – Sep 17 **355 Days**	**Year Seven*** 2031 – 2032 Sep 18 – Sep 5 **354 Days**
Total Days in Seven Years = 2539	Total Days in Seven Years = 2539	Total Days in Seven Years = 2541	Total Days in Seven Years = 2541	Total Days in Seven Years = 2540
+ 10 until Yom Kippur	+ 10 until Yom Kippur	+ 10 until Yom Kippur	+ 10 until Yom Kippur	+ 10 until Yom Kippur
2549 Days	**2549 Days**	**2551 Days**	**2551 Days**	**2550 Days**
Dates depicted are the start of Rosh Hashanah to the night before Rosh Hashanah of the next year. * Indicates a leap year, so you have to add another day for our extra day in February.				

Now let's look at the seven-year periods where there are 87 months from Rosh Hashanah to the seventh Yom Kippur (7 years plus 10 days). Because there is an extra month, there will be an additional 30 days, which brings our days to roughly 2,580 days.

2,580 days = 1,290 days until the stop of sacrifice + 1,290 days until the end

Again, this matches Daniel, with the final three and a half years of exactly 1,290 days. But again, the days aren't always exact. Like the 86-month period the 87-month period has between 2579 and 2581 days from Rosh Hashanah to the seventh Yom Kippur.

Years Starting with Rosh Hashanah that Have 87 Months				
2017	2018	2020	2021	2023
Year One 2017 – 2018 Sep 21 – Sep 9 **354 Days**	**Year One** 2018 – 2019 Sep 10 – Sep 29 **385 Days**	**Year One** 2020 – 2021 Sep 19 – Sep 6 **353 Days**	**Year One** 2021 – 2022 Sep 7 – Sep 25 **384 Days**	**Year One*** 2023 – 2024 Sep 16 – Oct 2 **383 Days**
Year Two 2018 – 2019 Sep 10 – Sep 29 **385 Days**	**Year Two*** 2019 – 2020 Sep 30 – Sep 18 **355 Days**	**Year Two** 2021 – 2022 Sep 7 – Sep 25 **384 Days**	**Year Two** 2022 – 2023 Sep 26 – Sep 15 **355 Days**	**Year Two** 2024 – 2025 Oct 3 – Sep 22 **355 Days**
Year Three* 2019 – 2020 Sep 30 – Sep 18 **355 Days**	**Year Three** 2020 – 2021 Sep 19 – Sep 6 **353 Days**	**Year Three** 2022 – 2023 Sep 26 – Sep 15 **355 Days**	**Year Three*** 2023 – 2024 Sep 16 – Oct 2 **383 Days**	**Year Three** 2025 – 2026 Sep 23 – Sep 11 **354 Days**
Year Four 2020 – 2021 Sep 19 – Sep 6 **353 Days**	**Year Four** 2021 – 2022 Sep 7 – Sep 25 **384 Days**	**Year Four*** 2023 – 2024 Sep 16 – Oct 2 **383 Days**	**Year Four** 2024 – 2025 Oct 3 – Sep 22 **355 Days**	**Year Four** 2026 – 2027 Sep 12 – Oct 1 **385 Days**
Year Five 2021 – 2022 Sep 7 – Sep 25 **384 Days**	**Year Five** 2022 – 2023 Sep 26 – Sep 15 **355 Days**	**Year Five** 2024 – 2025 Oct 3 – Sep 22 **355 Days**	**Year Five** 2025 – 2026 Sep 23 – Sep 11 **354 Days**	**Year Five*** 2027 – 2028 Oct 2 – Sep 20 **355 Days**
Year Six 2022 – 2023 Sep 26 – Sep 15 **355 Days**	**Year Six*** 2023 – 2024 Sep 16 – Oct 2 **383 Days**	**Year Six** 2025 – 2026 Sep 23 – Sep 11 **354 Days**	**Year Six** 2026 – 2027 Sep 12 – Oct 1 **385 Days**	**Year Six** 2028 – 2029 Sep 21 – Sep 9 **354 Days**
Year Seven* 2023 – 2024 Sep 16 – Oct 2 **383 Days**	**Year Seven** 2024 – 2025 Oct 3 – Sep 22 **355 Days**	**Year Seven** 2026 – 2027 Sep 12 – Oct 1 **385 Days**	**Year Seven*** 2027 – 2028 Oct 2 – Sep 20 **355 Days**	**Year Seven** 2029 – 2030 Sep 10 – Sep 27 **383 Days**
Total Days in Seven Years = 2569	Total Days in Seven Years = 2570	Total Days in Seven Years = 2569	Total Days in Seven Years = 2571	Total Days in Seven Years = 2569
+ 10 until Yom Kippur	+ 10 until Yom Kippur	+ 10 until Yom Kippur	+ 10 until Yom Kippur	+ 10 until Yom Kippur
2579	**2580**	**2579**	**2581**	**2579**
Dates are depicted from the start of Rosh Hashanah to the night before Rosh Hashanah of the next year. * Indicates a leap year, so you have to add another day for our extra day in February				

205

I am fully aware that these charts and calculations can make your eyes bleed. Before we get into any discussion, the important thing to note is that in any given seven-year period, the days come suspiciously close to an exact division of either a prophetic three and a half years (1260 days) plus the additional 1,290 days determined in Daniel or exactly 1,290 days both before and after the midpoint (in an 87 month scenario). God is amazing, and of course, doesn't want us to peg any given year as the "start" of the final seven years. He wants us ready at all times. What this discussion is intended to do is really fuel your faith to know that the days in scripture are literal, and if you spend enough time with them, they can work out in a way that is mind-boggling. So, saying that, we have a final question:

Can any of these Seven-Year Periods be the Final Seven Years Discussed in Daniel?

2549 Days (of the 86-month period): You can make an argument that God would count the day after Yom Kippur as part of the 2,550 total days (1,260 days before the "midpoint" + 1,290 days after the "midpoint") because that would be the final end of the war. So this could add up to our 2,550 days (2,549 + 1 if adding the day after Yom Kippur). This would be the same theory as the 2,579 days in the 87-month period (where we are looking for a total of 2,580 days: 1,290 days both before and after the midpoint). If you add in the day after Yom Kippur it would total 2,580 days, which would equate to two 1,290 day divisions, matching our 1,290 day count in Daniel.

2,550 Days (of the 86-month period): You could also make an argument that God wouldn't count the day after Yom Kippur – which would indicate a number of days between Rosh Hashanah and the seventh Yom Kippur of exactly 2,550 days (1,260 days before the "midpoint" + 1,290 days after the "midpoint"). This would be the same theory as the 2,580 days when you have 87 months (or three additional months added). There are some years that have exactly 2,580 days (1,290 days before the midpoint + 1,290 days after the midpoint).

2,551 Days (of the 86-month period): You could also make an argument where God would count up to the night before Yom Kippur because Yom Kippur is His return – which would subtract a day from the 2,551 days to equal our 2,550 days (1,260 days before the "midpoint" + 1,290 days after the "midpoint"). This would be the same theory as the 2581 days when you have a total of 87 months. If you count only up until Yom Kippur you get and exact count of 2,580 days, which leaves two 1,290 day divisions (1,290 days before the midpoint + 1,290 days after the midpoint).

In summary, what we need to understand is that in every given year the days from Rosh Hashanah to the seventh Yom Kippur could match Daniel's 70th week. The only difference is the days BEFORE the Antichrist sets himself up as god, which are never specifically measured in scripture. If it is during a seven-year period that has 86-months there would be 1,260 days, matching the prophetic year of 360 days per year. If it is during a seven-year period that has 87-months there would be 1,290 days, making the days equal on both sides of the "midpoint."

We did not cover the final feast of the Jews, but that feast will be fulfilled after the Millennial Reign of Christ. If you want more information on this feast please see my *Revelation in Black and White* study.

1 www.endtimepilgrim.org

Made in the USA
Columbia, SC
14 February 2021